Agrarian Reform
and Rural Poverty

Westview Replica Editions

The concept of Westview Replica Editions is a response to the continuing crisis in academic and informational publishing. Library budgets for books have been severely curtailed. Ever larger portions of general library budgets are being diverted from the purchase of books and used for data banks, computers, micromedia, and other methods of information retrieval. Interlibrary loan structures further reduce the edition sizes required to satisfy the needs of the scholarly community. Economic pressures on the university presses and the few private scholarly publishing companies have severely limited the capacity of the industry to properly serve the academic and research communities. As a result, many manuscripts dealing with important subjects, often representing the highest level of scholarship, are no longer economically viable publishing projects--or, if accepted for publication, are typically subject to lead times ranging from one to three years.

Westview Replica Editions are our practical solution to the problem. We accept a manuscript in camera-ready form, typed according to our specifications, and move it immediately into the production process. As always, the selection criteria include the importance of the subject, the work's contribution to scholarship, and its insight, originality of thought, and excellence of exposition. The responsibility for editing and proofreading lies with the author or sponsoring institution. We prepare chapter headings and display pages, file for copyright, and obtain Library of Congress Cataloging in Publication Data. A detailed manual contains simple instructions for preparing the final typescript, and our editorial staff is always available to answer questions.

The end result is a book printed on acid-free paper and bound in sturdy library-quality soft covers. We manufacture these books ourselves using equipment that does not require a lengthy make-ready process and that allows us to publish first editions of 300 to 600 copies and to reprint even smaller quantities as needed. Thus, we can produce Replica Editions quickly and can keep even very specialized books in print as long as there is a demand for them.

About the Book and Author

Agrarian Reform and Rural Poverty:
A Case Study of Peru
Tom Alberts

Initiated in 1969 after the establishment of Velasco Alvarado's military government, Peru's program for agrarian reform remains one of the few enduring examples of major planned reform in Latin America. Based on extensive data for land ownership, income distribution, and agricultural production, this book assesses Peru's experience with development planning since 1950 and discusses efforts to improve the standard of living of its rural population through changes in agrarian structure.

Dr. Alberts is a consultant for several international development agencies and for the U.N. International Labour Organization.

Agrarian Reform
and Rural Poverty
A Case Study of Peru

Tom Alberts

Westview Press / Boulder, Colorado

A Westview Replica Edition

Copyright © 1983 by Westview Press, Inc.

Published in 1983 in the United States of America by
    Westview Press, Inc.
    5500 Central Avenue
    Boulder, Colorado 80301
    Frederick A. Praeger, President and Publisher

Library of Congress Cataloging in Publication Data
Alberts, Tom, 1943-
    Agrarian reform and rural poverty.

    (Westview replica edition)
    Bibliography: p.
    1. Land reform--Peru. 2. Rural poor--Peru. I. Title.
HD1333. P4A4 1983   338.1'885   83-10326
ISBN 0-86531-962-6

Printed and bound in the United States of America.

10 9 8 7 6 5 4 3

Contents

Tables

ix

Figures

Foreword

In 1964 I started studying economics, greatly interested in economic and social development. After a few years I was convinced that the rural sector and agriculture were central to overall growth and development. I also felt it necessary to acquire first hand knowledge of developing countries. When an opportunity became available to work for the UN in Peru in 1968, I accepted the offer and arrived in December of that year in Lima. President Belaúnde had just been overthrown by a military coup and the new military government promised sweeping reforms. Very few people believed that these promises were more than rhetoric.

While I worked in Peru in 1968-1971, mainly in agricultural planning, I often wanted to sit down to reflect and analyze the rapid events which took place. The very interesting years in Peru were followed by three more years in Chile with its equally important social changes, not least in the agricultural sector. Even my work in development since has convinced me that many governments in developing countries are preoccupied first with modernization and industrialization. Rural development seems to be generally neglected in domestic economic planning for developing countries.

I have been writing this book on Peru since 1975. It was first published in 1981 in a limited edition. This is a slightly modified version of the work; the worst errors have been corrected and the bibliography has been updated to include several important Peruvian publications.

Unfortunately the main conclusions remain valid. Agriculture continues to be the major bottleneck for social and economic development in Peru. While there has been a slight growth in overall per capita output between 1970 and 1983, income distribution has deteriorated and value-added in agriculture has declined significantly on a per capita basis. Although agricultural exports were significantly higher than imports at the end of the 60s, imports took the lead at the beginning of the 80s. In 1978, Peru negotiated an agreement with the IMF and a debt relief programme was agreed upon by both the Paris Club and commercial banks. Still, in March 1983, Peru was following other Latin American countries by defaulting on foreign debt repayments. I predict that as the world economy starts to grow during 1983, Peru will soon be pulled out of the most pressing problems. It will then be possible to continue to neglect Peruvian agriculture.

Rural poverty continues to be a serious problem. Twenty years after the rural guerilla movements of the 60s, they are re-occurring. The answer has always been repression. My hope, though, is that the Peruvian peasant will be given a fair chance to participate in future development, through increased economic interest in rural areas.

Tom Alberts
Simrishamn
5 April 1983

1
Introduction

1.1   THE PROBLEM STATED

Uneven distribution of incomes and wealth is a characteristic of most Third World countries. Since the majority of the people live in rural areas, agrarian reform could help to equalize incomes and wealth, as well as to increase agricultural growth.

Peru is an important country in the discussion of agrarian reform. In October 1968 a military junta took power in Peru. Its main development objectives were, "... to accelerate the rate of economic growth, redistribute the income...[and to] assure the incorporation of the Peruvians, of all regions of the country, in the benefits of progress."[1] One of the key elements in the development strategy of the military junta was an agrarian reform. This is a case study of the Peruvian agrarian reform as a strategy to improve the standard of living of the rural population. It investigates to what extent the government was successful in accomplishing the objectives of redistribution and growth.

In our analysis the following 5 questions have guided the research:
1. What was agricultural growth prior to 1968?
2. What were the long-run tendencies in agricultural growth?
3. What prospects existed for a higher growth of agriculture as of 1968?
4. What was the income distribution in agriculture before 1968?
5. What were the effects of the agrarian reform on income distribution?

- 1 -

In several sections we will consider the relationship between the agricultural sector and the rest of the economy.
This study, it is hoped, will be a contribution to the general knowledge of the possibilities and problems of agrarian reform as well as of Peruvian development, and also
to the discussion on equity cum growth debate which has
taken place for about a decade.

1.2   OVERVIEW OF THE STUDY

In the next section 1.3 we will give some basic data on Peru. The reader familiar with Peru can proceed directly to
section 1.4 where we will summarize the equity cum growth
debate and relate it to the Peruvian experiment in the period 1968-75.

In chapter 2 we will present the development objectives of
the military government, and how the Government proposed to
accomplish these. In particular we will analyse the Government's approach to agricultural development and agrarian reform. Some comments will also be made on the situation prior
to 1968 so as to enable the reader to appreciate if there
was a change in the basic development objectives, and if so,
to what extent.

Having identified these overall development objectives, and
also the means to accomplish these, chapter 3 makes an overall appraisal of the results of the junta's reign. Two periods are considered, 1968-75 and 1975-80.

Chapters 4-6 mainly deal with the agricultural sector. In
chapter 4 we will make some theoretical comments on the concentration of landownership and its impact on the distribution of income within the agricultural sector.

The results will be used in chapter 5 which analyses the effectiveness of the agrarian reform in eradicating rural poverty.

Chapter 6 makes an appraisal of government policies towards agricultural growth and evaluates the results in terms of agricultural production.

In chapter 7 we will summarize our main findings in light of the five questions posed above. We will examine to what extent the military junta carried out a successful agrarian reform, with respect to social and economic growth objectives. The lessons of the Peruvian experiment give rise to our discussion of Peru's major development options for the years 1980-2000 and their implications for distribution and growth.

1.3   PERU AND ITS AGRICULTURAL PROBLEM

1.3.1 Adverse environmental conditions

Peru is a large country, more than twice the size of France. There are three natural regions: The Coast (Costa), the Andean Highlands (Sierra) and the Jungle (Selva). The Jungle is often sub-divided into the High Jungle (Ceja de Selva or sometimes also called Montaña) and the Jungle proper. The map on p. 4 outlines these regions. For planning purposes two other geographical divisions are often used. One divides the country into twelve agrarian zones. The other is the North-Center-South-Jungle division which is frequently also referred to in planning documents. In this study we will use both the division into natural regions, and the twelve agrarian zones. A complete list of the departments covered by the agrarian zones can be found on p. 6. Some comments on the particularities of each natural region will be of use for an understanding of the special problems surrounding Peruvian agriculture.

COLOMBIA

ECUADOR

Tumbes

Piura

Lambayeque

Amazonas

Cajamarca

La Libertad

San Martin

Loreto

SELVA
BAJA

BRASIL

Ancash

Huánuco

Pasco

Junin

SELVA
ALTA

Madre de Dios

OCEANO PACIFICO

Lima

Huancavelica

Ica

Ayacucho

SIERRA

Apurimac

Arequipa

Puno

BOLIVIA

Moquegua

Tacna

CHILE

National region boundary ——

Department boundary ++++

– 4 –

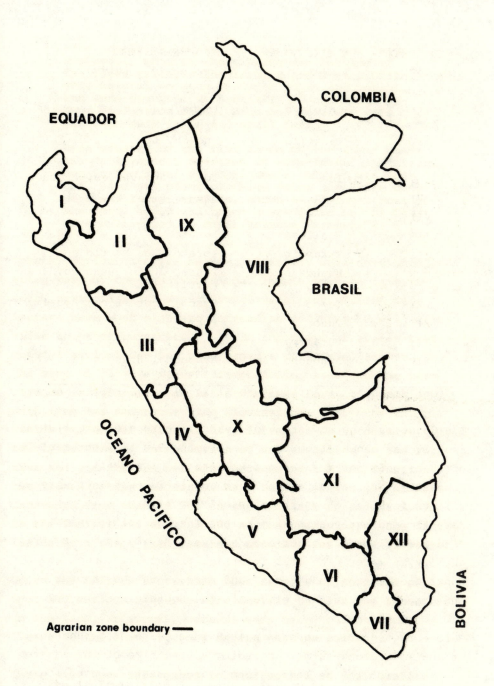

EQUADOR

COLOMBIA

I

II

IX

VIII

BRASIL

III

OCEANO PACIFICO

IV

X

XI

V

XII

VI

BOLIVIA

VII

Agrarian zone boundary ——

NUMBER OF AGRA- RIAN ZONE	NAME OF AGRA- RIAN ZONE	DEPARTMENT COVERED (completely or partially)
I	Piura	Piura, Tumbes
II	Chiclayo	Lambayeque, Cajamarca, Amazonas, La Libertad
III	Trujillo	Ancash, La Libertad, Huánuco
IV	Lima	Lima
V	Ica	Ica, Huancavelica, Ayacucho
VI	Arequipa	Arequipa, Ayacucho
VII	Tacna	Moquegua, Tacna
VIII	Iquitos	Loreto
IX	Tarapoto	Loreto, San Martín
X	Huancayo	Pasco, Junín, Huánuco, Huancavelica
XI	Cuzco	Cuzco, Madre Dios, Apurímac
XII	Puno	Puno
XIII	Pucallpa	Loreto, Huánuco, San Martín
XIV	Ayacucho	Ayacucho, Huancavelica, Apurímac, Cuzco

Source: Ministry of Agriculture (1976:2)

The Coast is a narrow strip of desert. There are some fifty-two rivers running from the Andes to the Pacific, but most of these only carry water a few months of the year. Irrigation necessary for coastal agriculture and it is used in the fertile valleys, as they are favourably located with respect to domestic and international markets. The possibilities to expand agricultural production are severely limited by the availability of water. The most important products grown on the Coast are, cotton, sugar-cane and rice in the North of Lima, and grapes, fruits, and olives in the South.

Before the agrarian reform in 1969 there were differences in product mix among farms, according to the size of the estates.

"Prior to the land reform, large estates controlled the best-watered lands. Areas of coastal minifundia

were generally located on the poorest and least
adequately watered lands along the margins of
the river valleys. The largest and most profitable coastal estates produced sugar and cotton,
and were operated as centrally managed wage-labour production units. Rice and potatoes were
grown on both large and small farms.

Rice estates on the flat lands of the lower coastal valleys were operated as wage-labour operations,
but in the upper valleys, where terrain was rug-
ged, land was often parceled among the share crop-
pers and labour tenants, known as colonos. Most of
the corn, beans and truck crops grown on the Coast
were cultivated by small private farmers."2)

Coastal agriculture had become relatively well-developed,
using most of the non-traditional inputs such as fertilizers, pesticides and agricultural machinery. Yields per
hectare have been high and increasing and compare well with
those in other countries.[3] It is important to stress that
coastal agriculture has been capable of dynamic growth. In
the case of rice, a major rice-producing area such as Lambayeque in agrarian zone II in Northern Peru, the area sown
with rice has undergone wide fluctuations since the thirties.
Yields (kilos per hectare) have increased in successive stages,
mainly because of introduction of new varieties in the thirties and the forties but also because of the introduction of
the transplanting technique. As a result yields per hectare
increased from about 1 700 in the thirties to almost 3 000
in the forties and about 3 500 at the beginning of the fifties.
Yields have since then remained constant for about 15 years.[4]

Up to the fifties there have been reports of shortage of labour and various measures were devised to bind the labourers
to the land. Frequently workers were brought down from the
Sierra to the Coast to work during peak periods.[5]

There have been references to destruction of soil quality

through inadequate production techniques in irrigated agriculture, resulting in, for example, saline soils.[6]

The Sierra is made up of three Andean ranges at elevations above 2 000 meters.

> "Between these ranges are high valleys and
> areas of relatively flat plains, the broadest
> and highest area of which is the Altiplano in
> the south. Areas below 3 500 meters are in-
> tensely cultivated, in many instances under
> irrigation, and support an extremely dense
> population."[7]

Yields per hectare have been stagnant and little technological progress has occured. Deforestation, in part because of demand from the mines, but also because of demand for fuel has led to erosion. Erosion has caused significant losses in agricultural land.[8]

Important Sierra crops are potatoes, corn, wheat and barley. Most of the crops grown in the Sierra are also consumed there. The major agricultural exports from the Sierra are wool and meat.[9]

The Selva (the Jungle) has long been the dream and hope of Peru.

> "Several times in the past the Peruvian govern-
> ment has fostered (more in word than deed) co-
> lonization in this region, but with little suc-
> cess. Inclemency, variability of soil resources,
> high settlement costs, and lack of social and
> economic infrastructure severely limit the con-
> tribution which this region can make to the na-
> tion's commercial agriculture and livestock pro-
> duction in the near future. Most colonization
> which has occurred to date in this region is in
> the 'High Selva' along the fringes of the Andes."[10]

1.3.2 Land Scarcity[11)]

Peru is large, 1 285 216 km^2, and in 1972 there were only 14
million people. One could, therefore, believe the country
to have an abundance of agricultural land. On the contrary,
the agricultural resource base is quite limited as the short
description of the three natural regions will have indicated.

Available data on arable land per capita show that land is
scarce in Peru. In Table 1.1 arable land has been divided
by total population and continental averages are presented.
Even an allegedly overpopulated continent such as Asia has
more arable land per capita.

Table 1.1 Arable land per capita in Peru and continental
averages

Country	Arable land per capita (hectare)
Peru	0.18
South America	0.50
Asia	0.20
Europe	0.30
Africa	0.60
North America	2.03

Source: FAO (1975)

New land can be incorporated in basically two ways in Peru.
In order to open up new land on the Coast large investments in
irrigation are required. In the Sierra only inferior land is
available. The second alternative is to develop the Selva.
It requires large investments and can only be accomplished
by a major redefinition of development strategy. The total
amount of land suitable for agriculture in this region is

not well known. Moreover, the kind of agricultural technology appropriate for its development is little investigated and not practically tested. [12]

The size of Peru made many believe that there were large un-tapped resources available for development. For example, in 1969 the Peruvian Office for Evaluation of the Natural Re-sources (ONERN), estimated that about 11 million hectares were suitable for intensive agriculture in Peru. By 1971 this figure had been reduced to 3.5 million. [13] According to these estimates there would hardly be any new land available. Even given the vast land area of Peru, only 2.7% of the country's area would be suitable for intensive agriculture. Consequently, in spite of being a large country, the Peruvian resource base for agriculture production is very limited. Much of the land suitable for agricultural production seems to be in production already on the Coast and in the Sierra. How much land and what quality is available in the Selva is still not clear. [14]

With some speculation, one can say that the high costs of ir-rigating new land on the Coast, and the relatively limited potential of the Sierra, could accelerate the Selva's deve-lopment.

1.3.3 Agriculture in the economy

Peru has undergone important changes. In the period 1940 to 1972 the population growth rate increased from below 2% to 3% and the Peruvian population more than doubled. The demographic data in Table 1.2 indicate the profound structural changes which have taken place in the Peruvian economy in the post-World-War II period. First, it should be noted that Peru has rapidly become urbanized. The re-lative share of the rural population has decreased, but

Peru has not yet reached the point where the rural population is decreasing also in absolute numbers. In Latin
America there are already several countries in which the
rural population is falling in absolute numbers: Argentina,
Chile and Venezuela. [15]

Table 1.2   Population in Census Years (thousands)

	1940		1961		1972	
	Number	%	Number	%	Number	%
Urban	2 197	35	4 698	47	8 058	60
Rural	4 011	65	5 209	53	5 480	40
Total	6 208	100	9 907	100	13 538	100
Coast		29		39		43
Sierra		64		52		47
Selva		7		9		10
		100		100		100

Source: Horton (1976), p. 77; and ONEC (1974)

The second major change is the shift of the population from
the Sierra to the Coast, where most of the economic growth
and investment have taken place. These demographic changes
are in part the responses to economic changes but are also
causes of these. It is extremely difficult to separate causes
from effects.

Another trend has been the decline in agricultural growth.
FAO data for example, based on official data, show that per
capita food and total agricultural production declined in
the second half of the sixties. For details see Table 1.3.
We will return to this question in chapter 6.

Table 1.3 Index number of total agricultural production, food production, per capita production, and production of selected agricultural commodities, 1952-1969 (1952-1956=100)

Year	Total Agric. Prod.	Food Prod.	Popul.	Per capita Total Prod.	Per capita Food Prod.	Production of Selected Agricultural Commodities									
						Wheat	Barley	Corn	Rice	Sugar	Potatoes	Cotton	Beef	Mutton	Pork
1952	97	99	96	101	103										
1953	98	100	98	100	102										
1954	103	103	100	103	103	100	100	100	100	100	100	100	100	100	100
1955	103	102	102	101	100										
1956	99	97	105	94	92										
1957	100	100	107	93	93	90	80	90	105	103	80	98	105	136	165
1958	107	106	110	97	96	97	87	96	76	111	79	99	118	144	190
1959	113	113	113	100	100	105	94	113	139	122	93	113	123	144	190
1960	116	112	117	99	96	100	105	113	129	121	87	125	125	148	195
1961	121	118	120	101	98	100	107	127	135	123	95	126	130	140	190
1962	125	119	124	101	96	99	89	153	145	125	108	141	112	156	210
1963	127	123	127	100	97	99	88	159	105	117	109	141	117	156	220
1964	132	130	131	101	99	93	88	167	136	116	117	131	135	144	235
1965	132	130	136	97	96	95	86	196	112	123	120	124	123	144	215
1966	138	139	140	99	99	91	85	183	140	117	115	114	148	156	210
1967	139	143	144	97	99	92	83	196	179	114	131	92	143	128	215
1968	131	134	149	88	90	73	71	177	111	97	121	99	142	128	215
1969	140	147	153	92	96	82	79	196	172	117	142	90	153	128	235

Source: FAO (1975). Taken from Horton (1976), p. 87; ONEC (1974), p. 172

Because of the poor performance of the Peruvian agricultural sector, and the relatively rapid overall rate of economic growth in the post-World-War II period in the economy, the agricultural sector's contribution to GDP has declined rapidly. At the time of the military coup in 1968 agriculture's share in GDP was about 15 percent, while in 1950 it was about 20 percent.[16]

Another salient feature and a consequence of this stagnation in Peruvian agriculture is the evolution of foreign trade in agricultural goods. In the fifties food imports were about 38 million US dollars, and represented about 15% of total imports.[*] Agricultural exports were quite important in generating foreign exchange. In 1951 Peruvian exports amounted to 253 million dollars of which 136 million dollars came from agriculture. For details of agricultural exports and imports see Tables 1.4 and 1.5.

By the time of the military takeover in 1968 the situation had changed dramatically. While in 1951 the share of agricultural exports in total exports was 54%, in 1968 it had dropped to 19%. Despite these share figures, still there occurred an increase in the dollar value of agricultural exports. Food imports on the other hand increased rapidly, from 38 to 128 million dollars in the same period, i.e. 1951 to 1968. The share of food imports (in total imports) increased from 14 percent in 1951 to 20 percent in 1968. Still in 1968 the value of agricultural exports were greater than food imports.

Due to the close links between the foreign trade of Peru

---

[*] Dollars will be expressed in current prices in this study, unless otherwise stated.

Table 1.4   Food imports and total imports (million US dollars)

	Total imports	Food imports	
		Absolute	Share in total (percent)
1951	280	38	13.6
1955	300	47	15.7
1960	375	54	14.4
1965	729	117	16.0
1968	630	128	20.3

Source: Total imports 1951 Boletín BCR (Enero 1968), p. 24
                        1955-68 -"-   -"- (Marzo 1975), p. 26
        Food imports 1951-65 share in total taken from Thorp
              and Bertram (1978), p. 277
        1968 total food imports from IBRD (1975), Volume II,
              Table E.3

Table 1.5   Agricultural exports and total exports
            (million US dollars)

	Total exports	Agricultural exports*)	
		Agricultural	Share in total (percent
1951	253	136	53.8
1955	271	119	43.9
1960	433	146	33.7
1965	667	162	24.3
1968	866	163	18.8

*) The sum of sugar, cotton, coffee and wool. These four
   export products represented over 95% of agricultural
   exports.

Source: BCR (1968), PP.44-45; BCR (1976), pp. 42-43

and the rate of economic growth, the agricultural sector
had become a bottleneck for overall economic growth. In
other words, if the rate of growth of the agricultural
sector had been higher it is probable that the Peruvian
economy would have been able to grow at a faster rate. A
higher rate of growth in agriculture has a direct effect on
GNP and also affects foreign trade and the Peruvian ba-
lance-of-payments, which largely determine growth potential.

We have emphasized some salient features of Peruvian agriculture. In particular the stagnation of production, increase in imports of food and the decline in the significance of agricultural exports. Concurrently Peru was rapidly being transformed from a predominantly rural country,
with its population concentrated in the Sierra, to an urban society with a major shift of the population to the Coast.

The other distinguishing feature of Peruvian agriculture
has been described as follows,

> "A further characteristic of Peruvian agri-
> culture is the markedly unequal distribution
> of land. Mention has been made of the small
> class of latifundistas, or large landowners.
> The mass of the farming population scratch
> out a subsistence from tiny plots of unpro-
> ductive, overworked land, or graze flocks
> on miserably poor pasture. Medium-sized farms
> run by middle-class farmers are the exception."[17]

A broad measure of land concentration is the physical extension of farms. Such a measure reveals an extreme concentration of ownership. According to the 1961 agricultural census
there were about 845 000 farms.[18] 1.3 percent of these covered no less than 84 percent of the farm land.

Since there are great differences in land quality, the size
of a farm is only a rough measure of its economic importance.
This is particularly so in Peru where regional differences,

such as soil quality and climate are very great. One hectare
of irrigated land on the Coast is obviously much more valuable
than one hectare of pasture land in the Sierra. One approach
for evaluating land ownership concentration, followed in several studies on Latin American agriculture, has been to
identify the employment-generating capacity of the land in
different regions for typical farms.*)

A family farm has been defined as: " Farms large enough to
provide employment for 2 to 3.9 people on the assumption that
most of the farm work is being carried out by the members of
the family.". It is further assumed that "... the farms should
have typical incomes, markets and levels of technology now
prevailing in the region."[19] Using this classification the
following figures apply to Peru.

Table 1.6   Size of family farm in Peru according to
             natural region

Region	Number of hectares
Coast	3 - 10
Sierra	
irrigated	3 - 10
dry farming	10 - 50
grazing land	100 - 500
High Jungle	10 - 20
Jungle	20 - 100

Source: CIDA (1966), p. 40

---

*) The CIDA aggregate data on land ownership concentration
based on such criteria do not differ significantly from
those of the 1961 Agricultural Census.

These figures provide a general conceptual framework for discussing land ownership in this study. However, as Owen has pointed out, family farms were not economically important in Peru. Eighty-four percent of the farms had about 6 percent of the farm land, meaning a small number of farm owners controlled most of the farm land in Peru.[20]

Peruvian agriculture was thus characterised by (i) oligarchic land ownership and (ii) limited opportunities for expansion of cultivated surface due to natural barriers. The pressures for new land could in part be relieved through migration to the cities, particularly on the Coast. Even so, the first part of the sixties witnessed increasing rural tensions and pressures for land. Massive land invasions on the big estates took place and guerilla movements emerged several times and were violently repressed.[21]

Rural tension was not a new phenomenon in Peru and Peruvian history testifies to the peasants' unsuccessful fights against the large estates. There was growing political awareness by the sixties that production stagnation and rural unrest were caused by distortions in land distribution. The idea of an agrarian reform became increasingly accepted by all political interest groups and parties, although differences arose concerning the mode of implementing the reform.

We may infer from the very uneven distribution of land and the lack of agricultural growth that the nutrition level in Peru was inadequate. This is confirmed from reports on the nutritional level in Peru. On the basis of agricultural production data food balance sheets were constructed showing low levels of caloric and protein intakes in Peru. In 1966, for example, a report claimed that:

> "Peru has a history of inadequate nutrition...,
> the per capita consumption of calories in Peru

was the lowest of any country in South America
...The per capita consumption of protein, the
essential building blocks for the body, was only 53 grams a day. This was next to the lowest
in all the countries of South America, and among
the lowest in the world."22)

There has been a great deal of controversy over the question
of food requirements. Clark and Haswell for example have
raised serious criticism against the FAO standards.[23] Factors such as climate, age, sex and type of work strongly
influence food requirements. In addition, national averages
have serious deficiencies in describing the general nutrition level.

Therefore, more informative food consumption surveys and
other sources of information are needed. One such study was
undertaken in 1960 based on a sample. It is not clear how
the sample was designed, so the results should be treated
with caution. According to this sample, the nutritional situation was quite serious. It was found that over 60% of
the Sierra rural families consumed less than 75% of the re-
commended diet of calories and proteins. These recommendations were laid down by the Ministry of Health in Peru.[24]
The nutritional situation of the Peruvian population has
been and remains precarious. Attempts to establish the magnitude of the problem always encounter both methodological
and statistical problems.

This brief description of Peruvian agriculture in the economy would be incomplete if we did not mention the problem
of unemployment and underemployment. Again, there are difficult methodological and statistical problems involved,
particularly when agriculture is discussed, because the production cycle in agriculture generates a cyclical demand for
labour which must be related to a constant supply of labour.

Several authors have pointed out the serious unemployment situation in Peru, for example the National Planning Institute (INP), and Thorbecke, while the Convenio studies indicated that there was no serious problem of overt unemployment.[25]

The studies mentioned attempt to measure the amount of open and/or disguised unemployment and are not primarily interested in causal factors. Although unemployment is very common in the developing countries there are specific variables which affect this situation, particularly the availability of land and its distribution.

Given the amount of land and the prevailing land ownership structure in Peru, there are differences in labour input per hectare. The larger estates have a lower input of labour per hectare than the smaller farms. On the aggregate level this means that overall employment is less than that which would have prevailed if land ownership was more even.[26] This relationship has been one important argument for agrarian reform since land redistribution would increase both employment and output and consequently lead to higher incomes more symmetrically distributed.[27]

The rural unemployment problem has been solved partly through the massive labour migration to the cities. Although migration has alleviated the rural problem, it has also transferred the problem to the urban areas where the unemployment situation has also become serious. To what extent this will be continued in the future is an open question. An agrarian reform could slow down rural-urban migration and alleviate pressures on urban labour markets.

It has been explained here that in Peru in 1968 there was an agrarian problem and that there existed a need for redistribution of agricultural land. The next section will review the recent discussions on the new emphasis on distribution among development economists.

1.4   REDISTRIBUTION WITH GROWTH

1.4.1 Introduction

During the first two decades after World War II most of the debate on development dealt with issues such as accelerating economic growth and industrialization. The world economy and trade were growing rapidly. The performance of the Less Developed Countries (LDCs) was uneven, though many countries did manage to attain high rates of economic growth.

However, a series of studies increasingly pointed out the negative side effects of the pattern of development taking place in the LDCs, such as rapid growth of urban areas, the slums, the mounting unemployment and disguised unemployment, the rapid growth of population and malnutrition. Many argued that a high rate of economic growth would in the long run make everybody better off, and consequently steps should be taken to accelerate the rate of growth.[28] The approaches in development economics have evolved however. It was becoming increasingly clear, among prevailing development patterns, that the poor majorities of the world would have to wait for generations for a permanent improvement in their standards of living. Moreover, with few exceptions, the gap between the industrialized countries and the LDCs did not seem to narrow, and often the reverse was taking place.

It is possible to identify two basic approaches in the debate that took place. The first line of thought emphasized the rapid rate of output growth in the Developed Countries (DCs) compared to the lower rate in the LDCs. Some argued that

this rapid development in the DCs was at the expense of the
LDCs.[29] The second line of thought concentrated on income
distribution issues. It has been argued that LDCs experience
more uneven income distribution than DCs, and that during
certain phases in the process of growth, the skewed distribution in the LDCs is worsened. The pattern or style of development was questioned and alternative development strategies were advocated.

Variables other than the level of output, such as nutrition,
education, health services and employment are obviously important in describing the standard of living. However, at
a given level of output, different income distributions are
correlated with these, i.e. an increase in the income share
of the 40% poorer strata would improve most other variables
in a positive way. Therefore, using the level of output and
the distribution of income as we do in this study, would
fairly well describe the standard of living of the poor in
terms of other key social indicators.[30]

1.4.2 <u>Some current issues</u>

The debate on economic distribution and growth has produced
a number of interesting hypotheses and conclusions. We will
review some of the current questions which have been controversial and which have an important bearing on this study.
Among these we will touch upon the following: Is there a
long-run relationship between the level of development and
the distribution of income? Is there a trade-off between
economic redistribution and growth? To what extent is it
possible to change the income distribution within a market
(capitalist) economy? Is the income distribution as a rule
more even in socialist countries? What are the pre-requisites
for economic redistribution in the agricultural sector?

The origin of the discussion on the relationship between economic development and income distribution can be traced back to the pioneering work of Simon Kuznets. In his famous presidential address to the Meeting of the American Economic Association in 1954 he stated that, "The scanty empirical evidence suggests that the narrowing of income inequality in the developed countries is relatively recent and probably did not characterize the earlier stages of their growth." A whole series of studies have subsequently been generated estimating the relationship between the level of development and income distribution. This is discussed further in chapter 3.3.1 when we discuss the income distribution in Peru.

The trend towards more emphasis on economic redistribution in the 70's is clear from the new focus of research. Thus, the World Bank has sponsored a series of studies in this field. A particularly important and well-known study is Redistribution with Growth by Chenery et.al. (1974). Earlier Adelman and Morris had been working on these issues which culminated in 1973 with their book: Economic Growth and Social Equity in Developing Countries. A reflection of the changing emphasis in development thinking is the article by Frances Stewart and Paul Streeten (1976) which emphasized the necessity of a multidimensional approach in development research. At present there seems to be consensus that the distribution of incomes and wealth can be changed and that these changes are not necessarily in conflict with high rates of economic growth. It is inevitable that theoretical and empirical studies of development and distribution frequently imply policy recommendations.

Some of the ethical and philosophical implications of redistribution policies were discussed by Deepak Lal in his

article from 1976 where he acidly critisized the World Bank
and other international agencies for being inconsistent.
He questions, "...whether there are valid ethical grounds
for universalist policies which concentrate on national
redistribution rather than on the international redistribution of incomes and wealth."[31]

Two questions evoke our attention. The first is the question of the possibility for change in the distribution of
incomes and wealth. Most authors, including several economists associated with the World Bank, seem to consider
that the political constraints are great in a market (capitalist) economy. In other words, although it is techni-
cally possible to design programmes which would improve the
relative income position of the poorer, while simultaneously
attaining a high rate of economic growth, the prevailing
political system would not permit these changes.

The debate has centered on growth and equality issues rather than the type of economic system to be adopted. Most
Western economists depart from the premise of the market
economy. Ahluwalia, for example, in an article in the American Economic Review, stated that,

> "...policy makers are perhaps best advised to
> think of the rate of growth as determining
> essentially the speed of transition through
> the different phases of development and in-
> equality: higher growth rates accelerate
> the transition without necessarily generating
> greater inequality than can be structurally
> expected in each phase."[32]

Thus Ahluwalia discusses the policy implications of his
research findings. In the same article he concludes, "Finally, we find that socialist countries display markedly
greater equality than others..."[33] Despite discussing policy implications Ahluwalia neglects the more profound
question of the choice of economic system.

Thus, the second question is whether a market (capitalist) economy can be politically adjusted to induce a high degree of equality. Deepak Lal in his article from 1976 was explicit in his criticism of international agencies:

> "In any case, it is probably politically naive to expect any substantial redistribution of assets in most developing countries (or in most countries, or in the world!) as is recommended by both Chenery et.al. and ILO. The radicals are at least right in stressing that revolution may be required to achieve a substantial measure of equality..."34)

The Marxist position was clearly stated by William Goldsmith in an article in Monthly Review,

> "What really influences the distribution of income, then, is ownership and control over the means of production - assets, in the words of Chenery and his associates. Only when property is socially owned and controlled, can distribution of income become seriously more equal. It is here that the new World Bank theory of income distribution becomes potentially most pernicious."35)

In any case, market (capitalist) economies do display a wide range of national income distributions at a given level of development.36)

When designing a development strategy which emphasizes economic growth with social equity one immediately will have to face the situation of agriculture and the rural population. There seems to be agreement among scholars that a necessary ingredient in such a strategy is an agrarian reform which among other things should eradicate extreme concentration of land ownership whatever the prevailing form of political economy.37) The relationship between the ownership of land and income distribution is explored further in chapter 4, in which some theoretical issues are considered.

Peru had an agricultural strategy of equity with growth for the rural sector. Under this policy, the Peruvian Govern-

ment implemented an agrarian reform, which was a necessary
condition for equity. The Peruvian experience is unique,
when compared with the agrarian reforms of Latin American
countries, such as Mexico, Bolivia, Cuba and Chile. Peru
and Chile are the only examples of specifically planned
agrarian reforms, involving massive land redistribution.
Peru, however, effected the only planned agrarian reform
which has endured Latin America's political upheavals. Nevertheless, the question remains whether agrarian reform
will necessarily lead to increased equity and/or an economically stronger agricultural sector. Given an agrarian reform, what other conditions are necessary for equity with
growth in the agricultural sector?

NOTES TO CHAPTER 1

1. INP (1968), p. 7.

2. Horton (1976), p. 5.

3. Horton (1976), p. 81.

4. Alberts (1977), pp. 39-40.

5. See chapter 4.2.2.2.

6. The World Bank estimated that as much as 150 000 hectares of coastal land have been taken out of production because of salinization and can be brought back to production. IBRD (1975), Annex II, p. 4. But if this land is brought back into production, water availability must be reduced in other areas. When land is abandoned the water is frequently diverted to other areas.

7. IBRD II (1975), Annex II, p. 1.

8. Ibid., p. 7.

9. Production data see for example 1961 Agricultural Census. Data on trade see the publication of BCR.

10. Horton (1976), p. 82. The Selva is to receive priority again during the government of president Belaúnde, 1980-85, according to the programme of Acción Popular (1980), p. 2.23.

11. See also chapter 6.3.

12. One attempt to use very capital intensive technique by the firm Le Tourneau was abandoned. Owen (1963) described these attempts in positive terms, pp. 8, 105-106.

13. ONERN (1971) and (1969). Taken from IBRD II (1975), Annex II, pp. 2-4.

14. One important attempt to investigate the development possibilities of the Jungle was a large pre-investment project of the United Nations Development Program, UNDP. In 1970 the summary report on the 3 million hectare region in the Selva had only been able to identify 213 000 apt for intensive use, and of these only 128 000 for crop production and the remaining 85 000, for grazing. It would seem as if most of this land was already under cultivation, but the report is not explicit. See Naciones Unidas (1970), pp. 12-13. "Most of the unused Class I-IV lands are in Class IV and in the Selva. For all practical purposes, not more than 0.3 million hectares of the high Selva are still available to be opened up." IBRD II (1975) Annex II, p. 3.

15. See for example Cepal (1977), p. 108. There are some data problems in Table 1.2 which were not discussed by Horton. The definition of urban and rural is different in the 1961 and 1972 Censi. According to some authors many urban persons in the 1972 Census should have been classified as rural. For a discussion of this see for example IBRD II (1975), Annex I, Appendix 1; and Statistical Annex section A. I have not made any corrections for differences in classification criteria between censi. However, Horton's figures were the preliminary results of the 1972 census and I have adjusted these in light of the final results. For a discussion of the ethnic composition in Peru see Owen (1963), pp. 10-12.

16. See Table 3.1 for details. There are some difficult problems which should be tackled by scholars studying Peru. One such area of research would be to investigate to what extent the price distortions in the Peruvian economy explain the apparent decline in agricultural sector contribution. Studies on other developing countries have arrived at the conclusion that, given the import substitution policies, the contribution by agriculture is greater than national accounts data would suggest. See for example Little et.al. (1970).

17. Owen (1963), p. 133.

18. In this introductory chapter we use the word farm. In subsequent chapters we will use the concept production units which seems to be a more adequate word.

19. Barrachlough-Domike (1966), p. 395. See also CIDA (1966), p. xxx.

20. In addition to Census data which have been the main source of information in various studies, there have been others using other sources of information. One of the most well-known is: "Los Dueños del Perú" by Malpica (1974). He gives data on the names of the most important families, farms and their extension. See also Valderrama and Ludmann (1979).

21. See for example CIDA (1965), pp. 469-481; Handelman (1975). Some guerilla leaders have published books on their experiences. See for example Béjar (1969); and Blanco (1972).

22. Shepherd (1966), p. 1. See also Convenio (1969), p. 80.
    The Convenio is an agreement between the Ministry of Agriculture and different public entities in the agricultural sector in Peru on the one hand, and the State universities of Iowa in the U.S. on the other hand.
    Ministry of Health studies on caloric and protein consumption in rural Peru in the fifties reported figures as low as 1 577 calories and 39 grams of protein per day. These are as low as those reported in Haiti. See Lundahl (1979), p. 418. Data on food consumption are often derived from national food balance sheets. Such sheets use agricultural production figures, import, and exports, etc., and finally the supply for human consumption is obtained. Agricultural

products for industrial uses, waste etc should have been deducted. Obviously, the quality of estimates of consumption of calories and protein are contingent on the quality of production statistics, and other statistical inputs for that matter. But it is quite clear that Peruvian agricultural production statistics are of low quality and consequently these data on nutritional levels are probably of low quality. In particular, yearly changes should be treated with extreme care.

23. Clark and Haswell (1970), chapter 2.

24. Chiriboga, et.al. (1960), p. 277. References taken from Shepherd (1966), p. 7. See also Coutu and King (1969), chapter 2.

25. According to INP the unemployment equivalent was 28.5% in 1970 while the figure for agriculture was 31%. INP I (1971), p. 15 and INP II (1971), p. 17. See also Thorbecke (1969). The Convenio study: "El balance de mano de obra actual y proyectada para la población económicamente activa an la agricultura" is based on two previous studies, one on labour demand and the other on labour supply projections. See Convenio studies in bibliography list. The CIDA study also stresses the unemployment problem. CIDA (1965), pp. 299-300.

26. The relationship between the size of farm and land use intensity has been studied in the case of Peru. See for example CIDA (1965),pp. 360-368; and Williams (1977).

27. See Griffin (1974), in particular pp. 34-45; ILO (1977), part I in particular pp. 20-21, 33; Cline (1970), chapter 2; Dorner (1972), chapter 4.

28. Adelman and Morris (1973), p. 1.

29. For a discussion of the dependency school in Latin America, see Blomström and Hettne (1979).

30. The concept "level of development" often describes two distinct aspects. First, it may refer to the level of output and second to the level of output and other socio-economic variables. We prefer to use the second interpretation. On the relationship between consumption of food and income distribution see FAO (1971); between education and income distribution Chenery et.al. (1974), pp. 27-30.

31. Lal (1976), p. 731; see also Sen (1978).

32. Ahluwalia (1976:1), p. 129. Almost identical in Ahluwalia (1976:2), p. 337. This bias of development economists is also pointed out by Leys (1975) writing on "Redistribution with Growth" (RwG) and its political assumptions. "First, it is assumed that the Third World countries in question will continue to be predominantly capitalist

societies,... Second, the report assumes that political power in these societies will continue to be based primarily on the private ownership of capital." In the same IDS Bulletin (August 1975), Richard Jolly, co-author of RwG replies and the remaining authors, viz Ahluwalia, Bell, Chenery and Duloy also give a comment in the same Bulletin.

33. Ahluwalia (1976:1), p. 132.

34. Lal (1976), pp. 736-737.

35. Goldsmith (1977), p. 54.

36. Ahluwalia (1976:2).

37. See chapter 4.2.1.

2
The New Development Strategy

2.1 INTRODUCTION

Practically all development plans produced in the Third
World have one central development objective, to increase
the rate of growth of the economy. Frequently, other development objectives are also included such as employment,
health, and distribution of income targets. Rarely, though,
is there a coherent and logical correlation between what Griffin-Enos has termed aspiration-goals-targets, and the means
to accomplish these.[1] In this chapter we will attempt to
identify the goals for development under the Peruvian government's Plan and describe their evolution. In later chapters we will examine the coherency within this evolution
and look at the final results of the Plan.

This chapter is organized in the following way. Firstly,
we will comment on the emergence of central planning in
Peru. Secondly, we will comment on how the income redistribution objective was introduced during President Belaúnde's
regime (1963-68). Thirdly, we will show that the income redistribution objective became a priority objective as of
1968, during the military junta. There was general agreement on income redistribution as a priority objective but
we will discuss areas of disagreement on the kind of equity
sought. Fourthly, we will focus the discussion on the agricultural sector. Fifthly, we will argue that the Development Plan 1971-75 was not viable, and, that there were several ambiguities in the conception of the agrarian reform,
leading to a contradiction between the type of reform and
the equity objective.

2.2   TOWARDS EQUITY AS A DEVELOPMENT OBJECTIVE

Formal central planning in Peru is relatively recent, although the public sector has always played an important
role in the economy. "Peru entered the 1960's with strong
traditions that had survived for centuries. The tradition
of a strong, centralized government dates back to the In-
cas."[2] It was not until the beginning of the 60's, however, that planning became institutionalized in the country.[3]

In order to understand the emergence of planning in Peru, it
is important to appreciate the changing political structure
in Peru. In the past there seemed to be agreement among scholars that: "Politically, Peru has been controlled for over
100 years by various combinations of the oligarchy, church,
and military."[4] The fundamental conflict in Peru which has
evolved since the Cuban Revolution in 1959, has been over
the distribution of incomes and wealth. The planning system
set up in Peru was advocated by groups in the Peruvian society questioning the status q o, and was opposed by the
oligarchy, and other important economic groups in control
of capital and land.[5]

The situation in the sixties has been summarized by <u>Lowen-
thal</u> thus,

> "Property and income distribution were exceptio-
> nally unequal...
> Industry, exports, and credit - like land - were
> controlled by small groups, members of a reduced
> number of Peruvian families or else foreigners,
> tied in with international firms. And national
> policies systematically protected the interests
> of Peru's dominant elites, domestic and inter-
> national." 6)

But as was described in chapter 1, rapid changes had taken
place in Peru and during the post-World-War II era economic
and urban growth rates were high. It became increasingly
necessary to redistribute incomes and wealth as Lowenthal
observed,

> "Pressures on Peru's elite began to mount from
> an increasingly urbanized and literate popula-
> tion that was insistently seeking a larger share
> of the nation's resources. Rural and urban land
> invasions, guerilla outbursts, student demonstra-
> tions, strikes, and increasing electoral support
> for reformist candidates reflected their demands."[7]

The change in the socio-political structure, and the challenge to the prevailing power structure was reflected in
Belaúnde's statement that,

> "This is a middle-class revolution and one which
> is not forgetting the peasants. It will change
> Peru for good. We are going to build a new Peru
> by fighting both great poverty and great wealth,
> by fighting illiteracy, and hunger,and by making
> citizens and customers of the Indians."[8]

The main emphasis of the development programme of Belaúnde
lay in, "Highways, irrigation works, specific economic and
fiscal reforms, and other projects..."[9] Belaúnde also proposed to decentralize some economic activities and,

> "Needless to say, this section of his platform
> appealed to the traditional upper class and the
> middle class of the Sierra. His emphasis on in-
> dustrialization and his newly gained confidence
> in domestic enterpreneurs sounded extremely at-
> tractive to the limited group of Peruvian indus-
> trialists and small mineowners, as well as to
> those working in their enterprises."[10]

The Belaúnde regime was applauded by the U.S. and international financial institutions. The IMF representative at the
Alliance for Progress meeting in October 1964 stated that,

> "To sum up, the Peruvian economy appears to be
> in an unparalleled position in its history for
> undertaking a programme of vast proportions that
> will ensure an improvement in the social struc-
> ture, in the country's productive capacity,and
> in the distribution of national income. The Fund
> urges the Peruvian authorities to carry on their
> economic and social development efforts in a
> climate of financial stability, the stability
> which they have so successfully provided in re-
> cent years, and declares itself willing and rea-

dy to lend its assistance to assure the continuity of external balance in the finances of
Peru."11)

The Belaúnde regime thus indicated an income redistribution
objective. However, any attack on poverty in Peru had to
include a programme of agrarian reform, and thus, one of
the key reforms of the regime was also an agrarian reform.
The 1967-70 Agricultural Development Plan stated that 2.2
million out of a total of about 17 million hectares were to
be expropriated and transferred to about 100 000 families.
In the agricultural sector there were about 1 000 000 families.[12] At that time 1% of the landowners controlled about
80% of agricultural land. Consequently, the targets were
quite modest in relation to the situation in agriculture.
Moreover, during the whole 1962-68 period only about 14 000
families received land through agrarian reform.[13] Therefore, there was very little practical importance attached
to the income redistribution objective, despite Belaúnde's
statement that, "We are going to build a new Peru by fight-
ing poverty and great wealth".

In summary, during the Belaúnde Government an income redistribution objective was introduced. There were some attempts
to accomplish this objective, but both the stated targets
and the policies implemented suggest that it had little priority.[14]

2.3   CHANGE IN STRATEGY - EQUITY FIRST PRIORITY

On 3 October 1968 the military deposed President Belaúnde.
Velasco, head of the army, became the new president, head-
ing the revolutionary council composed of the heads of the
armed forces. The new system was to be neither capitalist

nor communist. Therefore, it has been labelled the Peruvian experiment or model. The new emphasis of the regime on income and wealth redistribution was clearly stated by Velasco in several speeches. For example, "This would be no revolution at all if poverty continued to be the only heritage of the vast majority of Peruvians, and wealth, until today, the privilege and inheritance of the few."[15]

Below follows a systematic review of various official planning documents which demonstrates that(i) income redistribution was a priority objective; (ii) an agrarian reform was a necessary condition for redistribution; and (iii) economic growth was another priority objective, but was considered a logical consequence of the reforms to be carried out.

About a month after the military coup, the Government made public its first outline of a Long Run Development Strategy. The main objectives were to redistribute incomes and to accelerate economic growth.[16] The agricultural sector was to play a key role in this development strategy. As described by the National Planning Institute,

> "In order to achieve the planned objectives, a general strategy is required, which would define a pattern of development that favours the transformation of our economy and that emphasizes, simultaneously, the structural reforms and the creation of new development centers. The matter of structural reforms emerges from the necessity of incorporating in the national economic process the population presently excluded, living both in the rural sector and in the surrounding of the urban centers. It is convenient to define this matter, at least, with respect to five basic reforms.
> Firstly, to restructure agricultural property with a view to give our agriculture access to the modern techniques of production, and as a means of generating income for the rural population, converting them into consumers of industrial products.

Admittedly, the agricultural problem is not only
a problem of production, but at the same time
one of land tenure structure and inappropriate
use of land, which are important sources of the
inequalities of income found in this sector, with
enormous social and political consequences."17)

The other four reforms advocated were as follows:

(i)   a new mining policy to increase, the Peruvian share
        in profits, and, the role of the State in mining
        and production;

(ii)   a new industrial policy to successively change the
        import-substitution policy in favour of a more com-
        petitive export-oriented industry;

(iii)   a stronger State sector and changed methods of col-
        lecting revenues;

(iv)   financial resources channeled according to the needs
        of the productive sectors and improved social servi-
        ces.18)

Therefore, the strategy treated agrarian reform as a _neces-
sary_ condition for implementing the two objectives of growth
and redistribution.

This conceptual framework was maintained in the Medium Term
Development Plan, 1971-75. It contained 15 principal objectives. The first 4 of these objectives stressed the importance of the agricultural sector as follows:

(i)   effective participation of the national majorities
        in the basic decision making of the country, through
        intermediate institutions such as unions, co-opera-
        tives etc;

(ii)   acceleration and conclusion of the transfer of rural
        property in the whole country, as part of the Agrarian
        Reform;

(iii)   substantial increase of the health level of the Peru-
        vian population which will enable full development of

its physical and intellectual capacities;

(iv)   provision of social services to the marginal groups,
       in particular the remote rural areas, rearranging to
       this end the public expenses allocated for those ser-
       vices.[19]

In the sixth objective the growth objective was emphasized:

(vi)   maximum increase of production and productivity and
       major sectoral and regional articulation of the eco-
       nomy, the dynamics of which will be based on the ag-
       ricultural, fisheries, industrial and mining sectors.
       The action of the transport, communication and energy
       sectors will be oriented towards serving as support
       to the productive sectors, mentioned above, and con-
       tribute to the National Security.[20]

The general development Plan was complemented with Sectoral
Plans, and in the Medium Term Agricultural Plan, 1971-75,
the first part stressed the macroeconomic equity objective:

"A national objective is the transformation of
the actual pattern of development. The Agricultural Sector's main role will be to incorporate
productively the rural sector in economic activity, in such a way that it will be possible to
reduce progressively the rural-urban imbalance,
as well as the marginal rural sectors. At the
same time, the participation of the peasants in
making political decisions in the country will
be promoted, with the purpose of reaching a new
economic and social order. These two key medium-
term objectives should achieve a substantial
increase in the level of the rural income, and
promote intensive peasants' mobilization. Therefore, it will be necessary to complete the Agrarian Reform in order to achieve a better distribution of property and rural income, and the
transfer of political power from the landowners
to the peasants. Additionally, this process will
enable the removal of obstacles which prevent
the assimilation of the countryside to new techniques, and it will also favour a better use of
the production resources available in the sector."[21]

- 37 -

Again, as was the case of the General Development Plan, the
main objectives referred to wealth- and income redistribution. The production objective was present, but was viewed
as hopefully a consequence of the agrarian reform. There was
also a specific reference to a urban-rural imbalance. We will
discuss this further later in this chapter and in several
other parts of the study.

From this review of planning documents for the long-term and
medium-term the conclusions emerge that equity became a priority objective and that it was the most important one in relation to the growth objective. The documents do not, however,
explicitly deal with how a potential short-run conflict between growth and equity could be solved.

A great number of the proposed reforms of the Military Government were actually implemented. This definitely marks a break
with the past.

>"What was most striking about these reforms, and
>what quickly attracted attention throughout La-
>tin America, was not so much the content of the
>legislation (embodying as it did ideas and propo-
>sals which had been widely canvassed and occasio-
>nally legislated during the 1960's), but the fact
>that the Military Government proceeded to apply
>the new measures with a determination previously
>unknown in Peru."22)

For example, in a few years, 1968-74, Fitzgerald has estimated
that the State enterprises increased their share in GNP from
11 to 26 percent, while the share of foreign capital decreased
from 20 to 8 percent, and domestic capital from 30 to 21 per-
cent.23)

The Government extended its control and influence over new
spheres of the economy. Thus, by 1975, the state companies
Mineroperu and Pescaperu (holding the entire fishing sector)
were given responsibilities also for export marketing, and
most of the banks were either expropriated or came under

strict governmental control. The idea of workers' self-management, labour communities and social property, was reflected in a series of laws, but it never became implemented on a large scale in the economy.[24] The agrarian
reform was at the basis of the new development strategy.

Keeping in mind the equity objective and the structural reforms the Government intended to carry out, the following
growth rate targets, Table 2.1, were clearly unrealistic.

Table 2.1   Planned Growth rates and trends

	Growth Rates (percent)	
Gross Domestic Product	"Trend"	Target (1971-75)
(GDP)	3-4	7.5
Agriculture	2-3	4.2

Sources: "Trends": Guesstimates based on chapters 3 and 6
         Targets : GDP, INP (1971) Vol. I, p. 7
                   Agriculture, INP (1971) Vol. II, p. 18

As will be shown in chapters 3 and 6 the structural reforms
were not sufficient means, as the planners might have believed,
to increase the rate of economic growth. Economic problems
were mounting towards 1975 and were probably one cause for
later deemphasizing the equity objective. Consequently, in
the 1975-78 Development Plan hardly any mention at all is
made of equity as an objective.[25]

Still the reforms carried out in the 1968-75 period were significant and the Agrarian Reform did produce lasting effects
in the Peruvian economy. We will proceed to discuss some critical issues of the Peruvian agrarian reform which in the
course of the events came to play a decisive role in determining the final character of the reform and consequently also future rural income distribution.

2.4   WHAT KIND OF EQUITY: EMERGING CONFLICTS

2.4.1   Introduction

The new Agrarian Reform law was passed in June 1969 and was
ambiguous. The planning documents referred to earlier stressed
the equity objective, but the question of how this was to be
carried out was not fully addressed. The military claimed
that it was revolutionary, but the Peruvian Left at times argued that it served the interests of the landowners by com-
pensating them generously.

In the first part we will show that the agrarian reform was
not a reform which was to be implemented according to a predetermined plan. The implementation of the reform was condi-
tioned by a complicated interplay of factors such as the conceptual framework of the policy-makers, the distribution of
political power and economic development during the 1969-75
period. Secondly, we will discuss several topics in Peruvian
agrarian reform which had important bearing on equity and
growth, particularly the former.

2.4.2   Changing interpretations of agrarian reform

The long run development strategy which was published in 1968
stressed the need for an agrarian reform. Thus, after the military takeover in October 1968, the new leaders were con-
fronted with crucial issues during the elaboration of the reform law. The military were not specific in their response to
questions such as: how much land and how many farms were to
be expropriated; what kind of compensation was to be given to
the landowners; how many peasants were to receive land and
how; or how much were the peasants to pay for the land. The
military's lack of consensus resulted in a vague reform law.

A significant example of the controversy surrounding the
law's drafting were the changes which occurred within the
Ministry of Agriculture. The first minister of agriculture
was General Benavides who had close connections with the
big landowners.[26] The first draft of the new agrarian reform law which was discussed among high-level officials
was rejected by COAP, the advisory body to the president,
composed of high level officers. Subsequently, a few days
before the new agrarian reform law was published, General
Benavides was forced to resign and a more radical general
was named minister of agriculture, Barandiarán. Consequently,
the final Agrarian Reform Law, Decreto Ley 17716, of 24 June
1969, was much more radical, and, symbolically it was passed
on the "Indian day", which was now renamed "Peasant day" -
día del campesino.[27]

One of the conflicting issues of Peruvian agrarian reform
had been which land should be expropriated. Two positions
had emerged, leaving aside the extreme position of the pro-
ponents of no-reform. The first one was that only land which
was undercultivated was to be expropriated. This was the basic approach of the Belaúnde regime, and was proposed by the
Benavides group.[28] The second was that the power structure
had to be broken up through massive expropriation. Therefore
even economically important estates were to be included as
priority targets of the reform.

Two factors were of special importance to the latter position.
The first one was that the D.L. 17716 was to a large extent
influenced by a MIR proposal to the Parliament during the
Belaúnde regime.[29] The MIR was the revolutionary left which
had been involved in the guerilla movements in the beginning
of the 60's. There were similarities between the Belaúnde
law (15037 of 1964) and the one adopted in June 1969, the basic differences being that: "...the main provisions of the 1969

law are more radical, and most provisions are more easily
implemented than were those of the 1964 law."[30] The 1969
Law contained over 30 motives for expropriation and, if interpreted strictly, it would have permitted the Government
to expropriate at will.[31] The second factor is that the
way the agrarian reform was implemented during the first
months indicated the actual position of the Government. It
was, therefore, of particular importance that the military
Government decided to expropriate the sugar complexes on
the Coast during the first days after the new law had been
promulgated. This approach was in sharp contrast with the
agrarian reform under the Belaúnde regime, when the sugar
estates were exempted from expropriation.

In order to emphasize its determination to carry out a massive reform the military government occupied the sugar complexes thus making clear its determination to break the power
of the big landowners. This political move by the Government
probably was an important reason for success, because when
it was clear that the military succeeded in getting control
over these estates, the landowners of the remaining properties could not organize themselves to block the reform which
they had managed to do ever since the end of World War II.
There were also changes within the administration so that
agrarian reform officials who did not comply with the intentions of the Government were replaced by more "aggressive"
officials who would not yield to the pressures from the landowners in the different parts of the country.[32]

The final outcome of the agrarian reform was a product of several interacting factors of which the power struggle was one
important element. Mejía, writing on the general state of research on the Peruvian agrarian reform, has stated this as;

> "...without doubt, the most profitable result (of
> the research) is that of having shown that the ag-
> rarian reform, far from following a predetermined

'path' was modelled according to the concrete
dynamics of the antagonistic classes, or sectors of these. This proposition forces a review
of the ideological interpretations made by many
political analysts. In those interpretations of
the reform's significance two spheres of concrete
reality have often been confused: the one of the
intentions and the one of the realizations...
...Both of these erroneous research approaches
were founded in their incapacity to properly distinguish and consider, what the government pre-
tends or pretended to do, i.e. its project of
change, from what the government finally did, or
accepted to do..."33)

In other words, due to military infighting and lack of political experience, the Peruvian government defined the agrarian
reform over time, rather than determining its profile at its
outset. The expropriation of big landowners' properties initiated a political process which forced decisions of regarding particular agrarian policies to be taken under pressure.
The pressures of conflicting economic and political interests
overrode the social objective of increased equity.

2.4.3 Agriculture should finance Peruvian development

As late as in 1972 Dorner claims that, "The agricultural sector must also contribute both capital and labour to the non-
agricultural sectors in the process of development."34) Marxist
thinking, particularly that based on the experiences of the
Soviet Union, also stresses the role of the agricultural sector in financing industrial growth.35) Similar ideas were
also prevalent among Peruvian planners, although there was
never an in-depth discussion of the role of agriculture in
Peruvian development. One main line of thought, heavily influenced by United Nations Economic Commission for Latin-Ame-
rica (ECLA), was that rural income redistribution should
create a larger consumer market for industrial output. This

was clearly mentioned in the Long Run Development Strategy of the junta.[36)]

The Agrarian Reform Law touched the same theme and the Military Government introduced the Law claiming that the Reform should "...decisively contribute to the formation of a wide market and <u>provide the necessary capital resources for a rapid industrialization of the country;</u>"[37)] The law also contained mechanisms for transfering capital out of agriculture. One such example is that the beneficiaries of the reform, i.e. those peasants receiving land, had to pay for the assets received (land, cattle, machinery, buildings, etc). The former landowners received compensation payments, part in cash and part in bonds. These bonds could not be sold or in other ways used for payments with the important exception that the bondowner could exchange the bond with the Government against investments in industry. Thus, the law contained a possibility of transfering agricultural assets into industrial assets. How this was implemented will be discussed in chapter 5. The main mechanism for capital transfers out of agriculture was that agriculture should provide cheap food. This was accomplished through squeezing agricultural prices. This will be discussed further in chapter 6.

These examples show that the military Government thought that agriculture should finance industrial growth even though neither the law nor the plans outline the extent to which such financing can be extracted. In contrast, an income transfer from the <u>urban</u> sector to the agricultural sector would also have been necessary in order to satisfy the equity objective advocated by the junta. Average rural household incomes were lower than urban ones. Rural incomes were not improving since the agricultural sector was already using resources to finance urban development to such

an extent that agricultural production had stagnated. Therefore, even given the importance of economic growth, it can
be argued that resources should have flowed to the agricultural sector, rather than seeking to further exploit agricultural capital resources.

2.4.4 How much land to expropriate?

Already in 1969 it became clear that the large estates would
be expropriated and that it would not matter whether the
land was well used or not. The size of the farms was the
most important criterion for expropriation. As was mentioned
earlier, the Law contained a great number of articles which
could permit the Government to expropriate practically all
land regardless of size. Moreover the Law itself could obviously be changed by a military decree, and it was also modified during the course of events. Therefore, the question
of how much land was to be expropriated had not been decided
when the Law was passed and it continued to be an area of
considerable conflict within the military.

The first Medium Term Plan, 1971-75, quantified the targets
of the reform. For example about 13 million hectares and 26
thousand farms were to be expropriated.[38] However, by 1975
the Agricultural Planning Office (OSPA) had reduced these
figures to 10 million hectares and 14 thousand farms.[39]
Thus, there was a significant drop in the expropriation targets.

At the outset of the reform, the 1972 Agricultural Census data
were not yet available. These later indicated that, since
the Agricultural Census in 1961, the amount of agricultural
land had increased substantially, although mostly low quality
land. Hence, considering the availability of land, the agra-

rian reform became less radical because (a) expropriation targets decreased and (b) the area of agricultural land was underestimated.

One area of considerable conflict during the reform was to what extent the middle-size farms were to be expropriated. During the course of the reform it became clear that the Government would not touch these. The main priority became to expropriate the very big farms.[40] This explains the decrease in the number of farms to be expropriated.

2.4.5 Reform for whom and by whom?

Closely related to the question of how many farms and how much land to expropriate is the question of reform for whom and by whom. Since the reform of 1969 was initiated from above the Government had to decide on how the peasants were to participate in the reform.[41] We will comment on the question of participation in the course of discussing the question of the beneficiaries of reform (for whom). Before clarifying the issue of the beneficiaries of the reform some key characteristics of the reform need to be discussed. We will discuss the emphasis on collectivization, the implications of the objective "land-to-the-tiller" and the concept cabida (roughly translated, "fitting").

Both the 1964 and the 1969 agrarian reform laws dealt extensively with what kind of land was to be expropriated. Far less attention was given to the post- reform agrarian structure which should emerge, and the process which should take place from the pre- to the post-reform agrarian structure. This lack of attention created conflict. Development economists writing on agrarian reform frequently envisage that big estates are expropriated and divided into family farms.

This model was never considered in Peru for several reasons. One major factor was ideological. The Peruvian Left, strongly influenced by Marxism, considered a collective or cooperative organization superior to family farming. In addition to the political argument there was the common supposition, also shared by the military, namely, that there were important economies of scale in agriculture.[42] Within the Catholic church there was also a tendency for collective forms of economic organization, based on a certain hostility towards private capital. The Peruvian society, particularly during the Inca period, also had forms of collective organization which had survived in the Indian communities.

Thus there were many factors operating towards a collective form of production. Consequently both the Law and the way it was implemented gave priority to collective forms of farming. However, the actual policy contained a bias against the poor peasants who did not live on these expropriated farms. From an administrative point of view this is understandable as it was easier to remove the owner and hand over the control to the farm workers.[43]

Who were to be the beneficiaries of the reform? One important principle was "land-to-the-tiller", the slogan of many peasant uprising in Latin America. It was taken by international agencies, including the U.S. during the Kennedy administration and the Alliance for Progress. It was also one of the basic principles of the Peruvian agrarian reform. The implications of such an approach were probably never clear in Peru.[44] This principle meant that the peasants who worked on the land were also given legal title to the land, and could increase their income with the rent component. Since this component could be very high, the increase in incomes could be substantial. However, the concept of land-to-the-tiller ignored the fact that most peasants only had little land to work, since a relatively small number of large estates owned most of agricultural land. The equity objective would have required that land be transferred also to the landless and small owners, as well as to the workers on large farms, either forming new small farms or collective forms of production. The land-to-the-tiller concept is consequently not consistent with an equity objective in the Peruvian context.

Related to the land-to-the-tiller strategy was another concept, namely, cabida, which in English would mean "room for a certain number of people". It is based on the idea of an economic carrying capacity of a given area of land. The higher the predetermined average rural annual income is set, the smaller the number of families which can be settled on that area will be. The concept of cabida was used to reduce the target number of families to be benefitted from the reform, because the Government predetermined a relatively high target family income. Consequently each family would receive relatively more land. This will be discussed further in chapter 5.

It is thus possible to detect two main lines of thought in regard to the Peruvian reform. Both schools accepted collective forms of organization, but for different reasons. The first approach, henceforth called Conservative, attempted to minimize expropriation, and to maintain target incomes high (cabida). It stressed the land-to-the-tiller concept, deemphasized participation, and stressed the short-run negative effects of the Reform on production. We have already shown that expropriation targets were lowered. The second approach, henceforth called Radical, emphasized massive expropriation, was critical of the cabida concept and stressed that the reform should be carried out in a given region expropriating practically all land and integrating most peasants into the reform.

As has already been mentioned the agrarian reform was poorly defined and there were no legal constraints for expropriating properties. The law also contemplated "integrated rural settlement schemes", PIAR, which were consonant with the Radical approach. "Within each PIAR, not only estate lands but all lands are subject to land reform measures, including parcel concentration and integration."[45]

Thus conflicting interests were quickly brought to the forefront during the reform process. The attempts to steer the reform in one direction or another forced the Government to take decisions which eventually molded the reform. A few cases will illustrate its evolution.

The reform carried out on the sugar estates mainly benefitted the permanent workers. The families living outside the sugar plantations received no benefits at all. Thus at the end of 1970 out of 32 thousand workers about 8 thousand were not allowed to become members of the cooperatives set up by the Government.[46] Moreover, under the administrative set-up for the sugar estates the Government named the majority of the delegates to the Assembly of these cooperatives. The employees were divided into four groups, without regard to the size of each group's total population: field workers, factory workers, lower level administrative employees and finally, higher-level technical and administrative personnel. Each group elected the same number of representatives to the Assembly. The basic principle of one worker one vote was consequently abandoned and the possibility of the majority of the workers to participate in the decisions was heavily circumscribed by the Government.[47]

Another example will illustrate how the Conservative strategy came to prevail. In 1970-71 OSPA was actively engaged in the agrarian reform in Piura, located in the North of Peru, working closely with the zone officials (Agrarian Zone I). The concept used integrated all the peasants into different production units, and, in a longer perspective, created only cooperative production units. Small- and medium-sized farms were, in the long-run also to be incorporated into these co-operatives. The peasants participated actively during this first period with the public officials. However, this OSPA proposal in 1971 was not accepted by higher policy levels and the decision   benefitted   the permanent workers only. When subsequently the peasants were informed that the ex-propriated farms were to be adjudicated only to permanent farm workers, opposition became increasingly strong, and the military was forced to send troops to this part of the country to quell resistance to Conservative strategies.[48]

In December 1972, the conflict was made public in a document from one of the Indian communities in this region, Catacaos. The importance to the Government of the cabida concept, the lack of peasant participation, the Government concern with maintaining production levels, and the dual characteristic of Peruvian agriculture are some aspects which were touched upon by the Indian community in its political pamphlets as cited below:

> "Actually, Catacaos' previous farms are provi-
> sionally controlled by the earlier permanent wor-
> kers, known as 'the permanent workers', who also
> receive the benefits. Indirect control is carried
> out by the group of engineers working in these
> areas who also receive benefits. Ever since the
> discussions on these provisional adjudications,
> it could be anticipated that they would encourage,
> no doubt, demands that these adjudications become
> of a definite character. This would consolidate
> again the control, benefits and property of the
> land of Catacaos in the hands of a group of pea-
> sants. This group, although larger than the pre-
> vious owners, is evidently smaller in comparison
> with the total number of Cataquese peasants. Such
> a solution would not solve, on the other hand, the
> conflict of the expropriated land which is also

claimed by the Indian community. A questionable argument against the Catacaos case refers to the possibility of a 'decrease in the production' on the farms affected if they were to be adjudicated to the Indian community of Catacaos. In addition, this affirmation is based on conservative suppositions: 1) The productivity of labour in the Indian community is inferior to the one achieved by the 'permanent workers', and 2) the capitalist organization of agricultural production is more efficient than the communal organization of work. The 'permanent workers' are also comuneros and collective work has a long tradition in Catacaos, opposing the hierarchical division of work. Therefore, both suppositions are evidently ideological and abstract and are not based on reality. Another argument is based on the debated concept of cabida which gives priority to the economic value of the production rather than to the group of social values which presumably should impregnate a revolutionary Agrarian Reform."49)

In another document from February 1973 it can be seen that the Government had decided to benefit only the permanent workers and that the peasants insisted that the Government should honour the original proposal of integrating all the peasants and not only the peasants who were permanent workers.[50]

The Piura example demonstrates that attempts to integrate most of the peasants in the agrarian reform were stopped at higher levels, and that subsequently the peasants were forced to accept the principle of adjudicating land to the permanent workers. Of course, these workers did not object since their incomes would be far higher than would had been the case if they had had to share the land with more peasants. These policy decisions led to a conflict with the equity objective which can be clearly shown by using targets from the beginning of the agrarian reform and at the end of the Medium-Term Plan. In 1969 the targets were stated as benefitting 100,000 families yearly during the first five years of the reform. In 1975 the total target for the reform was 400 000 families.[51]

2.5   TOWARDS A REDEFINITION OF DEVELOPMENT OBJECTIVES

Equity had priority in the development strategy of the military government as it was outlined in the first Long Run Development Strategy, the Medium-Term Plans, 1971-75, and the speeches of the military. In order to accomplish these objectives a series of reforms and economic policies were designed and implemented rapidly. Probably the most important of these was the agrarian reform. In this chapter we have shown that it was not clearly defined and thoroughly planned at the outset. As an example of this, during the first nine months of the Government, different agrarian reform proposals were debated within government circles. When the Law was passed in June 1969 it was far more radical than that of the Belaúnde regime. It was a key decision of the military government towards fullfilling their promise of equity.

Moreover, already during its first month it became clear that the Government truly intended to implement the Law. This was the second crucial test of the Government's intentions. However, the extent to which the Government intended to guarantee its policies of equity was uncertain.

On the one hand the average rural income was very low, and to alter this, incomes and/or investments would have to increase in the agricultural sector relative to the non-agricultural sectors. On the other hand, one tenet of the agrarian reform was that agriculture should finance industrial growth. These two objectives of the reform were of course difficult to reconcile, and the Government never made it clear how it could be done.

There were other conflicting issues in the reform which were not decided on before the Law was passed. Therefore, a series of important decisions during its implementation gave the reform its definite character. Towards 1973 it was becoming increasingly clear that the reform was to be rather Conservative (in relation to the equity objective) and key target variables such as the area and the number of farms to be expropriated, and the number of families to be benefitted, were all reduced over time.

In 1975 president Velasco was replaced by general Maldonado, and the trend towards deemphasizing the equity objective was continued. Economic problems were mounting and successively more attention was given to stability measures. In the next chapter we will turn our attention to the economic results of the military Government both with respect to overall growth and income redistribution.

1. For a discussion of planning Griffin-Enos (1970), chapter 3, p. 32; Meier (1976), chapter XII.

2. Kilty (1967), p. 35.

3. Kilty (1967); de las Casas Moya (1978), chapter 2. The National Planning Institute was established in 1962.

4. Kilty (1967), p. 35.

5. Lowenthal (1975), pp. 24-31; Kilty (1967), p. 64.

6. Lowenthal (1975), pp. 23-24.

7. Ibid. p. 26.

8. Kilty (1967), p. 50.

9. Astiz (1969), p. 113.

10. Ibid. p. 114.

11. Kilty (1967), p. 78.

12. INP (1967), p. II-209. For a discussion on the number of rural families see the Appendix to chapter 5. We use Lipton's definition of an agrarian reform, "Land reform (agrarian reform, reforma agraria) comprises (1) compulsory take-over of land, usually (a) by the State, (b) from the biggest land owners, and (c) with partial compensation; and (2) the farming of that land in such a way as to spread the benefits of the man-land relationship more widely than before the take-over. The State may give, sell or rent such land for private cultivation in smaller units than hitherto (distributivist reform); or the land may be jointly farmed and its usufruct shared through co-operative, collective or State farming (collectivist reform).", in Lehman (1974), p. 270.

13. See chapter 5.

14. See also Webb (1977), chapter 6.

15. Cited from Webb and Figueroa (1975), p. 121 (my translation); Lowenthal (1975), chapter 1.

16. INP (1968), chapter 1. This document does not have numbered pages.

17. INP (1968), chapter 3. My translation. This development strategy is strongly influenced by the publications and policies of the UN Economic Commission for Latin America (ECLA and in Spanish CEPAL). See Lowenthal (1975), p. 25. See also Delgado (1965), pp. 29-53.

18. INP (1968), chapter 3.

19. INP (1971) Vol. I, p. 14. My translation.

20. Ibidem.

21. INP (1971) Vol II, p. 16. My translation.

22. Thorp and Bertram (1978), p. 301.

23. Fitzgerald (1976), p. 36.

24. Thorp and Bertram (1978), pp. 300-307; Fitzgerald (1976). For a discussion of workers' self-management see for example Knight in Lowenthal (1975), chapter 9.

25. INP (1975:2), pp. 27-28.

26. "This man was closely linked to the traditional right. Son of a major-general, who governed twice during this century to the approval of the oligarchy; owner of coastal land and industries...". My translation. Pease (1977), p. 61. See also Valderrama (1976), p. 46-150 on the prelude to the new law.

27. Horton gives a short and good history of the agrarian reform. Horton (1974), pp. 32-57. See also Lowenthal (1975), pp. 36-41.

28. "...he (Benavides) declared that uncultivated land would be affected by the agrarian reform." Pease (1977), p. 68.

29. Caballero (1975:1), p. 43.

30. Horton (1974), p. 49.

31. Private communication of an OSPA official in March 1976.

32. During field trips 1969-71 agrarian reform officials in some areas were expropriating land slowly. These were subsequently replaced.

33. Mejía (1978), p. 179. My translation.

34. Dorner (1972), p. 16. See also pp. 126-131 in the same work. Cf. Lipton (1977), chapter 4.

35. Ellman (1979), chapter 4.

36. See note 17.

37. Our underlining. Decreto Ley (1969), p. 1. English translation taken from Mann and Huerta (1969), p. 1. It is peculiar that in subsequent editions of the law this passage is not included.

38. INP (1971) Vol. II, p. 81.

39. Ministerio de Agricultura (1976:1), pp. 66-67.

40. The medium-size farmers became very active to protect their interests. See for example Pease (1977), p. 68 and pp. 194-203.

41. Griffin has stated that "It is becoming more and more widely recognised that rural development, to be successful, must be not only for the people concerned but also by them." ILO (1977), p. 34. He also refers to a study of Joost Kuitenbrouwer, Premises and implications of a unified approach to development analysis and planning. Kuitenbrouwer served as a UN expert in Peru at the time of the agrarian reform and actively advocated the need for peasant participation which the Government was lukewarm about.

42. In general economists do not accept the idea of economies of scale in agriculture in low-income countries. "While the idea of an optimal farm size is extremely popular, it is simply inconsistent with the vast bulk of empirical evidence, which shows constant returns to scale considering inputs actually used as well as greater utilization of available land as farm size diminishes." Cline in Frank and Webb (1977), p. 284. Lipton in Lehman ed (1974), pp. 288-295. On the experiences of socialist countries see Ellman (1979), chapter 4. Horton (1970) writing on Peru suggests that the relevant approach should be "economies of size". "In this case the objective of analysis is to determine the size of farm which minimizes average costs or maximizes productivity." p. 55. On p. 57 he argues that small farms are more efficient. See also chapter 4.

43. Horton has reported that peasants in the Sierra resented pressures to form collective enterprises. Horton (1976), pp. 18-19. See also Guillet (1979), pp. 175-183. See chapter 5 for data on how land was adjudicated.

44. The law gives priority to the permanent workers on the estates which were expropriated. See also Lehman (1978), pp. 343-344. Already in 1970 officials in the Ministry of Agriculture were discussing how to tackle the problem of the majority of peasants. In Peru the slogan was, "La tierra para quien la trabaja", during the reform. See also Figueroa (1977), p. 161.

45. Horton (1976), pp. 228-229. See also 228-233. Valderrama (1976), pp. 29-30 and 55; Giles (1972) Matos Mar (1976), p. 246.

46. Roca (1975), p. Anexo No 29. Also based on visits to the sugar estates in 1969-70 and contacts with researchers from the Catholic University.

47. Roca (1975), pp. 26-29; Guillet (1979), p. 196-200.

48. Internal document of OSPA 1971. Also based on discussions with Ministry of Agriculture officials in 1971, 1976 and 1977.

49. Catacaos (1972), p. 2. My translation.

50. Catacaos (1973). Many of the permanent workers belonged to the Ca-
    tacaos community.

51. FAO (1969), p. v. and Ministerio de Agricultura (1976:1), pp. 66-67.

3
Overall Development of Peru 1950–75

3.1 INTRODUCTION

In this chapter we will investigate to what degree the military junta was successful in implementing its overall
macro-economic objectives of improving the income distribution and of increasing the rate of economic growth. These
were, as abovementioned, the central development objectives
of the junta. Consequently, this chapter purports to answer
the following questions:

Firstly, has there been an increase in the rate of growth
in the economy after 1968? Secondly, has there been a significant improvement in the distribution of income, after
1968? Thirdly, to what extent have government policies been
responsible for these changes?

A fourth question is related to the debate on the equity-
cum-growth strategy. One of the key reforms advocated to
improve the income distribution has been an agrarian reform,
and we will also in this chapter analyse how an agrarian reform could affect the overall distribution of income in the
economy.[1]

3.2 OUTPUT PERFORMANCE 1950-75

3.2.1 Development trend 1950-68

National accounts statistics of some reliability did not become available until 1968 in Peru, and since then the Central
Bank of Peru has published such data. The Central Bank has
thus far published two studies of national account figures.
The first one covered the period 1950-67 and the subsequent

one, 1960-74.[2] There are some minor differences in these
two sets, but in general these sets of data are coherent
and represent a major improvement upon previously available
macroeconomic statistics. Unfortunately, in the first set,
the data are not given yearly. In addition, the Bank and the
National Planning Institute (INP) have released figures on
the Peruvian economy. Using this information, it is possible
to reconstruct roughly the performance of the Peruvian economy year by year since 1960 for some macroeconomic variables.

According to these figures, primarily relying on the Central
Bank data, the rate of economic growth in Peru was rather
impressive in the period preceeding the military junta. Between 1950 and 1968 the economy grew at 5.4% per year. (for
details see Table 3.1).

Table 3.1   Growth pattern and structure of the Peruvian
            economy 1950-75   (constant 1970 prices)

Sectors	Annual rates of growth/period			Structure (% of GDP)			
	1968/1950	1975/1968	1975/1950	1950	1960	1968	1975
Agriculture	3.4	3.3	3.4	20.4	18.5	14.6	12.7
Fishing	17.4	-11.0	8.5	0.4	1.4	2.6	0.7
Mining	6.9	-0.1	4.9	6.8	10.4	8.8	6.0
Manufacturing	6.5	7.1	7.3	16.7	20.0	23.6	26.2
Construction	2.5	12.6	5.3	6.3	5.0	3.8	6.1
Total "Produc- tive" Sectors	5.8	5.0	5.6	51.3	56.1	54.5	52.8
Others	5.0	6.0	5.3	48.7	43.9	45.5	47.2
GDP	5.4	5.5	5.4	100.0	100.0	100.0	100.0

Source: Brundenius (1976:2), p. 3.

During this period, i.e. 1950-1968, the rate of economic

growth differed between economic sectors. The most outstanding feature is the rapid growth of the manufacturing sector, increasing its share in GDP from 17 to 24 percent, while the agricultural sector share declined from 20 to 15 percent.*)

The rate of growth in the population was about 2.2% 1940-61 and increased to about 2.9% in the period 1961-72. Consequently, there should have been a large increase in per capita GDP since the end of World War II.[3]

Most scholars on Peru agree that the rapid increase in exports explains best this high rate of economic growth. Writing on the long-run development of Peru, 1890-1977, Thorp and Bertram arrived at the conclusion, "Peru's post-colonial economic history can be visualized as a series of major export cycles, and it will become apparent as we proceed that the export sectors have been central to the process of economic change in Peru even in the 1970s."[4] Studies focusing only on the Post World War II period also stress the importance of the export sectors. An Iowa mission study in 1967, with the assistance of Thorbecke, came to the conclusion: "...the growth of the Peruvian economy was export-led contributing to a relatively high rate of growth of income, a strong balance of payments and price stability."[5]

Fitzgerald has stated this in the following way:
> "Peru has an export-based dual economy: the dynamic factor in the modern sector is primary-export production, which provides the surplus from which the demand for modern industry and service sector is derived, accounting for the bulk of output, but only including a minority of the workforce."[6]

The close relationship between gross domestic product and exports is clearly seen in Figure 3.1. There is also a relationship, albeit much weaker, between the rates of growth of

---

*) For the poor performance of fishing during the military government see Thorp and Bertram (1978), chapter 12.2.

Figure 3.1   Peruvian exports and Gross Domestic Product 1950-1977

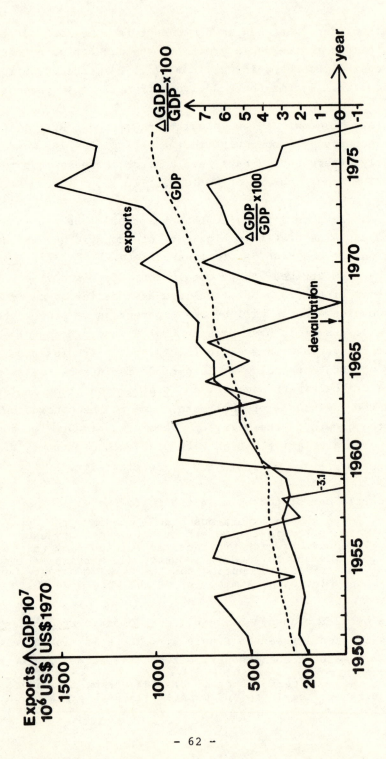

Sources: BCR (1968), p. 45; BCR (1976), p. 43; Memoria (1977), p. 25;
           Alberts-Brundenius (1979)

exports and of domestic product.[7]

Another important factor in explaining this growth was that
gross investment as a percentage of GDP, was quite high during this period (above 20 percent) as can be seen from
Table 3.2.

Table 3.2   Gross investments as percentage of Gross
            Domestic Product

Year	Investments (Percent of GDP)
1950	17.2
1955	22.5
1960	21.6
61	22.3
62	22.8
63	20.4
64	18.7
1965	18.6
66	20.1
67	19.8
68	13.9
69	13.3
1970	12.9
71	15.0
72	14.2
73	15.7
74	18.9
1975	19.7
76	17.8
77	15.1
78	13.6

Sources: BCR (1968), pp. 18 and 20; BCR (2976), pp. 20
         and 22; CIEPA (1979), pp. 47 and 52.

In summary, the period 1950-68 was rather good economically, although some difficulties were becoming evident. In
particular, there was a lack of investments in the export
sector which meant that the possibilities for a continuation of this export-led growth were diminishing. The above
cited Iowa macroeconomic projections for 1967-72 stated
that: "Under optimistic conditions, export earnings are expected to grow at a rate of 4% per year."[8] Consequently,
they concluded that, on a per capita basis, the economy
would stagnate during the 1967-72 period. Thorp and Bertram concluded that, "The years 1967 and 1968 brought the
Peruvian economy to a turning point. The process of economic growth was losing momentum;...
At the centre of the emerging crisis lay the failing dyna-
mism of the export sectors."[9] One of the main reasons was
the lack of investments in the export sector.[10] Therefore,
the military junta in 1968 faced the prospect of a lower
rate of economic growth, while pronouncing itself in favour
of increasing growth rates.

3.2.2 The first phase of the military junta 1968-75

The devaluation of the Sol in 1967 and the mounting economic difficulties in 1968 were probably some of the causes
for the military takeover in October 1968. One of the first
moves by the military government was to impose austere economic policies which subsequently, in 1969, were followed
by expansionary policies.[11]

As was mentioned above the medium-term economic prospects
were rather poor. In view of this it seems overly optimistic that the 1971-75 plan growth target was 7.5%.[12] The
figure appears absurd, if one considers all the reforms
·which the Government intended to carry out simultaneously.[13]

The explanation to the optimistic growth rate figures can probably be found in the development of the Peruvian economy since the coup in 1968 on the one hand, and the completion of the plans in late 1970 on the other hand. The yearly GDP growth rates increased from 0.0% in 1968 to 7.3% in 1970, and such a growth acceleration probably caused expectations of the military, and also many planning officials, to become too optimistic about the future. [14)]

The rate of economic growth in the period 1971-75 was 5.2% per year, clearly below the planned figure of 7.5%. In light of the proposed targets economic performance was failing. However, considering the foreseeable economic difficulties, economic performance was quite successful. The rate of economic growth was about the same in the period 1968-75 as the Post World War II period since 1950. (Cf. Table 3.1).

But how can we reconcile the relatively high rate of economic growth observed in the period 1968-75 with the claims that the Peruvian economy was moving towards stagnation? We would claim that stagnation was postponed mainly because of exogenous factors such as the improvement in the commodity terms-of-trade, and because of deliberate economic policies. These policies, however, caused serious disequilibria, and, when the full effects of the short-run economic policies worked themselves through the economic system a depression was developing. We will briefly comment on the following key variables in this respect: foreign trade, investments and public finances. We will thereafter treat economic performance of the Peruvian economy after 1975 to test the repercussions from earlier policies.

The dependence on the export sector for growth was increased during the military junta, because the development strategy which was implemented stressed the import substitution policies. They in turn, contributed to a continuation of a lack of investments in the export sector, and a re-allocation of investments to the manufacturing industry for domestic consumption. This industry was heavily dependent on imported goods, not only on capital goods, but also on raw material and on semi-elaborated inputs.[15] Also, the low growth of the agricultural sector forced the government to increase imports of food.[16] The evolution of key foreign trade variables has been summarized as follows,

> "Export earnings at current prices increased
> 71 percent between 1969 and 1974, but this
> increase was made possible only by the improve-
> ment. of world commodity prices; over the
> same period the quantum index of exports sup-
> ply actually dropped by 17 percent, while from
> 1969 to 1975 the fall was no less than 27 per
> cent. When the improvement in Peru's terms of
> trade was reversed in 1972, the continuing stag-
> nation of export production clearly spelt trouble.
> In 1975 export earnings fell while the rapid
> growth of import requirements continued."[17]

The other key variable was investments. In 1967 the rate of investments was about 20 percent dropping to about 14 percent in 1968, and remained at this level until 1973. Since then it increased until 1976 when it fell again to 14 per cent in 1978. Therefore, the possibilities to attain a higher sustained rate of economic growth were severely affected. For details see Table 3.2. The Government was not passive during this unfavourable development of investments. One of the objectives of the Peruvian government was to increase the role of the state sector. Thus while the share of the private sector in total gross capital formation was over 80 per cent in the 50's, its share started to decline in the middle of the 60's. By 1975 the public sector contribution was about equal to that of the private sector.[18]

This rapid increase in both the share and the level of public sector investment needed financing. Part of it was financed domestically and part of it through foreign loans.
Turning to the first source, there were attempts to increase taxes though not enough.In general there was a lack
of effective fiscal measures to increase taxes to finance
an increasing public sector share in investments. This together with the increase in spending on current account
were building up inflationary pressures.[19] Thus, while in
1970 the deficit, defined as the difference between central
government revenues and expenditures, was about 8% of total
revenues, by 1972 it had risen to over 20% and in 1975 to
35% and in 1977 to over 50%.[20]

The equity-cum-growth strategy made it absolutely indispensable to design a tax system which would have imposed the
tax burden on the rich. To what extent this was possible in
the Peruvian context and the proposed mixed economy strategy
is debatable. The capital owners would probably have reduced
investments further which would have necessitated even more
drastic measures by the junta. In the end the government
chose not to, or did not succeed to, increase tax revenues
to a level compatible with expenditures. Deficit financing
was increasingly relied upon, and inflationary pressures did
thus increase. The junta attempted to combat this by both
subsidies and price controls.[21]

In order to finance imports the Government also had to rely
on foreign borrowing. The results were that the foreign debt,
amortization and interest payments increased rapidly. After
1968 both the outstanding debt and debt repayments increased
very rapidly as can be seen from Table 3.3.

Table 3.3   Foreign debt of public sector (Million US dollars)

	(1) Debt repayments (Interests plus amortizations)	(2) Outstanding Debt End of the year	(3) Exports	(4) 1:3=4 percent	(5) 2:3=5 percent
1950	2	87	194	1.0	44.8
1955	12	152	271	4.4	56.1
1960	47	159	433	10.9	36.7
1965	49	379	667	7.3	56.8
66	87	533	764	11.4	69.8
67	--	-	757	-	-
68	202	713	866	23.3	82.3
69	142	854	866	16.4	98.6
1970	173	911	1 048	16.5	86.9
71	215	988	893	24.1	110.6
72	219	1 121	944	23.2	118.8
73	433	1 491	1 050	41.2	142.0
74	456	2 182	1 534	29.7	142.2
1975	474	3 066	1 315	36.0	233.2
1976	533	3 641	1 281	41.6	284.2
77	618*	4 252*	1 582	39.1	268.8

Sources: Columns 1 and 2: Suárez and Tovar (1967), Tables II and
         XI in Appendix; BCR, Memoria, various years
         Column 3: Boletín del BCR, January 1979, p. 28
*) Preliminary figures.

Since the volume of exports could not increase substantially,
due to lack of investment, export financing could only be
used during a few years. It was becoming increasingly difficult for the Government to borrow on the international markets, despite its growing need. The cumulative effects of a
fall of world market prices of major Peruvian export goods
and increasing difficulties to borrow on the international
finance markets set the depression in motion.[22] Inflationary pressures had been attenuated by a set of policies which

eventually became impossible to maintain. Such policies included the subsidies of imported agricultural goods, general price controls, lack of equilibrium in the exchange rate etc.[23]

This review of some key variables suggests that sooner or later the economy was to enter stagnation, or a serious depression. The Peruvian planners, however, working on the 1975-78 Plan apparently had not taken the economic constraints seriously and projected an aggregate growth rate of 6.5% yearly.[24]

The final results became painfully evident in the 1976-78 period when inflation accelerated to about 60% and GDP growth rates became negative.[25] See Table 3.4.

Table 3.4   Economic growth and inflation 1974-78

	Rates of growth (percent)				
	1974	1975	1976	1977	1978
Gross domestic product	6.9	3.3	3.0	-1.2	-1.8
Agriculture	2.3	1.0	3.3	0.0	-3.0
Inflation	17	24	33	38	58

Sources: BCR Memoria (1980), pp. 127 and 135.

These short notes on the economic performance during the first phase of the military junta indicate that the relatively good economic performance was mainly a consequence of favourable world market prices for Peruvian export goods and to a lesser extent of deliberate economic policies of the military junta. These policies had the effect of reactivating the economy after 1968, but were not sufficient to create the conditions for continuous growth. In fact their primary positive effects seem to have been of a short-run nature, and with negative effects in a longer perspective.

The very favourable development 1968-70 probably contributed to creating an atmosphere of undue optimism within the
junta, such that the necessary steps towards the implementation of the junta's strategy and objectives were never
taken. As the economic difficulties grew at an accelerated
pace, the junta was incapable of rectifying its course. Instead of designing a new set of policies to implement its
long-run objectives, the junta chose to relax its previous
objectives. This was never clearly stated, and the junta
propaganda was still emphasizing the "Peruvian model".

Already in the first phase 1968-75 the equity objective was
successively loosing in priority. In the second phase, as
of 1975, economic policies were increasingly designed to re-
establish equilibrium, with little, if any attention, given
to equity considerations.

3.2.3 A comparison of the two periods

The overall rate of economic growth in the two periods (1950-
1968 and 1968-75) was quite similar. One of the more important differences is that there was a significant drop in the
level of investments, something which jeopardized future
growth. Moreover, the rapid increase in the foreign debt, and
the consequent increase in foreign debt services also tended
to become a bottleneck for growth. In addition, the public
sector expanded rapidly its sphere of influence over the economy during this period, including the nationalization of
banks, copper mines, and the fishing industry. The public
sector rapidly increased its share in capital formation, but
never managed to increase its tax revenue to levels compatible with its economic activities.

In summary, the economic performance in the period 1968-75

was a failure with respect to development objectives because the growth rate did not reach the planned figure,
and the drop in investments constituted a serious obstacle
for future growth.

But, if the economic performance is judged against the stagnating tendencies of the Peruvian economy, the period 1968-
75 was a partial success in that the military junta managed
to maintain a high rate of economic growth, while simultaneously carrying out many structural reforms of which the
agrarian reform was probably the most important one.

3.2.4 Agriculture - continuation of a problem

We have thus far in this chapter not commented on the agricultural development during the whole period considered,
1950-78. As can be seen from Tables 3.1 and 3.4, agriculture has rapidly lost in importance in the Peruvian economy,
as its share in GDP dropped from over 20 percent in 1950 to
about 13 percent in 1975. This process continued after 1975.

It should be noted that elasticity of demand for food with
respect to income is high in Peru and demand projections at
moderate income growth rates of 4-5% suggest that food demand will grow at approximately the same rate, because in
addition to the population growth of about 3% the demand derived from increased incomes has to be added.[26] This high
elasticity of demand and the relatively high population
growth implies that agricultural sector growth at constant
relative prices ought to be significantly above that of population in order to meet demand. The rapid Post-War economic growth and the low rates of agricultural growth suggest
that agricultural exports must have declined and/or agricul-

tural imports grew. In chapter 1 we showed that food imports grew very fast and total agricultural exports grew
only slowly.

The structural dependency on world markets of Peru commented on earlier in this chapter implies that the agricultural sector became increasingly a bottleneck in Peruvian development. The agricultural problem was even more
serious if income redistribution takes place, because the
elasticity of demand for food with respect to income is
higher among lower income strata than for upper income
strata. The net effect on demand for food of economic redistribution, for a given income level, would be an increase in aggregate demand. In chapter 6 we will return
to the question of agricultural production.

We will now turn our attention to the second central development objective of the junta, namely, income redistribution.

3.3   TRENDS IN INCOME DISTRIBUTION

3.3.1 Overall distribution

Although there are no systematic studies on the distribution of income prior to 1961 in Peru, some estimates and
hypotheses have been put forward, usually using the 1961
census. For example, both Thorp and Quijano have claimed
that in spite of the very rapid economic growth, income
distribution deteriorated. While Thorp has suggested the
possibility of an absolute decline in real incomes for important groups, Quijano has even claimed a general reduction in the standard of living.[27] Webb has estimated the
trend in real incomes for the period 1950-66, and his data

shows that although the distribution in income has become
more unequal, data do not indicate an absolute decline.[28]

The possibility of a decline in absolute income levels of
the poor has provoked debate in the general discussion on
growth and distribution. There are basically two hypotheses
which predominate.

The first relates to the U-hypothesis and can be stated as
follows: As average per capita income grows, the income
shares of the poorer groups first decline and subsequently
increase. Kuznets' work on the time series on developed capitalist economies provides empirical evidence of this.[29]
Cross-country studies also indicate that this is the case.[30]
In summary, capitalist development is characterized not only by great inequalities but also by growing inequalities
during phases of low levels of development.[31]

A much stronger hypothesis has been set forth, and which
follows from the U-shaped hypothesis, namely, that the absolute income levels of the poorer strata decline during
certain phases of development implying even greater inequalities. This possibility has been subject to a great deal
of controversy. In 1973 Adelman and Morris claimed that,

> "...development is accompanied by an absolute as
> well as a relative decline in the average in-
> come of the very poor. Indeed, an initial spurt
> of dualistic growth may cause such a decline
> for as much as 60 percent of the population.
> The absolute position of the poorest 40 per-
> cent apparently continues to worsen as coun-
> tries move toward less dualistic growth pat-
> terns unless major efforts are made to improve
> and expand human resources".32)

This conclusion is again reaffirmed in the Adelman and Robinson study of 1978.[33]

Ahluwalia has repeatedly criticized this statement and Cline

in his survey article is also critical.[34] At this point
it is not possible to enter into a lengthy discussion of
these issues, but scrutinizing the data, and the methods
used, it seems that capitalist development does not preclude the possibility that during some phase of a growth
process, there may be an absolute decline in income levels
of the poorer strata. Even though this stronger hypothesis
is subject to heated debate the weaker one, viz. that the
income inequalities grow during certain phases of development has not been refuted, and most empirical work, either
using time series or cross sectional data, have produced
evidence of this characteristic of capitalist development.

Unfortunately there are not time series data on the income
distribution in Peru which would enable us to get a picture
of its development in 1950-68 and earlier and to compare it
with the period, 1968-75. There have been some studies, however, which shed light on the probable development of income distribution. After having established the tendencies
in overall income distribution, we will focus on the relationship between the agricultural/rural versus urban sectors.
We will investigate the contrasts in income distribution
within the rural sector as well as between sectors.[35] We
will then proceed to investigate to what extent the overall income distribution in Peru could be affected by income
redistribution programmes within the agricultural sector.
Lipton, has argued that the most important bias in development is not the vertical income differences, but rather the
great difference in the horizontal income distribution.[36]
Peruvian data will enable us to analyse this general problem.

It was not until the beginning of the sixties, after the publication of census data, that it became possible to make macroeconomic estimates on the income distribution in Peru. There
have been several estimates since then which have been used

in international comparisons, and before presenting any data, a short review of these estimates is useful so as to enable the reader to follow the evolution of data in this field. Brady (1968) and García (1969) were the first to publish data on the Peruvian income distribution. The García estimates were based on his earlier work at the Planning Institute (INP) on income distribution.[37] The INP released some of these estimates, and these have also been used in the discussions on Peru. Some of these are, for example, Adelman and Morris (1973) using the INP data and Paukert (1973) using the data of the above mentioned authors.[38]

It was not until the middle of the 70's that the systematic studies of Webb provided a set of significantly improved data on the Peruvian income distribution in 1961. The Webb estimate, Table 3.5, reveals a very high degree of concentration of income in Peru.

Table 3.5   Distribution of personal income in Peru
             by Quintiles in 1961

Income groups (Quintiles)	Personal Income (Percent of total)
0 - 20	2.5
20 - 40	5.5
40 - 60	10.2
60 - 80	17.4
80 - 100	64.4

Source: Webb (1977), p. 6. Also in Webb-Figueroa
        (1977), p. 29

These data on the income distribution in Peru in 1961 will serve as a reference point for comparisons with the situation in subsequent years.

Using the data in the Population Census 1972, Brundenius has estimated the income distribution in 1972.[39] The 1961 data are the Webb estimates, excluding property income. See Table 3.6.

Table 3.6   Distribution of personal income, excluding property income in Peru 1961 and 1972, by Quintiles

| Income groups (Quintiles) | Personal income (Percent of total) | | Difference |
	(1) 1961	(2) 1972	(3) 3=2-1
0 - 20	3.0	2.5	-0.5
20 - 40	7.0	6.5	-0.5
40 - 60	13.0	12.5	-0.5
60 - 80	21.5	20.5	-1.0
80 - 100	55.5	58.0	+2.5
	100.0	100.0	0.0

Source: Brundenius (1976:2), p. 9.

Another study by Amat y León and León provides important information on the distribution of family incomes in Peru 1971/ 1972. It is based on the national food consumption survey, ENCA, carried out in Peru from August 1971 to August 1972.[40,41]

Table 3.7   Distribution of family income in 1971/72 by Quintiles

Income groups (Quintiles)	Family income (Percent of total)
0 - 20	1.6
20 - 40	5.2
40 - 60	10.7
60 - 80	21.0
80 - 100	61.5
	100.0

Source: See Appendix to this chapter

These data, Tables 3.5-3.7, on the Peruvian income distribution unequivocally show its regressive nature. But what
can be said about its evolution over time? Table 3.6 indicates that there has been a reduction in the income share
of all groups, except that the richer 20% gained by a percentage of 2.5. If we compare Tables 3.5 and 3.7 the bottom
40% lost in their share, while the middle 40% gained and
the top 20% lost. How can these differences be reconciled?
While Table 3.6 should only include salaries and wages,
Tables 3.5 and 3.7 should include profits and rents, and
hence, it could be argued that there has been a redistribution of property income. Amat y León and León have suggested that they have underestimated such incomes, and if
so, the top income bracket(s) should be revised upwards.[42]
Taking all these pieces of information together it is clear
that at least the 40% poorer decreased their share in the
income distribution.

As was mentioned before, the debate on distribution and growth
has also involved the question, whether there has been an absolute decline in the real income of the poor in the developing countries. The estimates by Brundenius indicate that
all income strata have increased their average annual incomes, although the richer obviously have done so more rapidly. This follows from the fact that their share in total
income has increased, according to him.

If, we instead use the figures in Table 3.7, the income share
of the 20 percent poorer was as low as 1.6 percent in 1972
and 2.5 percent in 1961 (Table 3.5). In this group there
would have been a drop in their real incomes from 1961 to
1972 (about 25 percent).

But there are two problems which have to be faced when comparing these sets of estimates. One is the quality of statistics
and estimation procedures used. The other one is that Webb/

Brundenius base their estimates on income earners while Amat y León and León on households.

With respect to the statistical problem, both the Webb and Brundenius studies faced the central difficulty in estimating incomes, namely, that data on incomes in agriculture were either lacking or of poor quality. Webb attempted to overcome this difficulty by using secondary sources, while Brundenius opted for National Accounts data. The assumptions made by him, using National Accounts figures, which are of low quality and ultimately rely on production statistics, all imply that the Brundenius income estimates of the poor allow for a wide margin of error. One of these sources of error, the value and volume of agricultural production will be discussed in chapter 6, where it will be shown that there are good reasons to suspect that official data on agricultural production are grossly overestimated. This means that Brundenius data on income share of the poorer should be revised downwards for 1972.

Turning to the second problem, comparability, it is of course an advance that a national household study has been carried out. As Kuznets has stated it:

> "Distribution among individual recipients are highly valuable as constituent components, but they cannot substitute for distribution among consuming units, i.e., units which respond to and are affected by changes in the production system that constitute economic growth."43)

Since household incomes usually show less inequality than data from individual recipient distributions, this would tend to indicate that the personal income distribution data as estimated by Brundenius should have shown greater inequality and a fortiori because property incomes were excluded.44)
Since the Brundenius data show less inequality it seems reasonable to assume that his 1972 figures overestimate the income shares of the poorer strata.

In summary it can be argued that the income distribution in Peru is skewed, and that the poorer strata have received a declining share in the income. The stronger hypothesis of an absolute decline in their incomes cannot be rejected. There are pieces of evidence which indicate that there has been an absolute decline in their incomes, but that data does not permit more than a tentative conclusion.

In chapter 2 we showed that the income redistribution objective had increasingly become a priority development objective. The information on the evolution of the income.distribution in Peru from 1961 to 1972 shows a probable increase in the concentration of incomes. At least up to 1972 the government(s) failed to alter the prevailing distribution of income. Since there are no estimates on the distribution of income since 1972, we will have to rely on sources which provide partial information.

Brundenius using data on wages and salaries claims: "There are thus [in 1976] clear indicators that the real income for the majority of the labour force has been declining since 1973" [45] The observed decline in the period 1973-76 was continued in 1977. Another indicator, the real legal minimum wage rate for Lima decreased from 100 in 1970 to 95 in 1975 and to 57 in 1978. [46]

Figueroa has estimated the income distribution effects of the reforms of the military junta. He used the comparative statics method and arrived at the conclusion that only 3-4 percent of the national income was redistributed. The recipients, 23 percent, belong to the richer income strata. Consequently, the main effect of this income redistribution would be within the 25 percent richer strata, leaving the 75 percent poorer with little if any direct benefits of the reforms. [47]

We will now turn to a methodological question which is important. It could be argued that the reforms of the military junta as of 1968 will in the long-run produce equity, and hence, the observed trend in income distribution cannot be used to infer that this development will continue. Figueroa's estimates are therefore, particularly important because he attempts to estimate the potential effects of the structural changes in the economy on the distribution of income. Although his estimates may not be very precise they do indicate orders of magnitude.

A few words on the outline of this study may again help the reader appreciate the way we have approached the problem. The empirical data we have presented thus far give a partial indication of what has happened in the Peruvian economy with respect to growth and distribution. We will now show that the majority of the poor are located in the agricultural sector and that in order to achieve a substantial improvement in the overall income distribution massive transfers were required for this sector. It would not have been enough to redistribute incomes within the agricultural sector, i.e. vertical transfers. Transfers from the rest of the economy to the agricultural sector, horizontal transfers, were also needed.

In chapter 5 we will turn our attention to the agricultural/rural sector and show that only a minority of its population benefitted from the agrarian reform. In chapter 6 we will show that the agricultural sector has stagnated, even more than official figures indicate, and that the economic policies have discriminated against the agricultural/rural sector.

3.3.2 Agriculture - continuation of a problem

From the preceeding discussion, a salient feature of Peruvian development has been the extreme and growing concentration of incomes. Rearranging data into urban and rural
household incomes as in Table 3.8, shows also the very uneven distribution of income between the rural and urban
sectors and the predominance of Lima.

Table 3.8   Household income distribution 1971/72 urban
             and rural sectors   (current Soles)

	Average Household income (Soles per month)	Families (Percent)	Income (Percent)
Urban	7 300	46	73
Rural	2 200	54	27
Peru	4 500	100	100
Lima	9 900	20	44

Source: Amat y León and León (1977), Tables II.4 and II.5

There was a general tendency for average income to increase
with the size of cities, and we also found that Coastal incomes were higher than Sierra incomes. There was also a tendency for Selva incomes to be higher than corresponding Si
erra incomes. Another noteworthy aspect of this regional
distribution was that rural and urban incomes, excluding
Lima, are higher in the Centro Region.[48] Curiously enough,
the Selva region seems to be relatively more developed than
the Sierra.[49] We will return to this phenomenon when reviewing agricultural growth performance.

Several development economists claim that in developing
countries rural incomes are less unequally distributed in
relation to urban incomes.[50] Therefore, a surprising re-

sult in Peru is that the income distribution in the rural sector is more skewed than that in the urban sector. Above we noted (Table 3.8) that the average rural income was significantly lower than the urban ones, and in Figure 3.2 the rural incomes proved to be more unevenly distributed than urban ones.

Figure 3.2   <u>Lorenz curve of urban and rural family incomes</u>
            <u>1971/72</u>

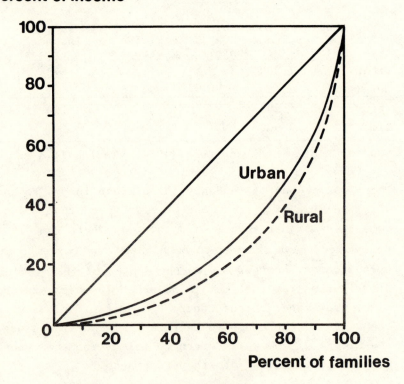

Percent of income

Ginicoefficient : Urban 0.48
              Rural 0.57
              Peru   0.59

Source: See Appendix

The very uneven distribution of incomes within the agricultural/rural sector indicates that the impact of a redistribution programme within the sector could have been substantial. It is also true that there is a very significant gap between urban and rural incomes, and implementing equity objectives requires not only vertical redistribution (within sectors), but also horizontal transfers(between sectors).[51]

In chapter 6, we will return to the question of the low rural income, and show that the most important reason for this is that agricultural production has stagnated. Data on the distribution of income between the rural and urban areas based on a random sample, are consistent with our agricultural production data which we have estimated from three agricultural censi in Peru and which show significantly lower volumes of output than the official data.

These data on the distribution of income within the rural sector may perhaps seem strange, because the agrarian reform should have had some impact on the distribution of income. We will argue in chapter 5 that only a smaller part of the rural population was benefitted by the agrarian reform, and hence, the post agrarian reform income distribution, albeit modified, remained almost as skewed as before.

3.4   SUMMARY

In this chapter we have investigated the overall tendencies in the Peruvian economy with respect to two variables, namely growth and income distribution. Since 1950 up to the coup in 1968, the overall economic performance was quite good. Towards the end of the sixties there were tendencies for the economy to experience a slower rate of growth, basically because of lack of investments in the export sector which had been the main motor for Peruvian economic growth.

It was suggested that the military government was overly
optimistic about the possibilities to increase the rate of
growth of the economy. However, the growth rate was maintained throughout 1975. We have shown that in part this was
more a result of rising world market prices for exports rather than a consequence of deliberate economic policies.
Moreover, economic policies tended to have negative repercussions on future growth and stability. The consequences
of government economic policies were lack of investment, a
rapid increase in foreign debt, and an incapacity to increase taxation sufficiently to meet development objectives.
Consequently, the economic performance after 1975 was de-
teriorating rapidly.

The data on the distribution of income in Peru show that in
1961 the distribution was very skewed. Available information
suggests that the income distribution worsened during the
period 1961-75, in contrast with the objectives professed by
the military junta in 1968. In fact, it is possible that
real incomes had deteriorated for the poorer strata. We have
also pointed out that the income distribution in the rural
sector is more uneven than that in the urban sector. In addition urban incomes are very much higher than rural ones.

The first phase of the military junta 1968-75, was to a large
extent a failure if its performance is judged based on the
junta's objectives of (a) increasing the rate of economic
growth and (b) improving the distribution of income.

In the next chapter we will make some theoretical comments
on the factors determining income distribution within an agricultural sector and the relationship between agrarian reform and agricultural growth.

In the following two chapters, 5 and 6, we will investigate to what extent the government acted upon these two objectives, growth and distribution, for the agricultural sector. The final appraisal of the relative success of the junta's policies will be treated at the end of this study.

APPENDIX TO CHAPTER 3

SOME COMMENTS ON TABLES A.3.1-A.3.3

Calculations of family income shares 1971/72

Table A.3.1 was calculated from the Amat y León and León
study in the following way. Their data on Peru, Table II.4
on p. 30 is reproduced in Table A.3.1. To obtain the income share for the population strata (in percent) in as-
cending orders of income shares; 0-20; 20-40; 40-60; 60-
80; and 80-100, the procedure followed was:

For the group 0-20, the 19% (column 3) poorer obtained 1.4%
of the income (column 5). In the following group 14.9% of
the families had 3.2% of the income. Hence each percent had
0.2% of the income. From this follows that 0-20% of the families had 1.4%+0.2%=1.6% of the income.

For the group 0-40, the 33.9% had 4.6% of the income. To
complete the 40% of the population we have to add 6.1%. In
the following group 10.6% of the families had 3.9% of the
income, and hence each percent had 0.368. From this follows
that the 6.1% had 2.2% which we add to the income, 4.6%+
2.2%=6.8%, obtaining the income for the 40% poorer.

For the group 0-80, we have that 77.9% had 35.5% of the income. The following 2.1% had 3.0% of the income, hence the
80% bottom of the population had 38.3% of the income.

The Lorenz curve and the Gini coefficient of concentration

The Lorenz curve presented in Figure 3.2 is commonly used
to describe the concentration of income. There are of course
a great number of ways to describe an income distribution,
but we have opted for the use of the Lorenz curve and the
Gini-coefficient. [See for example Szal and Robinson in
Frank and Webb (1977), pp. 491-530; Yotopoulos and Nugent
(1976), pp. 237-247; and Bronfenbrenner (1971), pp. 43-57.]
As with any single aggregate measure, the Gini coefficient
has advantages and disadvantages. The measure is obtained
by dividing the area between the Lorenz curve and the diagonal (the shaded area) OABO with the area under the triangle
OACO. See figure A.3.1 below.

Figure A.3.1 Income distribution curve

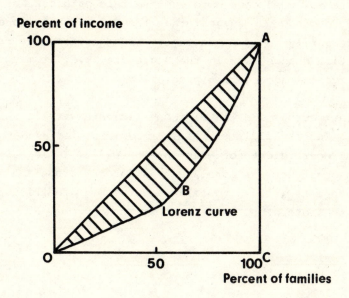

The closer the Lorenz curve is to the diagonal, the smaller the area OABO will be, and hence the smaller the Gini coefficient will be. When the Lorenz curve coincides with the diagonal, perfect equality, the Gini coefficient is zero. Theoretically with perfect inequality, the Gini coefficient will be one. Hence, it is an increasing function of inequality. A major deficiency with the Gini coefficient is that many different Lorenz curves can give rise to the same value of the Gini coefficient. (Szal and Robinson, Op.cit, p. 505).

Robinson (1976:2) has explored an interesting idea in explaining the U-hypothesis referred to in chapter 3.3.1. Dividing the economy into two sectors with different income levels and distributions, it could be shown that migration from one sector to the other can generate an aggregate U-curve of income distribution for the poorer strata. The data on Peru, however, are not good enough to explore this path further. The article does however suggest that the U-curve phenomenon does not necessarily imply a growing of inequalities, but rather composition changes within the aggregate, i.e. it may represent a typical aggregation problem.

The Lorenz curves and the Gini coefficients were calculated from the Tables A.3.1 and A.3.3. Table A.3.1 was used to construc the Gini coefficient for Peru in Figure 3.2. Table A.3.3 was used to construct the Lorenz curves for the urban and the rural sectors as well as to calculate the Gini coefficients for these sectors.

Table A.3.1   Peru - family income shares 1971/72

Soles/month	Families(%)	Cumulative	Income(%)	Cumulative
- 170	4.0	4.0	0.1	0.1
171- 670	15.0	19.0	1.3	1.4
		20.0		1.6
671- 1 330	14.9	33.9	3.2	4.6
		40.0		6.8
1 331- 2 000	10.6	44.5	3.9	8.5
2 001- 2 670	8.6	53.1	4.4	12.9
2 671- 3 330	6.9	60.0	4.6	17.5
3 331- 4 000	5.1	65.1	4.2	21.7
4 001- 4 670	5.2	70.3	5.0	26.7
4 671—5 330	4.5	74.8	5.0	31.7
5 331- 6 000	3.1	77.9	3.8	35.5
		80.0		38.5
6 001- 6 670	2.9	80.8	4.1	39.6
6 671- 7 330	2.2	83.0	3.5	43.1
7 331- 8 000	1.9	84.9	3.3	46.4
8 001- 8 330	0.9	85.8	1.7	48.1
8 331- 9 670	2.9	88.7	5.8	53.9
9 671-11 000	2.6	91.3	6.0	59.9
11 001-12 330	2.0	93.3	5.1	65.0
12 331-13 670	1.0	94.3	3.0	68.0
13 671-15 000	0.9	95.2	3.0	71.0
15 000-	4.8	100.0	29.0	100.0

Source: Amat y León and León (1977), p. 30

Table A.3.2   Distribution of family incomes in 1971/72
by Quintiles

Families	Income share	Cumulative
0- 20	1.6	1.6
20- 40	5.2	6.8
40- 60	10.7	17.5
60-880	21.0	38.5
80-100	61.5	100.0

Source: Table A.3.1

- 89 -

Table A.3.3   Distribution of urban and rural family income 1971/72 (percent)

Income Soles/month	URBAN Families Share in Total	URBAN Families Cumulative Share	URBAN Income Share in Total	URBAN Income Cumulative Share	RURAL Families Share in Total	RURAL Families Cumulative Share	RURAL Income Share in Total	RURAL Income Cumulative Share
- 170	0.7	0.7	0.0	0.0	6.7	6.7	0.3	0.3
171- 670	3.6	4.3	0.2	0.2	24.5	31.2	4.5	4.8
671- 1 330	5.8	10.1	0.8	1.0	22.6	53.8	9.9	14.7
1 331- 2 000	6.7	16.8	1.5	2.5	14.0	67.8	10.6	25.3
2 001- 2 670	8.1	24.9	2.6	5.1	8.9	76.7	9.4	34.7
2 671- 3 330	8.5	33.4	3.5	8.6	5.6	82.3	7.8	42.5
3 331- 4 000	6.8	40.2	3.4	12.0	3.6	85.9	6.2	48.7
4 001- 4 670	7.5	47.7	4.5	16.5	3.2	89.1	6.5	55.2
4 671- 5 330	6.7	54.4	4.6	21.1	2.6	91.7	6.1	61.3
5 331- 6 000	4.6	59.0	3.6	24.7	1.8	93.5	4.5	65.8
6 001- 6 670	4.9	63.9	4.3	29.0	1.2	94.7	3.6	69.4
6 671- 7 330	4.0	67.9	3.9	32.9	0.8	95.5	2.6	72.0
7 331- 8 000	3.1	71.0	3.4	36.3	0.9	96.4	3.0	75.0
8 001- 8 330	1.8	72.8	2.0	38.3	0.3	96.7	0.9	75.9
8 331- 9 670	5.5	78.3	6.8	45.1	0.8	97.5	3.1	79.0
9 671-11 000	4.8	83.1	6.8	51.9	0.8	98.3	3.9	82.9
11 001-12 330	3.9	87.0	6.1	58.0	0.4	98.7	2.0	84.9
12 331-13 670	1.7	88.7	3.0	61.0	0.4	99.1	2.6	87.5
13 671-15 000	1.7	90.4	3.4	64.4	0.2	99.3	1.9	89.4
15 001-	9.6	100.0	35.6	100.0	0.7	100.0	10.6	100.0
	100.0		100.0		100.0		100.0	

Source: Amat y León and León (1977), Tables II.4 and II.5

1. See chapter 4.2 for a discussion of policy recommendations to improve income distribution in the agricultural sector.

2. BCR (1968); BCR (1976). For a general discussion of data see Fitzgerald (1976), Appendix IV.

3. See e.g. Alberts and Brundenius (1979), chapter 3 for per capita growth rate calculations for different periods.

4. Thorp and Bertram (1978), p. 4.

5. Iowa (1967), p. 18. See also Thorbecke-Condos (1965) in Spanish, and by the same authors in English in Adelman-Thorbecke (1966), and also Thorp (1978). Goldberger commenting Thorbecke and Condos' article in English is sceptical about their evidence about the alleged export led growth. See p. 209.

6. Fitzgerald (1976), p. 1.

7. The export data are from the BCR and in current million US dollars. The GDP figures are from Alberts & Brundenius (1979), and were obtained from the BCR figures on GDP in 1970 prices. Using the official exchange rate in 1970 the series was converted into US dollars.

8. Iowa (1967), p. 2.

9. Thorp and Bertram (1978), p. 286.

10. Ibidem, pp. 286-294.

11. Thorp and Bertram (1978), pp 286-320; Fitzgerald (1976), pp. 62-63.

12. INP I (1971), p. 7.

13. For a discussion of the structural reforms see Fitzgerald (1976), chapter 3; Thorp and Bertram (1978), chapter 15.

14. The figures calculated from Brundenius (1976:2). The expectations are based on my interpretation of discussions with Peruvian officials while I worked in the country 1968-1971.

15. Thorp (1977) particularly p. 128; and Fitzgerald (1976), Appendix I. See also Thorp and Bertram (1978), chapter 15.

16. See chapter 6.

17. Thorp and Bertram (1978), p. 316.

18. Thorp (1977), p. 129; Fitzgerald (1976), pp. 20-23; and INP (1976:2),

p. 31. BCR Memoria (1976), p. 183. The Table 3.2 on investments include inventory changes, while the above cited sources have excluded these.

19. Fitzgerald (1976), chapter 4.2.

20. Calculated from BCR Memoria (1976), p. 38; and BCR Memoria (1977), p. 22. See also Thorp and Bertram (1978), pp. 310-311; and Fitzgerald (1976), pp. 42-47.

21. Thorp and Bertram (1978), pp. 309-311; Fitzgerald (1976), pp. 42-47. See also chapter 6.

22. Thorp and Bertram (1978), p. 314. See also BCR Memorias on new loans.

23. See chapter 6.

24. INP (1975) Vol. II, p. 89.

25. Latin American Weekly Report No. WR-80-13 on page 5 comments, "The recovery of the Peruvian economy since mid-1978 has been attributable almost for a remarkable improvement in its external sector."

26. See for example Convenio (1969); INP (1975) Vol. I; Amat y León and León (1977); and Amat y León (1970).

27. Webb and Figueroa (1975), p. 50.

28. Ibidem, p. 45.

29. "The scanty empirical evidence suggests that the narrowing of income inequality in the developed countries is relatively recent and probably did not characterize the earlier stages of their growth..." Indeed, they (various factors) would suggest widening inequality in these early phases of economic growth, especially in the older countries where the emergence of the new industrial system had shattering effects on long-established pre-industrial economic and social institutions." Kuznets (1955), p. 18. See also Kuznets (1963).

30. For example: Chenery et.al. (1974); Paukert (1973); Ahluwalia (1976:1), (1976:2); and Adelman and Morris (1973).

31. This hypothesis had been criticized, but the following examples reflect its general acceptability. Beckerman has attempted to refute the U-shaped estimates in Chenery et.al. (1974), but has to admit, "Thus, although the statistical correlations that, in Redistribution with Growth supported the Kuznets' hypothesis still appear to hold, it does seem that they were strengthened by that part of the hypothecated relationship (negative correlation) between incomes and inequality that applies only to the more developed countries." Beckerman (1977), p. 671.
See also Ahluwalia (1976:2), pp. 309-313, where he also carries out the regression analyses, excluding the developed countries. He finds

that the variables remain significant, but with lower correlation coefficients.
Paukert argues that: "The data presented in this article support the hypothesis expressed but not fully tested by Kuznets and Oshima that with economic development income inequality tends to increase, then become stable and then decrease." Paukert (1973), p. 121. See also Chenery (1979), pp. 456-469.

32. Adelman and Morris (1973), p. 189.

33. Adelman and Robinson (1978), p. 1.

34. Ahluwalia (1976:1), p. 134, Ahluwalia (1976:2), pp. 330-335; Lal is also critical of this hypothesis and has raised objections, Lal (1976) p. 729. See also Cline (1975), p. 378; and Adelman-Morris' answer (1975), pp. 401-402.

35. See also chapter 4.2.1.

36. Lipton (1977), p. 13.

37. For a discussion of these earlier estimates see Webb and Figueroa (1975), p. 28.

38. Jain (1975), cites these earlier estimates on p. 89, columns 1 and 3. Column 2 is on earlier estimates of Webb which was revised by him. See Webb (1977), p. vi. We have not been able to obtain the original source of the preliminary estimates reported in column 4.

39. See Brundenius (1976:3), pp. 39-49 for details, and in the shorter English version, Brundenius (1976:2), pp. 7-10.

40. See Encuesta Nacional de Consumo del Alimentos P-ENCA No. 2 on the design of the research project and of the sample.

41. The FAO advisor and other officials who have worked with the ENCA project consider it to be of good quality.

42. For a discussion of the sources of income see Amat y León and León (1977), chapter III. The underestimation of capital income is mentioned on p. 53. A very important finding is that contrary to many scholars' belief the subsistence economy is quite insignificant. In the poorest strata and in the rural area, the autoconsumption represents only 29% of total income. For Peru as a whole it represents only 3.6% in total income (p. 59). Obviously capital incomes have been underestimated since it in the ENCA study would only represent 2.6% in total family income (p. 59).

43. Kuznets (1963), p. 7.

44. That household incomes show less inequality see for example Kuznets (1963), pp. 7 and 18.

45. Brundenius (1976:2), p. 9.

46. CIEPA (1979), pp. 62-63.

47. Figueroa in Webb and Figueroa (1975), p. 140. See also Figueroa in Foxley ed. (1976), pp. 163-178, particularly p. 176.

48. Amat y León and León (1977), p. 25.

49. Ibidem.

50. Chenery et.al. (1974), p. 21; see also Lipton (1977), p. 54.

51. These concepts of income transfer were developed by the Peruvian economist Richard Webb. See Webb (1977), p. 73.

4
Theoretical Framework

4.1 INTRODUCTION

In discussions on agrarian reform two development objectives are practically always present, viz., income distribution and growth. This was also the case of Peru, and in
chapter 2 we discussed the overall development objectives
as well as those for the agricultural sector. Both equity
and growth were priority development objectives.

In chapter 3 we investigated to what extent the military
government was successful in implementing its general economic objectives. We showed that not only was the average
rural income lower than the average urban income, but the
rural income distribution was more skewed. In order to evaluate the Government's efforts at income redistribution, we
will now comment on the determinants of rural income distribution. Henceforth, we will limit the discussion principally
to the agricultural sector, rather than the economy as a
whole.

In chapters 5 and 6 the discussion of income redistribution
will be developed to analyse the relationships between agrarian reform and income distribution, as well as between agrarian reform and agricultural production.

4.2 INCOME DISTRIBUTION IN AGRICULTURE

4.2.1 Introduction

The study of income distribution has always been a principal aspect of any basic introduction to economics.[1] We have
touched briefly on its recent increased importance in the

writings of development economics in chapter 1.4. When we
discuss agrarian reform, we also must treat the development objectives of income redistribution and growth.

The methodological approach following here selects the most
important factors explaining the income distribution reigning
in a given agricultural sector. As we have noted, income distribution should be discussed in the context of the
entire economy. In most developing countries, as in Peru,
there exists a significant rural-urban income gap.

The World Bank study, <u>Redistribution with Growth</u>, stressed
that, "The basic fact that the poor are disproportionately
located in the rural areas and are engaged in agriculture,
or allied rural occupations is well established in conven-
tional wisdom and easily verified."[2]

<u>Lipton</u> has even gone so as far as to state that,

> "The most important class conflict in the poor
> countries of the world today is not between la-
> bour and capital. Nor is it between foreign and
> national interests. It is between the rural clas-
> ses and the urban classes. The rural sector con-
> tains most of the poverty, and most of the low-
> cost sources of potential advance; but the urban
> sector contains most of the articulateness, or-
> ganization and power."[3][*]

In chapter 3 we investigated the relationship between rural
and urban wages. In 1971/72, urban average household income was more than three times larger than the rural average income. Thus empirical data on Peru confirm these gene-

---

[*] Lipton is not a marxist scholar, and hence, his use of the
word "class" differs from that used by marxists. An interesting review of Lipton's book can be found in Discussion Paper
116 of the Institute of Development Studies at the University
of Sussex, in which Dudley Seers makes a careful review of the
book, and Lipton comments on this review. See also Byres (1979)
Currie (1979).

ral propositions on the urban-rural income gap.

The Peruvian economist Webb has developed a conceptual framework which is useful. He distinguishes between horizontal and
vertical transfer. "Income transfers can be considered vertical when they redistribute within a productive sector, or horizontal when the transfer takes place between productive sec-
sectors."[4] We will thus say that in general and particularly
in Peru, equity as an overall development objective implies
significant horizontal transfers from the urban to the rural
sector in Peru. We will discuss this further in chapters 5
and 6.

Moreover, we observed that   rural distribution was more
unequal than the urban income distribution. Therefore, there
exist large possibilities for income re-distribution. In this
section, as was mentioned before, we will concentrate on the
key factors which determine income distribution within the
agricultural sector.

At the core of the discussion of income distribution in agriculture are two notions. The first one is the distribution
of land ownership, and the second one is the concept of land
rents. As Clark and Haswell have pointed out, "A number of
instances can be found in low-income agricultures in which
rent may be expected to take nearly half of the gross product..."[5] Since this rent is high in many developing countries, the way it is distributed will have a decisive effect
on income distribution. The interest in rent and ownership
of land has long occupied economists. Ricardo, for example,
spent a great deal of his writings on this subject, when agriculture played a more important role in the economy of the
industrialized countries. The renewed interest of development economists, during latter years, in equity and growth

in developing countries, has again brought this issue to the centre of attention. Examples of the views of contemporary development economists are as follows:

Jacoby considered that land redistribution is the most important reform to improve the standard of living of the rural population.[6] Griffin has written several books on agricultural development and has also insisted on the need for agrarian reform. Thus in 1976 he writes,

> "It seems inevitable, then, that the principal component of a successful attack on poverty must be a redistribution of the stock of wealth. Given that the economies of the most underdeveloped countries are largely agrarian, it follows that a redistribution of landed property is almost certain to be of prime importance."[7]

Two years later he writes,

> "In the countries with which we are concerned, most of the poverty is in the rural areas and in most rural areas poverty is intimately related to the degree of land concentration. A reduction in the inequality of land ownership through a redistribution of property in favour of landless workers, tenants and small farmers would contribute directly to the alleviation of the most acute forms of poverty."[8]

Webb states that, "...land reform and other 'structural reforms' that transfer property ownership to workers are radical forms of vertical redistribution."[9] The World Bank sponsored study, Redistribution with Growth, argued that, "We consider an effective land reform to be a necessary condition for the type of strategy propounded in this volume..."[10]

In the ILO sponsored study, Poverty and Landlessness in Rural Asia, one major conclusion was,

> "A reduction in inequality, therefore, if brought about through a redistribution of landed property and supported by subsidiary measures such as the provision of credit and marketing facilities, is likely to raise total production and is certain to raise the incomes of the poor."[11]

Foxley et.al. in their introduction state that:

> "A critical factor explaining differences in
> personal incomes is the distribution of as-
> sets among individuals and families... An exa-
> mination of the alternative available for re-
> distributing assets will have to start by re-
> cognizing the basic differences between the
> problem in rural and urban areas. The most con-
> centrated asset in the rural sector is usually
> land. This is a productive factor which is di-
> visible and in the exploitation of which eco-
> nomies of scale are not important."12)

Adelman has come to the conclusion, based on systematic studies, both empirical and theoretical, that in order to achieve
significant improvements of the incomes of the poor certain
necessary stages in the implementation of a development strategy have to be followed. The first stage involves:"...radi-
cal asset redistribution, focusing primarily on land;..."13)

Cline argues that,

> "Agricultural policies are particularly impor-
> tant in affecting income distribution, in view
> of the concentration of the poor in the agri-
> cultural sector and considering the limitations
> of early absorption of the poor of excess la-
> bor by the industrial sector. Of the various
> agricultural policies, land redistribution is
> the most effective if properly managed."14)

Finally, Lipton states that, "Clearly, redistribution of land,
from big holdings to small, improves income distribution."15)

The logic of these arguments is that in many developing countries land ownership is concentrated and because of this the
income distribution becomes highly unequal. In order to change
the income distribution significantly a land reform is a necessary condition. Clearly, the way in which the expropriated
land is redistributed will determine the post-reform income
distribution in agriculture. However, the distribution of land
ownership does not give any information on how the income distribution is determined and which factors are important. We wil

concentrate on land and labour factors, but before we will first give some comments on the role of capital in agricultural growth.

The potential role of capital and technology in agricultural growth is very important. USA data are indicative in this respect. In the period 1929-1953 the main changes in the aggregates of US agriculture were as follows: available land and labour input decreased with 1% and 44% respectively. Simultaneously, inputs of intermediate products and, machinery and equipment increased 139% and 160% respectively. Capital, and of course modern technology, have become the most important factors in modern agricultural growth. [16]

In Peru, based on several case studies in 1962 carried out by CIDA, the value of land was by far the most important of the capital assets of a farm. See Table 4.1 for details. Still it should be mentioned that for the livestock estates the value of the cattle was about the same as for the land itself. Douglas Horton writing on the 60's maintains that, "Large landowners realized that sooner or later land redistribution was inevitable. The expectation of reform encouraged them to decapitalize their estates and to transfer their assets out of agriculture". [17] In 1970, the Convenio group investigated 150 farms and came to the conclusion that the value of the non-land part of a farm, was only 0.5-1.5 percent of the farm value (livestock excluded). [18]

From these pieces of information it is justifiable to conclude that land and labour have been, and still are, the most important factors of production in Peruvian agriculture. Thus, we shall simplify our analysis by considering only land and labour and no capital in our models.

Where land is concerned, we suggest that rent becomes impor-

Table 4.1   Value of fixed capital in 7 Peruvian farms in 1962*
(1 000 1962 Soles)

	LAND	BUILDINGS		MACHINES VEHICLES		TOOLS		OTHERS		IRRIGATION PUMPS AND WELLS	
	Value	Value	Percent of Land value	Value	Percent of Land value	Value	Percent of Land value	Value	Percent of Land value	Value	Percent of Land value
A. Sierra Farms											
(1)	8 006	540	6.7	858	10.7	171	2.1	197	2.5	–	–
(2)	6 000	193	3.2	595	9.9	56	0.9	483	8.1	–	–
(3)	160	50	31.3	–	–	3	1.9	2	1.3	–	–
(4)	35	15	42.9	–	–	6	17.1	–	–	–	–
B. Coastal Farms											
(5)	45 000	151	0.3	3 295	7.3	88	0.2	134	0.3	320	0.7
(6)	34 180	2 580	7.5	2 200	6.4	200	0.6	800	2.3	1 200	3.5
(7)	900	3	0.3	241	26.8	7	0.8	–	–	10	1.1

Note: Farms on the Coast usually have a higher price because of (a) better land and (b) easier access to main markets.
See chapter 6.3.

*) Excluding livestock and plantations.

Source: CIDA (1966), p. 86 and p. 152

tant, when land is scarce. Land scarcity implies a price
of land and a rent. If land were a free good, the price
would be zero and no rent would exist.

In poor economies a major peasant objective is to produce
food for survival. There is always a cost involved in this
production, labour.[19] To incorporate new land implies at
least a labour cost. The extent of availability of virgin
land is another element determining land scarcity, its
price and rent. The other variable in this context is labour. The degree of land scarcity is measured by the amount
of standardized land available to the rural population.*)
The general argument is that in Peru land is scarce because
(a) the cost of incorporating new land is high, implying
high land prices; (b) the amount of land already available
to the rural population is little, and moreover the relationship land/labour has been declining because of population growth in the 20th century[20]; (c) the landowners monopolized the use of land, leaving part of it underutilized,
thus making land even scarcer; and (d) there is little of
known potentially good quality land available. (See chapter
6.3)

These are the main factors which contributed towards the
very uneven distribution of rural income in Peru, referred to
in chapter 3. Simultaneously, a counteracting factor was at
work in the Peruvian economy: the population movements to
the urban areas and the Coast. These large migration waves,
to some extent, attenuated the above mentioned situation.

---

*) Land is of different quality depending on such factors as
soil quality and climate. Therefore it is not appropriate to
use the cultivated area available to the rural population as
an index of land scarcity. However, lack of statistics often
forces the investigator to use such data for lack of better.

The next section will formalize some of the above mentioned relationships, by the use of microeconomic theory.

4.2.2 Some formal considerations[21]

In this section we will use microeconomic theoretical tools, by means of the comparative static method, to illustrate the importance of the ownership of land as a factor determining the distribution of income. The first part is mainly based on perfect competition assumptions. In the second part, various non-competitive assumptions are introduced which are intended to highlight some of the main features in agriculture where land ownership is very concentrated. This section concludes with a discussion of how the neo-classical paradigm may be adjusted to analyse this type of agriculture.

4.2.2.1 Perfect competition cases

Let us assume that there is a fixed amount of land in the economy $(\bar{R})$. The output price of the agricultural good $(\bar{P})$, and the wage rate $(\bar{w})$ are given. In Figure 4.1 the wage rate is given by the line ww. The x-axis measures the number of labourers employed (L) per unit of time, while the y-axis the amount of the good produced (Q) during the same period. There is no capital.[22]

The ABD curve, value marginal product of labour VMP_L, shows the value of the incremental output obtained by adding one labourer. It is the marginal product of labour (MP_L) multiplied with the price of the good (P), or $MP_L \cdot P$.

Rent (profit) maximization (we will use the term rent through out this chapter) is obtained at a point where the cost of employing the last labourer equals the value of his produce. In this model the labour cost is constant, w, and the rent maximization criterion, $w=VMP_L$ is obtained at point B in Figure 4.1.

Figure 4.1   Value Marginal Productivity (VMP) of labour per unit of land

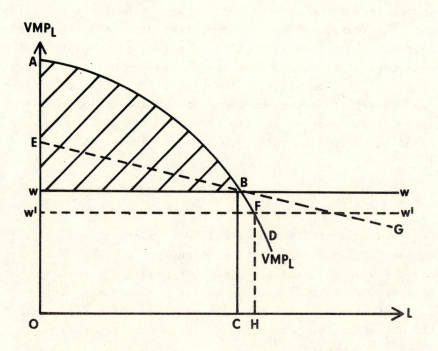

Thus the value of the total product is given by the area OABC, and is distributed so that the shaded area wAB is rent and OwBC wages, per unit of time, e.g. yearly. Assuming that the landowner maximizes his rents (π), the solution is obtained in the usual way in equations 1-5:

1. $Q = f(L)$;   Production function

2. $\pi = P \cdot Q - w \cdot L$;   Rent function

3. $\pi = P \cdot f(L) - w \cdot L$;

4. $\frac{d\pi}{dL} = P \cdot \frac{dQ}{dL} - w = 0$;   First order condition for rent maximization

From equation 4 we obtain the following necessary condition for rent maximization discussed above:

5. $w = P \cdot \frac{dQ}{dL}$

The rent rate will thus depend on (a) the shape of the production function, (b) the price of the good and (c) the wage rate. If the value marginal productivity curve instead were flatter, such as the dotted line in Figure 4.1, the rent derived would <u>ceteris paribus</u> be less, the area wEB.*) Also, a lower price of the agricultural good would shift the ABD curve downwards and would reduce rents. Consequently, a higher price would increase rents.

The shape of the production function probably varies greatly in Peru. Since land quality and climate factors tend to be more favourable on the Coast than in the Sierra, for a given labour input production should be higher on a given amount of land on the Coast in comparison to the Sierra.[23] Also, the price paid for agricultural goods tend to be higher on the Coast, because of lower marketing costs, due to lower transport costs.[24] Thus the information available suggests that rents and consequently land prices are higher on the Coast than in the Sierra.[25] In the model developed here the ABD curve approximates Coastal agriculture while the EBG curve approximates Sierra agriculture.

A lower wage rate, w'w', increases rents, employment (if un-

---

*) It does not necessarily pass through point B.

employment exists) and production. In the model, rents increase by $wBFw'$, total production by $BFHC$ and employment by CH. The share of rent in total production also increases.

This simple model brings out some essential factors determining income distribution. It is in the interest of the landowner to obtain labourers at the lowest wage possible, in order to capture a larger rent. The agricultural workers on the other hand would of course prefer to capture the rent component in addition to their salaries. The Latin American peasant's slogan "Land or death", is a testimony to the intensity of the struggle for land ownership and its rents.

If land became a free good, the agricultural labourers would of course move onto the land and capture the rent component themselves. Moreover, in such a situation there would be no supply of excess labour, wages would be correspondingly high, and rents zero.

At a zero wage rate, rent, production and employment reach their maxima. For a number of reasons, the most obvious that the labourers would die because of starvation, this wage rate will never occur in reality. (The minimum wage rate possible will be discussed in 4.2.2.3). Still a high concentration of land ownership and little land available could push wages down so that the rent component becomes very high. Therefore, even in a competitive rural economy, the income distribution may be very unequal. Moreover, a high degree of concentration of land ownership means that markets are no longer competitive. Landowners can use their economic power to increase their incomes and wealth. Different methods are available, and the results may be different, but there will still be similarities: high rents, low wages, negative effects on employment and output. We will now turn our attention to some such cases, belonging to the category of imperfect competition.

4.2.2.2 Imperfect competition cases

If landownership, including control of water supply in irrigated agriculture, is concentrated, labourers are forced to
seek employment on the big estates to supplement their incomes.[26] We will concentrate on a few important ways of how
the landowner can increase his rents. As the landowner's monopsony power successively increases in purchasing of labour
services, we approach cases of coercion. In the following
section we develop such a model of "forced" labour.

In Peru available land has been concentrated among a reduced
number of large producers. Thus for example, in 1961, 1.3% of
the production units covered no less than 84% of total area,
while the "subsistence sector" accounted for more than 1/3 of
the production units had less than 1% of the land. This concentration of land ownership will be discussed further in
chapter 5.2. In addition to this concentration of land ownership, though closely related, the landowners had various ways
of controlling the use of labourers, ranging from slavery in
the 19th century to various tenure arrangements and indentured
labour known as engancho in Peru. The landowner advanced money
and/or goods to the peasant and this legally binding debt was
perpetuated, enabling the landowner to control the wage rate.

> "Once the peasant was in the hacienda, his debt
> was even more inflated as the owner had the
> monopoly of the only existing storeshop or
> tambo in which the peon bought goods at in-
> flated prices. In this way, the Indian's debt
> became endless, so also his bondage to the
> sugar hacienda."[27]

The mechanisms for the functioning of the system of obtaining
cheap labour have varied, although its feudal characteristics have broken down over time, particularly with the
rapid growth of the urban industrial centres after World War
II.[28]

The monopolization of land can be described as follows. If there is only one landowner, and the rest are labourers, labourers would not have any alternative employment opportunities. Thus there would be a new supply curve of labour pushing down the wage rate. In turn, there would be a shift in income distribution in favour of the one landowner. An extension of this is of course that since the landowner is in a monopsony position in the labour market, the landowner can increase his profits even more.[29]

The production function, equation 1, and the rent function, equation 2, are the same as in the former case.

1. $Q = f(L)$;

2. $\pi = P \cdot Q - w \cdot L$;

Wages on the other hand increase the more labourers the landowner employs, equation 3.

3. $w = g(L)$, where $\frac{dw}{dL} > 0$;

The total costs to the landowner, $w \cdot L$, will thus increase as he employs more labourers because of the increase in the number (L) and because of the increase in wages (w). The marginal cost of labour to the landowner is given by equation 4.

4. $\frac{d(w \cdot L)}{dL} = w + L \cdot \frac{dw}{dL}$;

Maximizing his rents, equation 2, we obtain:

5. $\frac{d\pi}{dL} = P \cdot \frac{dQ}{dL} - w - L \cdot \frac{dw}{dL} = 0$;

6. $P \cdot \frac{dQ}{dL} = w + L \cdot \frac{dw}{dL}$;

Equation 6 states that the necessary condition for rent maximization is that the value of marginal product equals the marginal cost of employing labour.[30]

In Figure 4.2 these relationships are shown. The value marginal productivity curve, VMP_L, shows the incremental value in production of employing an extra labourer. From the supply curve of labour, S_L, is derived the marginal cost of employing an extra labourer, MC_L. If the landowner employs an extra labourer he has to offer a higher wage to this labourer as well as to all the others employed, thus the expression in equation 4. This appears again on the right hand side in equation 6 for the condition of rent maximization. This condition shows that the landowner should continue to employ workers until the value of what the last worker produces is equal to the marginal cost of employing that worker. In Figure 4.2 this condition is satisfied at point C, and the landowner will employ L^O workers, paying a wage rate of w_O. The value of production is OCL^O, and total wages paid Ow_OBL^O, and the difference constitutes the rent.

Figure 4.2   Rent maximization under monopsony of labour input

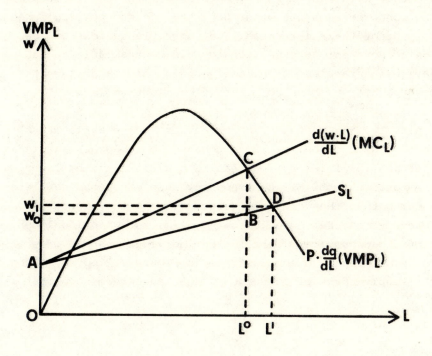

In perfect competition L' labourers would be employed at a wage rate w_1. Comparing the two situations we find that in the monopsony case wages, employment and output are less than in perfect competition.

Thus far we have considered (1) perfect competition on factor produce markets; (2) perfect competition on the produce market and monopsony on the factor market. There are of course a number of other possibilities as for example: (3) monopoly on the produce market and perfect competition on the factor market; (4) monopoly on the produce market and monopsony on the factor market. Cases 1-4 represent extreme cases, perfect competition and monopoly/monopsony. There exist a number of intermediary cases. These have been studied in detail by other authors and shall not be reviewed here.[31] A general discussion of markets and price policies will be carried out in chapter 6.

In general the Peruvian peasants have been almost powerless. The landowners on the other hand have formed powerful unions to protect their interests. The sugar plantations on the Coast represent an exception to this general rule and there have been examples of collective bargaining and wages have been pushed up above competitive equilibrium level.[32]

Typically, the Peruvian labour market in the agricultural sector is monopsonistic. This means the landowner has further possibilities for increasing his/her rent, by lowering the total wage bill. The monopsony case discussed earlier assumes that the wage rate paid to the last labourer is paid to everybody. But, the landowner, familiar with local conditions, can probably identify the individual labour offer curve, at least to some extent. In Figure 4.2 moving along the supply curve of labour, S_L, the landowner knows that at

the wage rate w_O he will obtain L^O of labourers. But he also
knows that most of the labourers would be willing to work at
a wage less than this one. If he could identify how much each
of the workers requires in order to work for him, he would
not have to pay every worker the same wage and could lower
the total wage bill. This type of behaviour belongs to the
general category of price discrimination. If perfect discrimination exists, the landowner could reduce total wages paid
from Ow_OBL^O, to $OABL^O$, thus gaining Aw_OB. In general, wage
discrimination tends to affect the poorer workers hardest
since they belong to the bottom part of the supply curve of
labour.[33]

Thus far our discussion has focused mainly on monopsony in
the factor market and perfect competition in the produce
market (case 2). There have been cases of monopoly on the
produce market (cases 3 and 4). "In the Sierra, as the high
inter-Andean valleys are known, produce markets tend to be
isolated and may be largely served by the output of a few
big landowners."[34] It would be in the interest of these
producers to reduce output to capture monopoly profits.
Bottomley (1971) in his conclusions states,

> "In South America, for example, it seems pos-
> sible that large landowners may choose to li-
> mit land-use in order to obtain monopolistic
> premiums in their rents, and that, whether they
> do or not, the extent of land-use is almost cer-
> tainly associated with the breadth of the pro-
> duce market."[35]

The Coast on the other hand, with access to both major urban and world markets and a good transport system, belongs
to the category of a competitive produce market. The possibilities of monopsonistic practices have also been less,
because of urban growth and rapid expansion of irrigated
agriculture. Therefore, case 3, monopoly on the produce

market and perfect competition on the factor market, does
not seem particularly relevant in the Peruvian context.
Case 4, has existed in the Sierra. Case 2 has existed both
in the Sierra and on the Coast.

The discussion thus far has been based on the assumption of
free association. The economic actors, the landowner and
the labourers, enter into contracts on their own free will.
As we have moved from perfect competition in all markets
to monopsony and price discrimination on the factor market,
the analysis is suggesting the existence of coercion. In the
next section we will proceed one step further in the discussion and assume that the landowner can at will fix the wage
rate, and discuss some such cases.

4.2.2.3 Rent maximization and "forced" labour

In this section we will assume that the landowner has a pool
of under- and/or unemployed workers at his disposal and is
free to set the wage. The underemployed are supposed to
live on small plots at the subsistence level. The amount
of work the labourers will be able to perform is assumed
to depend on the food intake, and hence output will be
largely determined by the number of labourers employed and
the amount of food they eat. In the first part we will review some of the literature and empirical findings, and
thereafter proceed to formalize some important aspects of
the discussion.

The relationship between the amount of food intake on the
one hand, and the amount of work a labourer can perform
on the other, is well established in economic development theory. Thus in 1957 Leibenstein wrote, "The amount
of work that the representative labourer can be expected

to perform depends on his energy level, his health and
his vitality, which in turn depend on his food intake."[36]
In 1965 Shoup explored this idea further and argued that
agricultural production could increase through consumption,
and that the production increase could be greater than the
consumption of food necessary to generate this production
increase.[37] Since then various studies have been made
exploring different functional relationships. One such idea
is the existence of a low nutritional equilibrium trap.[38]

Another line of reasoning which is of particular interest
to our discussion is the hypothesis,

> "First, it often pays the employer to offer a
> wage to workers above that which would be de-
> termined by the ordinary forces of supply and
> demand, since in this way he can take account
> of the 'fact' that, over a certain range,
> higher wages result in greater efficiency and
> lower costs."[39]

Griffin has strongly critisized this hypothesis.

> "Surely, if labour productivity is a func-
> tion of consumption this is an argument
> either for a redistribution of income and
> wealth (and hence of consumption) within
> a capitalist system or for determining the
> distribution of consumption on the basis
> of collective decisions."[40]

He further proceeds to state,

> "There is no reason whatever to think that
> in an economy in which average incomes are
> low and the distribution of income is highly
> unequal the market will ensure that all em-
> ployed workers receive an income high enough
> to ensure their efficiency and adequate nu-
> trition."[41]

There are, however, several observations which should be
made about this statement. The first is that efficiency
of work does not necessarily imply adequate nutrition. It
is well accepted that a positive relationship exists be-

tween food intake and the amount of work a labourer can perform per unit of time, but there is no general agreement on what constitutes an adequate nutritional level. <u>Clark and Haswell</u> have for example critisized the FAO standards of nutrition as being exaggerated.[42] Also, the notion of an adequate nutritional level is related to variables such as calories, proteins,and their combination, vitamins, minerals, type of work performed, age, sex, bodyweight and climate.

Also, it is well established in economic theory that there is a positive correlation between income (wages) and consumption of food, but the elasticity of demand tends to be decreasing as income increases (Engel's law). In Peru several studies have been made showing that caloric and protein consumption increases as income grows and that the elasticity of demand decreases as income increases.[43] In Peru, as in other poor countries, the whole family income is not spent on food and the general rule is that as income grows a proportionately smaller share is allocated to food. It can however safely be assumed that there is a relationship between the wage rate and the nutritional level.

Assume that there exists labourers (L) and the amount of work one labourer is able to perform per unit of time (E) depends on the amount of food he consumes (C_F), or

1. $E = \phi\,(C_F)$;

Then, one labourer will be able to perform different amounts of work depending on the consumption of food. The total labour input will thus depend on (i) how many labourers are employed and (ii) how much food they eat. The amount of food one labourer consumes depends on the wage rate he receives (w), per unit of time, or

2. $C_F = g(w)$;

Thus the amount of work the labourer can perform (E) can be
written as a function of the wage rate:

3. $E = f(w)$;

The exact shape of equation 3 is not the same in all places
and at all times. Though, in general, theory and empirical
data suggest that at low wages the curve rises rapidly because (a) the labourer has a high marginal propensity to consume food, and (b) because the food is used directly by his
body to perform work. Furthermore, as wages increase (a) the
marginal propensity to consume food declines and (b) there
is a region of proportionately smaller effects of consumption
of food on work units.

The type of curve suggested, of equation 3, has been drawn
in Figure 4.3. The amount of work (with a constant intensity) performed by the worker (E) is measured along the y-
axis and the wage rate along the x-axis. It is assumed that
at very low wages, OD in the figure, he is not able to perform any work at all, "resting metabolism".[44]

As the wage increases the amount of work supplied increases
first rapidly along DB_and subsequently the increase in work
becomes smaller and smaller for each unit of wage increase.
The line HF is the maximum of work which normally can be obtained from a worker and the DBG curve approaches it probably asymptotically. At very high wages the DBG curve
might turn downwards again.

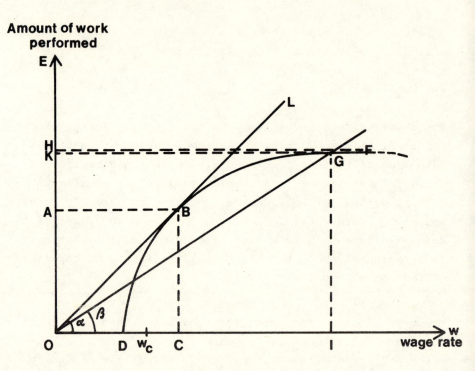

Figure 4.3 The relationship between malnutrition and rent maximization

It is easy to obtain the cost per unit of work supplied. At point G, the amount of work supplied is OK and the wage paid is OI. Thus the cost per unit of work is OI:OK. As can be seen the greater the angle, β, or OK:OI, the smaller the cost per unit of work supplied. The minimum cost is obtained at point B, where the ray OL is tangent to the curve DBG, angle α.

We imagine that the producer wage policy is to maximize the amount of work-units supplied per wage unit paid. Thereafter he employs the number of workers he needs at this wage rate. The amount of work supplied, by a worker was,

3. $E = f(w)$;

The amount of work units per wage unit paid is:

4. $\dfrac{E}{w} = \dfrac{f(w)}{w}$;

Taking the derivative of equation 4 we obtain,

5. $\dfrac{d(E/w)}{dw} = \dfrac{w \cdot \dfrac{df}{dw} - f(w)}{w^2}$;

First order conditions for maximum require equation 5 to be zero and rearranging we obtain,

6. $\dfrac{dE}{dw} = \dfrac{f(w)}{w}$, or $\dfrac{dE}{dw} = \dfrac{E}{w}$;

The left hand side of equation 6, $\dfrac{dE}{dw}$, shows how much more work is obtained for an increase in the wage rate. This depends on the slope of the curve DBG in Figure 4.3.

The necessary condition for maximizing the supply of work per cost unit is obtained where the ray from the origin is tangent to the curve DBG, as in point B.[45] Having thus established the wage rate and the cost per unit of work, the producer employs the needed number of workers from the existing pool of unemployed.

Returning to Griffin's statement on the relationship between wages, efficiency and adequate nutrition, mentioned earlier, the difficulty remains to specify what is an adequate level of nutrition. If an adequate level of nutrition is understood by the flatter segments of the curve DBG, rent maximization under "forced" labour will produce inadequate diets. Moreover such a situation is possible even under competitive equilibrium. That wage rates can be very low in competitive equilibria was discussed earlier, 4.2.2.1.

However, very low wages are bound to have effects in the long run and one probable outcome is that key demographic variables are affected such as population growth, mortality rates, infant mortality just to mention a few. The Peruvian history is an important example in this respect. In Peru since the colonization in the 16th century there have been numerous methods of gaining control over the Indian population. It can even be argued that one overall objective of the power structure has been to secure the maximum work at the lowest possible cost from the Indian population.[46] Available data suggest that from the colonization and up to the end of the 18th century, a time span of over 250 years there was a drastic decline in the Peruvian population, in spite of the European immigration.[47]

4.2.3 Summary and conclusions

In this section we developed simple models to explain some key factors determining income distribution in the agricultural sector, assuming only two factors of production, land and labour. We organized the section by beginning with a perfect competition case, discussing the effects of concentration of landownership, and the availability of land and labour. We proceeded further by introducing different non-competitive situations. Throughout this section we made various comments on the degree of landownership concentration and land scarcity. The following main conclusions emerge from this section.

Even in a competitive economy land rents occur if land is

scarce. For a given amount of land, the higher the degree
of land ownership concentration the higher the rent component is. Landowners thus have a collective interest in controlling the total amount of land availabe and its distribution. By reducing the total amount of land available to the
rural population, the landowners can improve their economic
position vis-a-vis agricultural labour.

If land ownership is very concentrated, a number of alternative non-competitive situations can occur. The theory
of monopsony pricing was used to show that the landowners
have several possibilities to increase their rents further. Another result is that employment, production and
wages become lower than in a competitive situation.

However, the neo-classical paradigm misses the central
point of the close relationship between ownership of land,
distribution of political power, and control over labour.
Barraclough and Domike have stated this as:

> "These land tenure institutions are a pro-
> duct of the power structure. Plainly speak-
> ing, ownership or control of land is power
> in the sense of real or potential ability
> to make another person do one's will. Po-
> wer over rural labour is reflected in te-
> nure institutions which bind workers to
> the land while conceding them little in-
> come and few continuing rights...
> The most common technique used to tie the cam-
> pesino to the farm is to cede him a small parcel
> of land for his home and garden while seeing to
> it that he has no alternative opportunities to
> obtain land or employment."48)

In the last part we developed a mode to cover cases when landowners can "force" the labourers to work. It was suggested
that chronic malnutrition may exist. However, competitive

equilibria can also produce such situations characterized
by malnutrition if land is very scarce. Clearly, in all
cases redistribution of land to the labourers should improve
their incomes and nutritional level.

From the preceding discussion it should be clear that the
distribution of land is one of the most important factors
explaining the distribution of income within the agricultural sector in traditional agriculture. Development economists concerned with income distribution problems agree that
in order to improve the income distribution an agrarian reform is necessary. How this was done in Peru will be discussed in the next chapter.

In chapter 1 we mentioned that land ownership was extremely
skewed and that land is scarce in Peru. In this chapter we
have elaborated several models which suggest that if land
ownership is concentrated and land is scarce income distribution is skewed. These conclusions are confirmed by the
data on income distribution in Peru discussed in chapter 3.*)

4.3 AGRARIAN REFORM AND PRODUCTION

Development economists agree that the ownership of land on
the one hand, and the distribution of income on the other

---

*) This section suggests a very unequal distribution of in-
come in the rural sector in Peru. The data in chapter 3 confirm this as well as the data on land ownership mentioned in
chapter 1 and discussed again in chapter 5. It would be of
great interest to know how this income was used. How much was
consumed and saved; and how much was invested in agriculture
and in other sectors? Unfortunately little is known of these
key variables in Peruvian agricultural development. We will
discuss investments in agriculture in chapter 6.

hand are directly related. Most agree that agrarian reform affects production, but there is no general agreement on what effects agrarian reform has on agricultural production. As Dorner has stated,

> "The relationship between land reform, increased investment and productivity are not always direct and positive, especially in the short run. Some countries without any land reforms have registered sharp increases in agricultural output, while others with major reforms have lagged behind."[49]

The time horizon is particularly important when making statements on the effects of agrarian reform on production as well as when causal relationships are specified. Frequently agrarian reform is a consequence or forms part of other major social changes and whatever happens to production cannot analytically be isolated from other changes. Citing Dorner again, "Reform, especially when associated with major political and social revolutionary upheavals, can be a disruptive process."[50] After having reviewed several cases he reached the conclusion, "The extent to which reform alone can be credited with or blamed for these production consequences is difficult to measure. Many other complex and interrelated factors influence the levels and shifts in farm output."[51]

In 1971 Cline reviewed the effects of an agrarian reform in Brazil and made a theoretical survey of the different hypotheses. His conclusions were,

> "The principal determinants of the effect of land reform on production are: (a) the existence or non-existence of increasing returns to scale for inputs actually used in agriculture; (b) the relationship of land utilization to farm size*);

---

*) On the concept of land utilization see note 54.

(c) the amount of unemployed labour which would
be absorbed in land reform; and (d) the relationship of the savings ratio and of willingness to
adopt technical change, to farm size."52)

Subsequently he writes, "The author finds it difficult to
state a priori, which of these influences are the more important."53)

However, a few years later he states that,

"...land distribution should increase output...
The central thrust of the arguments is that
large estates underutilize their available land
resources while at the same time the latifundio-
minifundio landholding structure compresses excess labor into the very small properties (minifundia) and into an underemployed landless labor force. Poor utilization of land on large
farms results from various factors: 'labor market dualism' in which the effective price is
higher for hired labor on large farms than for
family labor on small farms; land monopoly and
monopsony over labor in larger estates; the holding of land as a portfolio asset rather than for
production; and the fact that production partly
for own consumption provides small farms with
greater market certainty than large estates. The
resulting misallocation of resources within agriculture means that output could rise from the
combination of underutilized labour on small
farms and in the landless labour force with
underutilized land on large farms.
...Numerous other studies, particularly those
concerning Latin America, reach similar conclusion..."54)

As can be seen from the above, one of the more important arguments suggesting an increase in agricultural production is
that,

"In many countries one finds that output per
unit of labor is higher on the large farms
and output per unit of land is higher on the
small farms. In these circumstances, total
output would increase if the small farmers

- 122 -

were given more land and the large farmers
were induced to cultivate their land more
intensively."55)

Griffin has continued to state this several times and thus in
1978 he wrote:

"Moreover, a redistribution of land through
the creation of smallholdings is likely to
reduce poverty indirectly by increasing production and total income.
The reason for this is that small farmers
typically use production technologies, cropping
patterns and rotation systems which are more
productive than those used by large farmers."56)

Regarding the quoted arguments one can briefly say that
partial analysis, involving comparative statics, such
as the inverse relationship between size of farm and the
part of land cultivated, can shed some light on possible
effects, but it will not lead far into predicting post
reform production levels.

The second one which concerns us here is that the lack of
agricultural growth in Peru could be explained by the land
ownership which prevailed prior to the reform in 1969 and
thus, on this account, there should be an increase in production, as can be suggested by theory. The lack of growth
could also be explained by the development strategy pursued by Peru since World War II with its heavy emphasis on
urban-industrial growth. More of this will be discussed in
chapter 6. Therefore, empirical observations of key variables such as land use intensity, investments, and technology
can be explained by both the land tenure situation which
prevailed and by the development of the economy in general.

In addition to these questions of a methodological character there is another one of relevance of theory. Most discussions on agrarian reform operate within a framework of

large landowners being expropriated and the land transferred
to the small and landless peasants. In Peru, as will be discussed in chapter 5, the land was not transferred to these
groups. Therefore, often theoretical deductions are not necessarily correct in the context of Peruvian development.

That an agrarian reform is necessary for equity has strong
support in theory. That an agrarian reform is a necessary
condition to increase production has some support in theory,
but theory suggests that it is not a sufficient condition.
That agrarian reform cum growth is possible nobody disputes,
though its short-run effects can be disruptive for agricultural production.

In chapter 6 we will review agricultural production in a
longer time perspective to attempt to identify the key factors which operated. We will also investigate whether necessary conditions for increased growth were present, and also
study, using what data are available, if there were short-
run production problems in agriculture.

1. Samuelson (1964), p. 5; Lipsey and Steiner (1966), pp. 4-5.

2. Chenery et.al. (1974), p. 19.

3. Lipton (1977), p. 13.

4. Webb (1977), p. 73.

5. Clark and Haswell (1970), p. 159. See also Table XXXIX.

6. Jacoby (1971), chapter 6.

7. Griffin (1976), p. 10.

8. Griffin (1978), p. 155.

9. Webb (1977), p. 73.

10. Chenery et.al. (1974), p. 119.

11. ILO (1977), p. 34.

12. Foxley et.al. (1977), pp. 69-70.

13. Adelman (1975), p. 308.

14. Cline (1975), p. 392.

15. Lipton (1977), p. 106. See also Lipton: "Towards a Theory of Land Reform" in Lehman ed. (1974), pp. 269-313.

16. Kendrick (1961), pp. 305-307, 347 and 367; Tostlebe (1957), pp. 50-51. Cf. Strauss (1969) and Chang (1949), chapter V.

17. Horton (1974), p. vii.

18. Convenio (1970:4), pp. 41-43. Cf Table A.5.8.

19. See Boserup (1965) for how labour inputs varies in different agricultural systems.

20. The relationship between labour and availability of land on the one hand, and the distribution of income on the other hand is well established in economic theory."A higher population density generated by faster population growth is likely to produce a higher rental share, which in turn generates greater inequality given the typically concentrated pattern of land ownership", Ahluwalia (1976:2), p. 327. See also ILO (1977), p. 23; Clark and Haswell (1970), chapter X. The notion of land

scarcity is related to the cost of bringing land into production. Bottomley (1971), p. 2 and chapter 4; Clark and Haswell, Ibidem.

21. This section relies extensively on two books. The first one is Income Distribution Theory by Bronfenbrenner (1971) and the second one is Factor Pricing and Economic Growth in Underdeveloped Rural Areas by Bottomley (1971). The mathematics of this section has been kept at a minimum, in order not to burden the main line of the argument unduly. In particular the properties of the functions have not been made explicit and only necessary conditions, not sufficient, have been derived in profit maximization. The term used throughout this section is rent maximization. Any standard book in mathematical economics such as Microeconomic Theory:A Mathematical Approach by Henderson and Quandt (1958) and Mathematical Analysis for Economists by Allen (1967), will give sufficient information in this respect.

22. According to Harry G. Johnson this is a Ricardian approach: "It is important to the understanding of Ricardian theory to note that capital appears only indirectly, in that none is used in the productive process. Labour does all the work, and only labour and land enter the production function; but capital enters indirectly by supporting labour during the production period". Johnson (1973), p. 14.

23. See chapter 6.3.

24. See chapter 6.4.

25. See Table 1 of this chapter.

26. For a discussion of different forms and origin of land tenure in Peru see CIDA (1966). The bibliography list contains several books on this subject and in particular Barraclough and Collarte (1972), Dorner (1972), Eguren (1975), Griffin (1969), Malpica (1974). The Instituto de Estudios Peruanos (IEP) has published several studies mainly of sociological and anthropological character such as Matos (1976), Spalding (1974), Mejia and Diaz (1975). For a microeconomic treaty see for example Bottomley (1971).

27. Flores-Saenz (1977), p. 121. See also the above note for references. Brundenius (1972), pp. 20-23 on the origin of the Encomienda system which tied the peasant to the land of the large landowner. Also Matos (1976), pp. 21-26; Horton (1976), pp. 38-39.

28. The question of feudalism has been debated,particularly by the Peruvian left. Beginning with the seventies it became generally accepted that Peruvian agriculture was not feudal. See for example Montoya (1970).

29. For the mathematics see for example Henderson and Quandt (1958), p. 195. For a detailed discussion of imperfect competition see Bronfenbrenner (1971), chapter 8;and Bottomley (1971).

30. Rearranging 6 we obtain $P \cdot \frac{dQ}{dL} = (1 + \frac{dw}{w} \frac{dL}{L})$ which is the form used by Bronfenbrenner in his discussion on imperfect competion and exploitation. Bronfenbrenner (1971), p. 189.

31. Bronfenbrenner (1971); Johnson (1973).

32. The sugar plantation workers were largely unionized after World War II, and there were many strikes. The sugar estates became higly mechanized during the sixties, as a consequence of labour unrest and high wages. Outside the sugar estates, on the Coast and in the Sierra, the Peruvian peasants were little organized. Attempts to form unions were repressed. CIDA (1966), pp. 259-263; Roca (1975), pp. 21-26; Astiz (1969), pp. 191-230; Malpica (1974). I visited several sugar estates in 1970 and recorded great differences between wages paid to unionized workers and non-unionized workers, on the sugar estates. Some data of this visit is reproduced in Alberts (1977), pp. 70-71.

33. "The analysis in section 13 implies that both employers and elastic-supply workers gain from discrimination, as compared with uniform monopsony wage setting. They share joint interests in keeping the disadvantaged workers down, so long as monopsony exists. When it comes to breaking down the monopsony itself, however, the two worker groups have a common interest, with management on the other side." Bronfenbrenner (1971), p. 203.

34. Bottomley (1971), p. 12.

35. Ibidem, p. 165.

36. Leibenstein (1957), p. 94; Clark and Haswell (1970), pp. 1-26.

37. Shoup (1965). These ideas were further explored by Mirrlees (1976); Stiglitz (1976); and Bliss and Stern (1978).

38. Shoup (1965); Turnham and Jaeger (1971), p. 91; Alberts (1968).

39. Griffin (1978), p. 139. See also Bottomley (1971), which explores this idea in his book. The hypothesis is stated on p. 1 and p. 7.

40. Griffin (1978), p. 141.

41. Ibidem.

42. Clark and Haswell (1970), chapter 1.

43. The National Food Consumption Survey (ENCA), in 1971/72 provides most valuable information in this respect. The basic data were further elaborated by Amat y León and León (1977). See also Amat y León (1970), reviewing earlier consumption surveys.

44. Shoup (1965), p. 175. Both Shoup (1965), p. 176 and Lundahl (1979),

p. 440, relate production to consumption. We have preferred to separate the production function from the labour input function. In Figure 4.3 we could have added a segment where a proportional increase in the wage rate results in a proportionately greater amount of work performed, as in Shoup (1965) and Lundahl (1979), but it would not add any to the substantive arguments here. There is of course a problem of measurement here which we do not go into in this analysis.

45. The model developed here is based on Alberts (1968). Bottomley (1971), pp. 22-24, arrives at the same relationship. For a proof that this condition is a necessary one for rent maximization under unlimited supply of labour see Bottomley,Ibidem.

46. See footnotes 25 and 26. Chewing coca has the effect of reducing hunger feelings and this practice is widespread in the Peruvian Sierra. See also Blanco (1974), pp. 109-115,for an interview illustrating a landowner-peasant situation.

47. Reliable demographic data on Peru, up to the Census in 1940, are scarce. There is no disagreement between scholars that there was a drastic reduction in the population between 1525 and the end of the 18th century. According to Roel (1970), the Peruvian population was about 12 million in 1525, 8.2 in 1555, 1.8 in 1586 and in 1793 the Indian population was about 609 000. In 1974 the Peruvian Government, through its Statistics Office (ONEC) presented a study: "La Población del Perú" as a contribution to the UN Population-year. It carefully avoids the fall in population after colonization but putting different pieces together it is possible to reconcile the Roel data with those of this study. On p. 7, at the end of the 18th century the ethnic composition was 12.6% whites and 3.7% negroes. The total population is not given. But on p. 9 it is claimed that the population more than doubled between 1791 and 1862, and on p. 8 the total population for the latter year is given, 2 482 000. Half of that is 1 241 000. Deducting the non-Indian population (12.6% + 3.7%) an estimate of the Indian and the mestizo population is obtained, 1 039 000 which is, as is to be expected, higher than the Roel estimate of 609 000. But why does not the ONEC study show the figure from 1791? Probably because that would show the drastic decline in the Peruvian population from the time of Colonization up to 1791 which is politically still a sensitive issue. See also Spalding (1974), p. 140; and Wachtel (1972), p. 83, Oman (1978), pp. 72-80.

48. Barraclough and Domike (1966), p. 398.

49. Dorner (1972), p. 110.

50. Ibid, p. 111.

51. Ibid, p. 113.

52. Cline (1970), p. 55.

53. Ibid, p. 57.

54. Cline in Frank and Webb (1977), p. 282. As has been pointed out by Cline the concept of land use intensity can have several meanings. The terminology used in this study follows the custom established by many development economists. "Intensive land use refers to the Ricardian sense of the term, rather than the more recent use of the factor intensity concept. By current usage, land intensive methods would refer to combinations of much land with little labour and capital. By intensive land use this study means just the opposite". Cline (1970), p. 11 note 2. This terminology is also followed by, for example, Bottomley (1971), pp. 52 and 165; Griffin (1978), p. 155; and Cline in Frank and Webb (1977), p. 282.

55. Griffin and Enos (1970), p. 129. For Peru see CIDA (1966), chapters V-VII; and Williams (1977).

56. Griffin (1978), p. 155, see also chapter 6; Griffin (1975), pp. 137-140; Griffin (1974), chapter 2; ILO (1977), chapter 1; Lipton (1977), pp. 106-107.

5
Redistribution For Whom?

5.1   INTRODUCTION [1]

In chapter 4 we discussed how various forms of land ownership determine the distribution of income in agriculture.
In this chapter we turn to the questions (1) of the beneficiaries of the agrarian reform.   First we will give a
brief description of the agrarian reform efforts leading
up to the new agrarian reform law in June 1969.

(2) We will use the 1961 agricultural census to establish
how much agricultural land was available, and how it was
owned. This census was the basic source of information to
the government, and the objectives as well as the targets
of the agrarian reform were established on the basis of
this census. We will also use the agricultural census of
1972 to give some additional information on the likely evolution between 1961 and 1972 of key agricultural variables.

(3) On the basis of the information thus obtained we will
comment on the new agrarian reform law and the targets set
forth by the Government to implement the reform. We will
review the data on the reform with respect to the number
of recipients of land (hereafter called beneficiaries) and
with respect to the recipients' sociological characteristics. Having established the number of beneficiaries, we
will investigate the amount of land they received.

(4) We will discuss some issues relevant to the interpretation
of the distributionary effects of the agrarian reform. It
has been claimed that the financial conditions imposed on
the beneficiaries were such that they led to a rapid decapitalization of agriculture, and that the income redistribution effects thus were rather few. We will investigate if
and to what extent this is correct.

(5) Using some scattered pieces of information on the co-
operative agrarian reform enterprises we will review the
data on income distribution for these, before and after
the reform.

After having established who were the main beneficiaries
of the reform, we will conclude the chapter by discussing
the groups which were neglected by the reform and still remain unaffected. Finally we will summarize our main findings in this chapter.

5.2   THE BENEFICIARIES

5.2.1 Pre-1969 agrarian reform attempts

The question of land has long occupied a central place in the
Peruvian discussion and increasingly so after the land invasions in the early sixties. Already in the twenties, José Carlos Mariátegui, the well known Peruvian marxist writer, was
writing on the feudal character of Peruvian agriculture in his:
"Siete ensayos de interpretación de la realidad peruana".[2]
The APRA party had also advocated an agrarian reform, as far
back as in the twenties, but progressively and particularly
in the sixties it sided with the more conservative elements.[3]
However, few actual land transfers occured until 1963 when
massive peasant occupations took place in several places in
Peru. These land occupations were subsequently legalized
through special decrees.[4]

In 1964 president Belaúnde signed the first major agrarian reform law, frequently referred to as the law 15037. Horton has
succinctly stated the effects of this law.
> "Land reform was not actively supported by either
> the Executive or by Congress; the Reform Agency

was inadequately financed and staffed; and the
land reform bureaucracy was controlled by officials who were sympathetic to estate owners.
Consequently, very little land redistribution
took place under the 1964 law. Instead, the
government attempted to defuse the peasant mo-
vement by promising land redistribution and by
threatening not to give titles to land invaders."[5]

In October 1968 a military junta deposed of Belaúnde in a
non-violent coup. The political events leading up to this
coup and its causes have been described in other literature.[6] Suffice to say that after a few months it became
evident that the military junta represented something quali-
tatively different in Peru, but it was uncertain what the
Government intended to do. Great divergences existed among
the military policy makers. As was mentioned in chapter 2,
this lack of definition could also be observed in the Ministry of Agriculture where different factions were operating and subject to a variety of pressures.

At the beginning of 1969 it was becoming clear in Government circles that the military junta intended to implement
an agrarian reform and that it would set out to eliminate
the owners' oligarchy in the agricultural sector (see chapter 2 for details),

In analysing the 1979 Agrarian Reform Law, frequently referred to as D.L. 17716, the Iowa Mission stated that it;
"...is nearly as extensive as its 1964 predecessor, with
196 articles (compared to 248 for 1964) divided into six-
teen Titles (15 in 1964), with nine Special Dispositions
(2 in 1964)..."[7] Therefore, we will not burden the reader
with an extensive review of the law. The interested can refer to the bibliography which gives references both in English and Spanish titles. Since 1969, the law has been amended
several times although not substantially.

The main objective of an agrarian reform can be to increase production and/or to accomplish equity. The introduction of the law,is, therefore, interesting because of its strong emphasis on re-distribution. The content seems to fit quite well with proposals of equity or basic needs development strategies.

> "**That** the fundamental objective of the Revolutionary Government of the Armed Forces is to promote higher living standards for the less favored sectors of the population, compatible with the dignity of the human person by realizing the transformation of the economic, social and cultural structures of the country;
> That the serious structural imbalance of the agrarian order has generated extreme conditions of rural social injustice.
> That all the sectors of the population have demanded the transformation of the agrarian structure of the country;
> That, besides constituting an instrument for realizing rural social justice, the Agrarian Reform should decisively contribute to the formation of a wide market and provide the necessary capital resources for a rapid industrialization of the country;
> That, therefore, it is absolutely essential that an authentic Agrarian Reform be carried out that responds to the unanimous interest of the Peruvian people, to the Fundamental Objectives of the Revolution, and to the needs of the integrated development of Peru;"8)

Although we will not discuss the law in detail, there are some characteristics which must be stressed.

1. Expropriation procedures cannot be stopped by legal maneuvers of the big farmers.
2. One of the more important criteria for expropriation is size and that no exemptions are granted in this respect.[9]
In many countries with more conservative regimes only poorly cultivated land has been subject to expropriation. The previous law, 15037, also had this feature.
3. When a farm is expropriated, the whole farm, including

buildings and machinery is expropriated.

The Chilean agrarian reform, 1965-1973, permitted the owners to retain a "Reserva", often the best land with machinery and buildings. This left the beneficiaries in a
difficult position to get started, because of lack of ma-
chines, tools, storage etc. In Peru in the case of the sugar
complexes on the Coast, it was not clear where the line was
to be drawn, since several of these also produced alcohol and
paper. In the end the whole agro-industrial complex of the
sugar estates was expropriated.[10]

4. Only part of the expropriated farm was paid in cash, while
the balance was paid in non-marketable bonds. We will return
to the financial aspects of the reform in section 5.3.

5. The estates were not to be broken up, and the production structure was to be maintained intact. Co-operative
forms of production were assigned priority.[11]

6. The Government allocated money for expropriation and
assigned necessary personnel to the agrarian reform department.

7. The Agrarian Reform Law was supplemented with a water
act which repudiated inherited water rights and stated that
water was to be used according to social and economic criteria, leaving these criteria's definition to the public
sector.[12]

5.2.2 Land ownership in 1961 and 1972

In order to analyse the effects of the reform on land ownership, it would be desirable to know the evolution of
land ownership during the pre-reform period, and contrast
it with the post-reform period. Unfortunately, the only systematic data available refer to the situation in 1961 and
1972, corresponding to the agricultural censuses of those
years.[13]

There are some important methodological questions which
should be answered. The Census data are based on the production units and not on the ownership structure. It is
for example impossible to obtain information from the Census data on how much land a particular individual or cor-
poration owned. What was registered was the physical extension of the production unit and not individual or cor-
porate ownership.[14] Also important is that frequently the
smaller production units did not own the land but rented
it from larger farms. Because of this, the Census data underestimated the ownership concentration of land in Peru.
The way land has been rented was very complex and has
been documentated in several studies including the CIDA
tenure study on Peru.

There were about 840 000 production units in 1961 (Table 5.1).
In order to analyse the data, the following classification
scheme is used: subsistence*) sector up to 1 Ha; small farmers 1-5 Ha's; medium size farmers 5-100 Ha's; and large
producers more than 100 Ha's. Table 5.1 shows that the subsistence sector accounted for more than 1/3 of the number
of production units, but less than 1% of land area in both
1961 and 1972. The small producers also show a similar as-
simetry: while the number of small producer units represented almost half of the total, their share of the area was
about 5%. The medium-size farmers, accounted for almost 16%
of the units, and covered slightly more than 10% of the area.
The large producers with 1.3% of the units occupied an area
of almost 84%.

We see that in 1961 there existed an extreme concentration

Table 5.1   Land tenure in Peru 1961 and 1972

Size (Ha's)	Production Units				Area covered			
	1961		1972		1961		1972	
	Number	Percent	Number	Percent	Hectares	Percent	Hectares	Percent
- 1	292 920	34.7	483 350	34.8	129 092	0.7	185 132	0.8
1- 5	406 507	48.2	600 425	43.2	907 096	5.1	1 375 316	5.8
5- 20	107 853	12.8	231 840	16.7	887 574	5.0	2 036 421	8.6
20- 100	24 638	2.9	59 592	4.3	953 307	5.4	2 182 599	9.3
100- 500	7 684	0.9	11 279	0.8	1 551 039	8.8	2 150 668	9.1
500-2 500	2 612	0.3	2 785	0.2	2 642 106	14.9	2 924 225	12.0
2 500-	1 026	0.1	1 017	0.1	10 651 831	60.1	12 790 788	54.3
TOTAL	843 240	99.9	1 390 288	100.1	17 722 045	100.0	23 545 149	99.9

Source: INP (1965), p. 2; ONEC (1975), p. 1

Average area per production unit (hectares)

1961	21.0
1972	16.9

of ownership of land. It is, hence, interesting to analyse
whether this situation still existed in 1972. The total
number of production units increased from 840 000 to almost
1.4 million, and, indeed, the tenure structure in 1972 was
similar to that in 1961.

It may seem odd that the 1972 land tenure situation was so
similar to that of 1961, since the agrarian reform could
have had a strong impact on land ownership. There are two
important reasons why this similarity occurs. First, the
expropriated estates were not subdivided, and hence, the
production unit remained intact, and was consequently counted as such in the Census. Second, different forms of indirect exploitation such as share-cropping and renting the
land were prohibited. Those peasants who rented the land,
were, in the process of the reform, given legal titles to
the land they worked. For census purposes these units also
remained intact, although the legal status of the farmers
had changed.

5.2.3 Government targets and implementation of agrarian reform

At the time of the promulgation of the Law there were no targets for how much land and how many farms were to be expropriated,nor for how many farmers were to be benefitted, and
at what rate the reform was to be implemented. It would have
been almost impossible for the Government to state precise
targets, but some guidelines should have been promulgated.
The Government found it difficult to state targets given the
lack of basic data on how many families lived in the agricultural sector, the extension of the farms, etc. In September
1969 a FAO mission was told that the target of the military
junta was to benefit 500 000 families during the next five
years.[15] This motion was subsequently defined to mean 100 000

families yearly during the next five years.[16] The total target "volume of the agrarian reform" depended on general policy decisions and was subject to changes. A review of the targets, as expressed in several official documents, illustrate this (Table 5.2). The reduction in the number of farms and the area indicates that there was a shift in policy orientation.[17]

Table 5.2   Agrarian reform targets in different documents

Source	Year	Expropriation		Adjudication*		
		Area (1000 Has)	Farms number	Area (1000 Has)	Families number	Area per family (Has)
Development Plan 1971-75	1970	12 677	26 193	12 677	336 032**	37.7
Agricultural Planning Office OSPA	1975	10 150	14 500	10 000	400 000	25.0

Source: INP (1971) Vol. II, p. 81; Ministerio de Agricultura (1976:1), pp. 66-67

*) The sequence in the reform is as follows. Land, machinery, buildings, cattle etc are expropriated. During a certain period the estate is administrated by the State and subsequently   handed over to the beneficiaries. A contract is signed between the Government and the beneficiaries, and the assets are thus adjudicated to the beneficiaries.

**) There have been some confusion among policy makers and officials in interpreting and making the law operational. This figure was based on setting a minimum target income per family, and allotting land on a per family basis until that target income is reached. Feder (1973), pp. 51-53. Interpreting the law strictly one estimate was that only some 80 000 families could be benefitted. See Convenio (1970:4), p. v. See also Chapter 2.4.5.

As can be seen from Table 5.2 the area to be expropriated, for example, has varied between 10 and almost 13 million hectares; and the number of farms to be expropriated between 14 and 26 thousand; and the number of families to be benefitted shows a variation from 340 to 400 thousand.

In Table 5.1 it was shown that average size of the produc-

tion units was 21 and 17 hectares for the years 1961 and
1972 respectively. The target of the junta was to allocate
25-38 hectares per family, well above the existing average.
This meant that only part of the agricultural population
could benefit from the reform. In terms of the key development objective, equity, it is clear that the targets are in
conflict with the objectives of the Government.

Having identified the targets of the government let us turn
to the results of the agrarian reform for the planning period
ending in 1975. In order to be able to use the data in
a systematic and explicit way, we will use the 1975 targets,
i.e. 10 million hectares expropriated and adjudicated, 14 500
farms expropriated and 400 thousand families to be benefitted.

Contrasting the targets for the total volume of the reform
and the situation at the end of 1975 the following table,
5.3, has been constructed.

Table 5.3   The state of agrarian reform as of 31 December
              1975 in relation to targets*)

	Expropriation		Adjudication		
	Area (1000 Ha's)	No. of farms	Area (1000 Ha's)	No. of families	Area per family (Ha's)
1. Target	10 150	14 494	10 150	400 000	25
2. Accom- plished as of 31 a) cember 75	7 426	9 740	6 210	254 000	24
3. as percent of 1	73.2	67.2	61.2	63.5	

Source: Table 5.2; Ministerio de Agricultura (1976:1), pp. 66-67

a) Includes 1.0 million Ha's and 548 farms expropriated; 0.4 million Ha's
adjudicated to 13 538 families in the 1962-1968 period.

*) Expropriation and adjudication data usually differ because of the se-
quences in the reform process. See note to Table 5.2. At the end of a reform,
on a yearly basis, adjudication figures are much higher than those for expropriation.

It is clear from Table 5.3 that in terms of stated targets of
of the reform, the advance was substantial. No less than
73 percent of the area had been expropriated, and over 250
thousand families had been benefitted.[18]

Still these accomplishments are below the original figure
of 500 000 families. Moreover, there were about 1.4 million
families in the agricultural sector during the first half
of the seventies of which about 1 million had less than 5
hectares. This demonstrates the modesty of the reforms obtained.[19] Practically none of these families received land,
because the major part of the large estates was handed over
to the permanent workers with some minor additions to their
labour force. The estates were then formed into new co-operative production units. The average amount of land allocated
on a per family basis coincided fairly well with the revised
targets, about 25 hectares. However, the proportion of good
quality land was higher in the expropriated land than in the
remaining part of the agricultural sector. (For statistical
details see Appendix to this chapter).

What has happened since 1975? There has been a continuous
modification to the timing of the implementation of the Reform.[20] (See footnote for the situation at the end of 1975).
In 1975 there was a significant change in the Government,
President Velasco was ousted, and as of 1976 the "second
phase" of the junta began. Pressures were strong within the
Ministry of agriculture to accelerate and conclude the agrarian reform.[21]

By the end of 1978 the agrarian reform had nearly terminated
land expropriations. In spite of the successively more conservative influences, the agrarian reform targets of 1975
were maintained. By October 1978 almost 370 000 families had
been benefitted by the reform and 8.6 million hectares had

been transferred.[22)]

We will now address some controversial issues of the Peruvian agrarian reform whereafter we will make our appraisal and concluding remarks.

5.3 THE ECONOMICS OF FINANCING THE REFORM

5.3.1 Introduction

The financial transactions of the Peruvian agrarian reform have evoked a lot of debate. This can be expected, since these issues touch the basis of the distribution of power, wealth and income in Peru.

Strangely enough there has been little economic but an abundance of sociological and political literature analysing the Peruvian agrarian reform. Economic appraisals have been frequently made on shaky theoretical basis and/or with little empirical support. The Peruvian left has violently attacked the reform claiming that it served the interest of the big landowners, the industrial and financial bourgeoisie, and that the objective was to transfer the surplus from agriculture to industry.[23)]

A little of historical background will help the reader to follow the discussion. In 1966 a Peruvian agrarian official stated, when discussing full compensation for expropriation of the big estates; "This compensation is indispensable if we want to maintain unhurt the principle of private property which has been the base for the most outstanding economic success which history knows. (Particularly in agriculture)..."[24)]

These lines are illustrative of one important current in Peruvian thinking, namely of full compensation. However, Dorner writing on agrarian reforms has noted that, "If compensation is at full market value, it may be impossible to meet the distributional requirements of reform. Thus, in this sense land reform must always be in part confiscatory."[25] Even, when writing on the new Law 17716 the Iowa mission noticed in 1970 that the landowners would not be fully compensated but proceeded to state: "A preliminary observation is that compensation provisions can be accepted as satisfactory 'just compensation' per se..."[26]

The political constraints imposed during the Belaúnde regime resulted in generous compensation schemes to the former landowners which led to high costs to the Government. One line of thought among policy makers of that time was to attempt to reduce these costs in different ways.[27] One such proposal was "The furthering of direct transactions between [those whose land was] expropriated and beneficiaries [such that they] would redound in considerable savings in agrarian reform costs."[28] There seemed to be a widespread belief in Peru that the agrarian reform inevitably would be costly and attempts were made to show that although the financial costs were relatively high the economic benefits obtained by far would outweigh these.[29] How much the landowners would receive was a political decision. There is nothing per se which makes an agrarian reform costly in terms of compensation to the former owners.

Still the military had to face several problems. First, the Government could not pay the landowners full compensation in cash, because of a fiscal constraint. Full compensation payments would have resulted in a large budgetary deficit and caused inflation. Therefore a system of partial cash payments and an agrarian bond system was inevitable. Second, the general idea prevalent among a number of the decision makers was that of "just compensation". The Government could only

- 143 -

finance this through a budgetary squeeze in the public sector, or through the beneficiaries' own payment, which would have compromised the income redistribution objectives pronounced by the Junta. Third, the Government thought that agriculture should "...provide the necessary capital resources for a rapid industrialization of the country". How was this to be implemented? In chapter 6 we will discuss the agricultural price policies which were used to tax the agricultural sector. A more direct way to extract capital from agriculture could be to require the beneficiaries to repay quickly for most of the assets they received. At the beginning of the reform in 1969 it was not clear what the Government intended to do.

This short introduction, in part explains why we address the following questions which have been debated.

1. Have land repayments contributed to a general decapitalization of the agricultural sector?
2. Did the obligation of the beneficiaries to pay for the assets they received conflict with the economic redistribution objective of the Government?
3. Were the former owners generously compensated by the reform?
4. Did the bond system enable the former owners to convert their agricultural assets into industrial capital?
5. Did the compensation to the former owners lead to financial difficulties for the Government?

Before discussing the above we will define various aspects of the financial system of the agrarian reform.

There are three major categories of agents:
(i) The beneficiaries of the reform, those who receive the assets. The expropriation-adjudication procedures included the

transfer of the assets of the farm to the beneficiaries. The degree of their control and ownership varies, but in general the Government retained a close control over the use of these assets which have to be repaid to the Government.

(ii) The public entities intervening in the process, such as the Ministry of Agriculture, the Agricultural Development Bank and the National Planning Institute. Henceforth they will be called the Government. The Government intervened directly in the transfer of the assets from the former farm owners to the beneficiaries. It stipulated the conditions by which the beneficiaries were to pay the Government for the assets received, and also compensated the former farmowners for the assets expropriated.

(iii) The former farmowners, henceforth referred to as ex-owners. These ex-owners received compensation for the assets expropriated. The conditions, however, were decided by the Government.

One important point raised by Dorner is

> "...whether payments for land are indeed 'unreasonable' is a matter to be judged in terms of historical circumstances. Present owners or their ancestors often gained access and ownership to the land by reason of their favoured power position. In many cases present market value reflects investments in infrastructure, much of it created either by the underpaid labourers who are the reform's intended beneficiaries, or through government investments financed by general tax revenues only part of which were collected from present landowners."[30]

Peruvian scholars have argued along similar lines, as have peasant unions.[31] This is certainly a relevant question in the case of Peru.

As stated there are three agents involved. The transfer
from ex-owners to the beneficiaries of the assets involve
stock variables, (land, cattle, machinery etc), while the
transactions taking place between the beneficiaries and
the government, and the government and the ex-owners, involve flow variables (beneficiaries' payments to the Government, amortization of the agrarian bonds). Theoretical
problems immediately emerge. How are we to evaluate the
effects on the beneficiaries? The transfer of a certain
amount of assets such as land, cattle, machinery etc, will
enable the beneficiaries to produce and obtain an income.
Part of this income has to be used to repay the Government
for the assets obtained, over a time period of 20-25 years.
The rates of interest charged and the rate of inflation
will also play a decisive role in this context. We will return to this later in this chapter.

The economic effects on the three groups of agents involved
are not independent of changes in policy instruments. For
example, the Government may choose to maintain a given system of the financing arrangements of the agrarian reform,
while changing other policy variables. For example, if the
Government finds the rates of amortization too high, it may
choose to reduce the amortization payments directly or instead reduce taxes on wage payments. This may benefit the beneficiaries as much and even stimulate employment.[32]

In this context it is useful to discuss the effects of inflation. A given rate of inflation, as measured by e.g. consumer price index or the implicit GNP deflator, could easily
disguise different effects on the three agents (changes in
relative prices). For example, the price of fertilizers has
increased drastically, while the overall rate of inflation
has been less. Obviously this should have a very negative
effect on the beneficiaries using fertilizers.[33]

The financial set-up was decided in 1969 when the rate of
inflation was moderate (less than 10% p.a.). All rates of
interests were set lower than the rate of inflation, and
since no adjustments were made for the effects of the inflation the real values declined. In view of the very sharp
increases in the rate of inflation since 1972, these real
values have fallen rapidly over time (See Table 5.6).

Ex-owners have received compensation for the assets, usually
the major part in bonds and the balance in cash. The real
value of the bonds decreased over time. A rate of inflation
of for example 20 percent per year would have reduced the
real value of a 100 000 US dollars bond to about 33 000 US
dollars in five years.[34] The real value of compensation
for expropriated assets, bonds, and beneficiary payments
have therefore dropped very rapidly. In fact, perhaps the
most decisive element in the financial flows has been the
very high rates of inflation that have prevailed in the Peruvian economy.

Let us now turn to each of the agents involved to investigate
how the financial transactions have affected them.

5.3.2 The beneficiaries

One difficult issue to resolve is the question of what meaning can be assigned to the "value" of the assets of the expropriated farm. This expropriation value, based on self declarations of the ex-owners before the reform, was in most
cases the same value as that adjudicated to the beneficiaries
of the reform. Since this value has to be related to some
hypothetical value in order to be able to estimate the degree
of confiscation, it is difficult to estimate. It seems at
least plausible to assume that the value registered by the

agrarian reform authorities was less than the market value that would have prevailed in a competitive equilibrium.[35]

We will not make a detailed account of how the repayments
are calculated. The general way the system functions is as
follows: The beneficiaries receive the assets, and the
price fixed for these is not greater than the value registered when the assets were expropriated. The interest
rate charged varied from 2-4% for land, depending on the
region: the Coast 4%, the Sierra 3%, and the Ceja de Selva 2%, and for building, machinery, cattle, etc the rate
of interest charged was 7%.[36]

The debt is to be paid back in 20 years with up to a maximum of a 5 years grace period. The rate of interest is added
to the debt, and this sum is then divided into 20 annual
installments.[37]

The aggregate debt repayments depend, inter alia, on the
rate of implementation of the reform as well as the volume
of the reform. There are two sets of estimates available,
and since they agree fairly well these have been reproduced
in Table 5.4. The Convenio estimate projected an increase
in debt repayments to a maximum of about 690 million current Soles as of 1982. For 8 years they were to remain constant. The Ministry of Agriculture estimate, from 1975, showed
a slightly higher repayment burden, reaching a maximum in
1981 of about 720 million current Soles. The difference can
probably be explained by the fact that the agrarian reform
came to expropriate more of first class land than the Convenio estimated, and hence, the Ministry of Agriculture figures for debt repayments are somewhat higher.

Table 5.4   Projections of beneficiaries' payments
             to the Government (Current Soles)

	Projection	
Period	Ministry of Agriculture $(Soles \cdot 10^6)$	Convenio
1969–74	1 132	1 152
1975	539	385
76	603	496
77	633	548
78	670	580
79	709	613
1980	722	646
1981–90	7 224	6 838
1991–2000	n.a.	2 991

Source: Ministerio de Agricultura (1976), statistical Table
        26; Ministerio de Agricultura (1975:2), Table 8. See
        also (1975:1), Table F-6 for the years 1975-76; Con-
        venio (1970:4), p. 57

To what extent would these payments from the beneficiaries
tend to contribute to a general decapitalization of the agriculture?   Using estimates on agricultural production we
have constructed the following table:

Table 5.5   Beneficiaries repayments and value of agri-
             cultural production (1970 prices, Million Soles)

	1975	1976
1. Value added in agricultural production	39 816	41 130
2. Value of beneficiaries repayments	298	249
3. Beneficiary payments as percent of 1	0.7%	0.6%

Source: 1) BCR Memoria(1976), p. 184; 2) Table 5.4 and Table A.6.

Note: Agricultural production statistics are very poor. This will be
      discussed in chapter 6. In 1975 beneficiaries' payments were
      actually less. See Table 5.9, but it seems as if the 1975 re-
      payment record was particularly low so we have used the data
      of Table 5.4 instead.

- 149 -

Table 5.5 conclusively shows that the debt repayments of
the beneficiaries of the reform cannot have been a major
cause for decapitalization of Peruvian agriculture. In
1970 a study by Van de Wetering, using aggregate data,
showed that the debt repayments would only represent a
few percent in the value added of the farms, and that the
beneficiaries' income would more than double after the reform.[38]

Still, this conclusion does not preclude that some of the
reformed units have encountered financial difficulties, and
some of the reasons have been: (a) difficulties in maintaining former levels of production; (b) Government enforced
price controls of output; (c) increased tax enforcement (because of closer control); (d) increased wages and salaries.[39]

There are, however, no reports indicating a general difficulty of the beneficiaries to repay the debt, although there
was massive opposition to these payments.[40]

The share of debt repayments in total incomes has varied
and in some cases has been quite great. Thus, for example,
the beneficiaries (3700) in a valley North of Lima, claimed
that each of them had to pay Soles 5 000 per year which
amounted to working 55 days each year in repaying the debt.
They finally demanded as have many others, "No pago a la
Deuda Agraria", no payment of the agrarian debt.[41]

Granted that some temporal difficulties may occur, in a longer perspective the debt repayments will hardly be of real
significance, because they are not to be adjusted for the
rate of inflation. Since inflation has been high in the latter years and without signs of slowing down, the real value
of the debt repayments has decreased rapidly.

The following Figure 5.1 shows the real value of 1 Sol in different years assuming different rates of inflation. As can be seen a rate of inflation of 10% would in 10 years reduce the real value of repayments to 35% of the original. In other words after 10 years the 700 million Soles of a yearly debt repayment of the beneficiaries would only amount to 245 million Soles (1970 prices). That this depreciation of the real debt repayment is occuring rapidly can be seen from the rates of inflation in Peru during later years in Table 5.6. The rate of inflation has risen from about 6% per year in 1969-71 to over 30% in 1976.

Figure 5.1   The real value of X Soles over 10 years at different rates of inflation

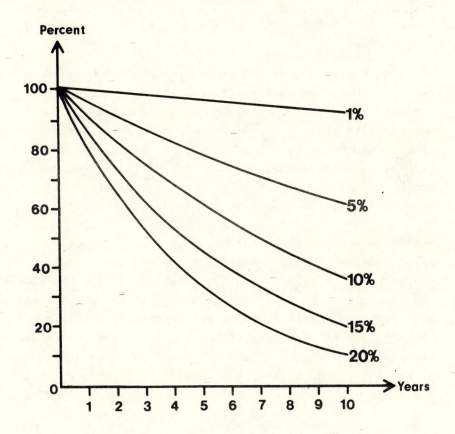

Table 5.6   Indicator of Peruvian inflation

| Year | Yearly rates of change in percent | |
	General Index	Food and beverages
1969	6.2	5.6
1970	5.0	3.1
71	6.8	6.8
72	7.2	7.4
73	9.5	10.1
74	16.9	18.8
1975	23.6	32.8
76	33.5	32.1
77	38.0	40.3
1978	57.8	59.7

Source: BCR, Boletin February (1977), p. 37 and February (1979), p. 32

Important is also that the expropriation-adjudication values were based on 1968 self declarations, before there was a clear threat of a reform. The longer the time period is between 1968 and the adjudication, the greater the difference between the "real" value of the assets and expropriation-adjudication values will be.[42] There have been some tendencies to re-evaluate the assets, but thus far, only to a minor extent.[43]

The Government on the other hand had insisted on making the beneficiaries repay the debt and had suspended credit, and used other coercive methods of securing a high debt repayment record. In fact in 1975 more than 90% of the accumulated debt had been repaid.[44] This is surprisingly high, because historically, defaulting on debts to the public sector has been common. (A Convenio study even considered that defaulting could be as high as 50%).[45] There was also a positive relationship between the economically better endowed production units and the better repayment records.

Let us now return to the second question posed in this section, viz, has the obligation of the beneficiaries to pay for the assets received led to a conflict with the economic redistribution objective of the Government?

In answering this question it should be recalled that rural incomes are much lower than urban incomes, so that from this point of view, it can be argued that transfers out of agriculture are contrary to the objective of equity. The beneficiaries of the reform, however, tended to belong to the higher income groups in the rural areas, so that on this account the repayment scheme does not seem to be inconsistent with the objective. Moreover, the poorer farms usually received better conditions (longer grace period and lower rates of interest). Finally, the real value of the repayments are falling rapidly. In summary, it is argued that this scheme is consistent with the equity objective of the Government.

5.3.3 The effects on the former owners

The repayment to the ex-owners is affected by how the assets are valued and by the terms regulating the payments for their assets. We have already commented on the first element, and we will now discuss the second one.

According to the law, only a part of an expropriated estate should be paid in cash: the balance in bonds. The bigger the farms and the less intensively exploited, the smaller is the share in cash, and this seems to agree fairly well with notions of equity. As can be seen in Table 5.7, the cash/bond

evolution for the period 1962–76 shows that these legal
intentions were also implemented. Strangely enough, earlier reform attempts (1962–69) do not display a significantly higher cash proportion.

Table 5.7 The relationship between compensation in cash
and in bonds to former owners (million current Soles)

	1 Cash	2 Bonds	3 1:2=3 Cash/Bonds
1962–69 (old law)	137	392	0.35
1969	217	182	1.19
1970	457	4 874	0.09
71	267	752	0.36
72	408	1 475	0.28
73	549	1 283	0.43
74	365	540	0.68
1975	501	778	0.64
1976	567	1 005	0.56
1969–76	3 331	10 889	0.31

Source: Ministerio de Agricultura (1977:1), various tables;
Ministerio de Agricultura (1978), various tables

In the 1971–75 Medium-Term Plan for the agricultural sector
the relationship between cash and bonds was estimated to be
0.4 and the result for the 1971–75 period was also 0.4. In
this case there was a close correspondence between the
Plan and the results. The planned amounts were estimated for
the planning period to be 8 300 million in cash and 20 000
million in bonds. The results for the whole 1969–76 period
fell far below and were 3 300 and 10 900 million respectively.

The following four factors are particularly important in e

laining the confiscation involved:
1. Agrarian bonds were non-transferable[46];
2. The nominal rate of interest paid is rather low (4-6%)
(implying a negative real rate, because of the inflation);
3. The redemption period is rather long (20-30 years);
4. There is a maximum for amortization + interest payments
on the bonds, and the balance is paid in shares of the public sector enterprises (also non-transferable for 10 years).

Rather than to enter into complicated calculations based on
the legal regulations a few figures will indicate the real
value of the part of repayment which was made in bonds. Firstly, the redemption period of 20-30 years rapidly depreciated
the real value of the interest and amortization payments. (See
earlier on the beneficiaries). Secondly, not all of the amount
due was paid in cash and the data on the distribution between
what has been repaid in cash and what has been paid in industrial shares are illustrative:

Table 5.8   Public sector payments to agrarian reform bondholders (Million current Soles)

Period	1 Total due to ex-owners	2 Paid in cash	3 (2:1)x100 Percent of total	4 Paid in shares	5 (4:1)x100 Percent of total
1969-74	878	151	17	727	83
31-12-74 to 31-05-75	177	72	41	105	59

Source: Ministerio de Agricultura (1975:2), Table 2

One idea contained in the law and which has been very much
debated refers to the possibility of converting the agrarian
bonds into industrial shares in private firms.[47] The re-
quirement was that the bondholder should provide new capital

amounting to the same amount as the discounted value of the bond, 36 percent - 80 percent of the nominal value.[48] In view of the rapid inflation this should have been an attractive alternative, but as of date hardly any firms have been formed using agrarian bonds. In part this was due to the uncertainty surrounding the Peruvian experiment, and hence a certain reluctance to invest new capital. Moreover, the Government as a rule did not approve the investment schemes presented by the bondholders.[49]

In summary the real value of the bonds has declined very significantly because of inflation. It cannot be sustained that the former owners were generously compensated, if the principle of "full compensation" is accepted. The mechanism to confiscate involved two elements. The first was that the accounting value for expropriation seemed to be significantly lower than a "market value". The second is that the real value of the cash flows received has decreased rapidly. Very big asset holders have been hit relatively harder than smaller ones, because there was a maximum set for amortization and interest payments.

5.3.4 The effects on the Government budget

Before discussing fiscal effects it is necessary to stress the fact that only the financial flows from expropriation-adjudication have been considered. There are many costs which the Government incurred during the reform such as administration costs. These have been substantial and accumulated costs at the end of 1974 represented no less than 69 percent of the cash outlays for expropriation.[50]

Again, the rapid inflation has depreciated real values. Al-

ready in the design of the economic set-up the rates of
interests to be paid to the former owners, and by the beneficiaries were set lower than the rates of inflation
prevailing. Moreover, at the moment of expropriation, the
maximum cash payments to the former owners as well as the
maximum payments of coupons and interest on the agrarian
bonds also reduced the need to finance the reform. See Tables
5.7 and 5.8. All these clauses in the law indicate that the
Government was aware of the difficulty which generous repayments to the former owners would have entailed. Apart
from this there was also an objective to confiscate from
the large landowners the partial value of their assets.
These mechanisms of maximum cash payments indicated that
the Government had an anti-oligarchy attitude when the Law
was passed in June 1969.

On the basis of various documents of the Ministry of Agriculture it is possible to obtain a fairly good picture of
the evolution during the period 1969-75. In the first column of Table 5.9 the amount of cash paid to the ex-owners
at the moment of expropriation is given. To this is added
the amounts paid in cash for interest and coupons of the
agrarian bonds. The total, column 3, gives the public sector outlays. In column 4, the beneficiaries' payments are
given, and they constitute the public sector receipts. The
difference (column 4 - column 3) represents the net financing needs for the Government for the different years.

In order to appreciate the importance of the deficit to finance, the Central Government expenditures for the period
1969-75 are given in column 6. As can be seen from column 7
this deficit should have played only a minor role. In 1969
it represented 0.6% and in 1970 1.1% of the expenditures of
the Government. In the subsequent years it dropped significantly.

Table 5.9 Cash flow of the agrarian reform for the public sector 1969-75 (Million current Soles)

| | Public sector outlays | | | Public sector receipts | | | |
| | 1 | 2 | 3 | 4 | 5 | 6 | 7 |
	Cash in expropriation to ex-owners	Cash for interest and redemption payments on bonds to ex-owners	Total outlays 1 + 2 = 3	Receipts from beneficiaries	Balance to be financed 3 - 4 = 5	Central Government expenditures	Balance to be financed as per cent of government expenditures (5:6)x100=7
1969	217	–	217	4	213	34 334	0.6
1970	457	–	457	6	451	42 124	1.1
1971	267	1	268	165	103	49 485	0.2
1972	408	17	425	275	150	56 467	0.3
1973	549	37	586 } 1 046	n.a. } 682	n.a. } 364	67 411 } 150 061	n.a. } 0.21
1974	365	95	460	n.a.	n.a.	82 650	n.a.
1975	501	194	695	216	479	118 487	0.4

Source: Column 1: Table 5.7
Column 2: Ministerio de Agricultura (1977:2), Table 13
Column 4: IBRD (1975), Volume II, Annex 5, Table 2; Ministerio de Agricultura (1976), statistical Table 28
Column 6: BCR (1974), p. 204; and BCR Memoria (1976), p. 38

The net financing need of the Government, column 7, should
have dropped even more after 1975. First, the rate of inflation had increased the Central Government's overall receipts
(in current prices) while payments from the beneficiaries
and to the ex-owners were not adjusted for inflation. Second,
the grace periods of the beneficiaries will come to an end
and their payments will increase relatively more than the
payments to the ex-owners. Third, because major expropriations have ceased and column 1 will be close to zero.

In Peru, the prevalent idea in the 60's was that an agrarian
reform necessarily must be costly to the Government. Against
the background of this general belief the figures in Table
5.9 are rather astonishing. In spite of the importance of
the agrarian reform in Peru, and in spite of its velocity,
the National budget was hardly affected by the financial
flows of the agrarian reform. This was in part because the
agricultural sector had lost importance in the economy and
in part because of the design of the reform by the Government. Particularly the agrarian bond scheme was important
in minimizing compensation payments to the ex-owners.

5.3.5 Some theoretical comments related to Figure 4.1

In chapter 4 we developed a simple model to illustrate the
importance of land ownership in determining income distribution. In figure 5.2, figure 4.1 is reproduced. Comments here
will illustrate a few of the points raised in the preceding
section. The discussion on the repayment scheme of the beneficiaries of the reform can be related to the rent ABw. If
the repayments expressed as an annuity were the whole of
this area, ceteris paribus, the economic redistribution effects of the agrarian reform would be nil.

Figure 5.2 <u>Agrarian reform and income distribution</u>

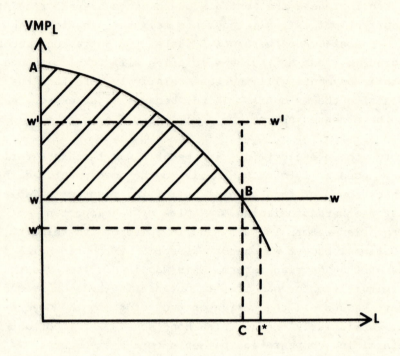

Our estimates on the repayments suggest that (i) they formed
only a part of the shaded area and (ii) they were rapidly
decreasing over time. <u>Ceteris paribus</u>, the agrarian reform
was increasingly permitting the labourers to capture an increasing share of the rent. This increase in the beneficiaries' incomes could be distributed in two distinct ways. The
first one is that they could award themselves higher wages
such as the wage rate w' and the registered surplus would be
much smaller, if any. If this occurred the reformed units
could even have registered losses on current accounts, and
some could have been unable to repay the agrarian debt. The
second one is that the profits obtained could be distributed

among the members. This option reduces the liquid surplus to be distributed among the members because the major part had to be allocated according to the laws in existance.[51] The beneficiaries seem to have preferred the first option which was restricted by the government through predetermining wages to be paid. For evidence of this see next section.

One argument in favour of agrarian reform is that labour input (and production) would increase after the reform, from C to L*, because the family opportunity cost of labour w* is lower than that of the landowner, w. At present we have too little information to argue this point.

Another important question is to what extent there has been any shifts in the marginal productivity curve of labour (MP_L). This remains also an open question. But, as we will discuss in the next chapter, investments have been low and declining. Increases in output would have to have been accompanied by investments in agriculture.

5.4   SHORT-RUN GROWTH OF INCOME, PRODUCTION AND EMPLOY-
       MENT ON CO-OPERATIVES

One central thesis of our study is that the agrarian reform only benefitted a smaller part of the agricultural population, such that major problems remain in the sector. We will now turn to their behaviour during the first years of the reform to investigate if the beneficiaries' income did increase and also look at their output performance. The main sources of information have been Horton (1974, 1976) (who has investigated in detail 27 co-operative production units) and Roca (1975) who studied the most important sugar estates.

The major part of the land expropriated under the Peruvian

agrarian reform was subsequently handed over to different cooperative enterprises. Table 5.10 summarizes the information on pre- and post reform incomes of a sample of the co-operative enterprises. The real income of these workers has improved substantially in these years, although the differences are great. We also note that Coastal incomes were significantly higher than Sierra incomes, both in the pre-reform and the post-reform period. On this account the reform has been successful in raising the real incomes of the family members of the co-operatives. There are, however, two points which need to be stressed.

Table 5.10   Blue collar workers annual income levels before and after agrarian reform. Sample of co-operative enterprises (1970 Soles)

	1		2		3
					$(\frac{2-1}{1}) \times 100$
	Pre-reform (1969)		Post-reform (1973)		Income Increase
	Value	Index	Value	Index	(percent)
Sierra Enterprises					
Agricultural	6 800	100	11 600	100	71
Livestock	12 600	185	14 700	127	17
Coastal enterprises					
Non-sugar	21 000	309	30 500	263	45
Sugar*)	44 000	646	103 000	888	134

Source: Horton (1976), p. 324; Roca (1975), pp. 44 and 46.
*) 1968 and 1972 respectively

Note: The original values (1968 and 1969 Soles) were converted into 1970 Soles. For the sugar estates only the blue-collar workers who were members of the co-operative have been used. For all except the sugar estates fringe benefits have been imputed and valued at market prices. The incomes have been rounded to the nearest 100 Soles.

First, within the co-operative enterprises there also remain great differences among different social groups. The
difference between blue-collar and white-collar workers
has been reduced substantially. (See Table 5.11).[52]

Table 5.11   Sugar estates annual income according to work
             categories in 1968 and 1972 (1970 Soles)

	1968		1972		Increase in in-come 1968-72 percent
	Income	Ratio	Income	Ratio	
Blue collar workers	43 945	100	102 984	100	134
White collar workers	94 386	215	150 714	146	60
Part time workers	16 397	37	25 819	25	58

Source: Roca (1975), pp. 44 and 46

Note: In Roca's Table 3, p. 44, the average blue-collar income corre-
      sponds to that in his Table 9 on p. 54. But in his Table 4, p. 46,
      the blue-collar income differs from that in his Table on p. 54.
      We have, therefore, used his basic Tables 3 and 4 and have our-
      selves elaborated his basic raw data. We have used his 1968 Soles,
      and have converted these into 1970 Soles. See also Ibid, p. 108,
      for a discussion of deflator used in his study.

Second, a crucial problem in agrarian reform is the question
of how many families are to be settled in the enterprises.
The overall policy within the Ministry of Agriculture has
not been consistent. There have been some pressures to include not only the permanent workers on the enterprises, but
also temporary workers, particularly in the case of the sugar estates. The permanent workers have, in general, zealously
opposed such attempts, because this would lower their incomes,
- dividing the cake among more members.[53] The part-time workers have an interest in becoming members of the enterprises
because their wages as non-members of the enterprise are significantly lower than those of the members. In view of the
fact that the employment opportunities outside the sugar
estates are scarce, the incomes derived from "part-time" work

constituted in fact the major part of their annual income. The figures in Table 5.11 are indicative of this [this was one of the major problems identified in the report of a Government Commission (1975)]. In addition, there were the Peruvian workers who would like to have worked at the sugar estates, but who could not obtain work.

A case study of the important co-operative Túpac Amaru II, located in the Sierra, reported that,

> "Wage differentials between co-operative members and non-members during the same period [1971-72] were on the order of two to one. By 1977, however, the ratio jumped to twelve to one. Aside from creating large increases in fixed costs for labour in the co-operative, these increases had the farther effect of creating class divisions. This pattern has occurred elsewhere in Peru leading to the creation of an agrarian reform elite in the rural sector."[54]

Figueroa has also argued that the reform would only benefit the relatively well off. To get an approximate idea of the situation we can use the data on income distribution from the Tables in the Appendix to chapter 3, on family incomes. According to this sample survey 54% of the rural families had an income of 10 600 Soles or less in 1971/72 (1970 Soles). In 1973 the beneficiaries' incomes on co-operative enterprises varied between 11 600 and 103 000 Soles.[55] These scattered pieces of information on income distribution suggest that the beneficiaries' income had risen substantially within a relatively short-time span, but that there were great differences among enterprises and regions. Most importantly, the majority of the rural population have been excluded from income rises.[56]

There are furthermore a few controversial issues in land reform which we will briefly comment here. First, it has been claimed that an agrarian reform would as a rule initially decrease the level of output. Or in a milder version, that the marketable surplus would be reduced, because the beneficiaries of the reform, having a higher elasticity of demand for food with respect to income, would increase their consumption of food. This would reduce marketable surplus, although production remains constant. We do not have data enough to permit a full discussion, but, in the Peruvian context, because the beneficiaries belonged to the upper income strata and their elasticity was probably not particularly high, we do not believe the reduction of marketable surplus to be of significance.

Second, one of the arguments in favour of an agrarian reform has been the positive effects it would have on employment. The labour input per hectare is higher among smaller farms than on bigger and re-distributing land would thus supposedly increase labour input. This is of course closely related to the whole complex of the role of technology in development.

There exist some data which permit us to give preliminary answers to these questions. However, these refer to the development in the very short time period, 1969-75, and later years development may be different.

We will discuss agricultural output in some detail in the next chapter, so we will only give brief comments here. Horton (1974 and 1976) has stressed that many of the co-operative enterprises found that the former owners had divested.[57]   He summarizes: "Reliable production data for recent years are not available, but it does not seem that the land reform process has caused major disruptions in the production of most agricultural and livestock commodities."[58]

In a survey (1975) of the opinions of the teachers attached

to the Agrarian University La Molina (The sample included 43 teachers both in and outside Lima. Over half of them made weekly field visits.), two-thirds believed that agricultural production had declined both inside and outside the reformed enterprises.[59]

Horton considered that in the reformed enterprises the production had increased somewhat:

> "On the 'average' reform enterprise the mix
> of crop and livestock production had inten-
> sified somewhat since the reform and the to-
> tal value of agricultural production had inc-
> reased slightly; employment had remained about
> the same and investments in social infra-
> structure and productive facilities had
> increased substantially."[60]

5.5 THE RURAL POOR AND THE AGRARIAN REFORM

Our general knowledge about the large estates and the agrarian reform enterprises is far more extensive than about the rural poor. The behaviour of the large latifundios has been studied, but the small farmers and the landless workers have received less attention. This was the situation prior to the reform in 1969, and since then, practically all studies have concentrated their attention on that part of agriculture involved in the agrarian reform. Fitzgerald goes so far as to claim that "...the 'traditional sector' is neglected by available statistics."[61] Who were the non-beneficiaries? How did they live and how did they earn their incomes? What were the relations between the non-beneficiaries and the reformed enterprises?

Family-size farms, as we have noted earlier, had not been important in Peru. With the disappearance of the landed oli-

garchy these have come to play an increasing role in Peruvian agriculture, and have been able to articulate their
interests. Bayer has even claimed that these will constitute a new important capitalist class in Peruvian agriculture.[62]

In the Appendix to this chapter we have shown how difficult
it is to estimate the number of families living in the agricultural sector. It is even more difficult to get an approximate answer to the questions we have posed above. In particular there is hardly any information on the landless workers outside the co-operative enterprises.

Still, a major part of these rural poor probably cultivate
very small pieces of land. Several years ago Barraclough
and Domike claimed that: "The number of landless peasants
is growing and the rapid subdivision of agricultural units
which were already too small is creating more minifundios.
Consequently the clamor for land is continually growing."[63]
This is probably also a correct description of the situation in the post-reform era of Peru.

For lack of better information we will use the census data.
From Table 5.1 it can be seen that the number of small landholdings has been growing rapidly in Peru. Between 1961 and
1972 the number of production units of less than 5 hectares
increased by some 384 thousand and simultaneously the average size decreased from 1.5 to 1.4 hectares per unit.[64] With
respect to the subdivision of land, again very little has
been published. The two agricultural censuses permit us to
identify the situation in 1961 and in 1972. As can be seen
from Table 5.12 the number of pieces of land or plots per
production unit was on average 3.4 in 1961 and increased to
4.0 in 1972. Looking at the disaggregated data it can be
seen that the fragmentation process has been particularly

Table 5.12   Subdivision of production units in Peru
in 1961 and 1972

Size of pro-duction unit	1961		1972		Percentage change between 1961-72	
	Number of pieces of land per unit	Average size of land piece (hectares)	Number of pieces of land per unit	Average size of land piece (hectares)	Number of pieces of land per unit	Average size of land piece (hectares)
- 1	2.95	0.15	3.59	0.17	+ 21.7	+ 13.3
1- 5	3.87	0.58	4.89	0.46	+ 26.4	- 20.7
5- 20	3.9	2.1	4.2	2.1	+ 7.7	± 0.0
20- 100	3.0	13.0	2.6	14.0	- 13.3	+ 7.7
100- 500	2.3	87.2	2.4	78.0	+ 4.3	- 10.6
500-2 500	2.4	416.8	2.5	400.5	+ 4.2	- 3.9
2 500-	2.7	3 917.6	2.7	4 618.6	± 0.0	+ 17.9
TOTAL	3.4	5.9	4.0	5.0	+ 17.6	- 15.3

Source: INP (1965), p. 2; ONEC (1975), p. 1

rapid among the smaller farms. In the stratum of less than
1 hectare, the production unit had almost 3 plots in 1961
and in 1972 no fewer than 3.6. In the stratum of 1-5 hectares, the number of plots were almost 4 in 1961 and in
1972 almost 5. In other words, for an average size farm
there has been an increase in the number of plots.

In summary, taking these pieces of information together we
find that between 1961 and 1972 the total number of production units has increased and the average size has decreased.
For a given size of a farm we find that in 1961 the smaller
farms were more subdivided that the larger farms. In 1972,
again for a given size of a farm, the smaller farms had become even more subdivided.

What are the economic implications of the Minifundio problem?
In the first instance the smaller the farm, the smaller its
income-generating capacity. In part this could be compensated
by investments and technological innovation. But, the institutional framework in a Latifundio-Minifundio system has excluded the minifundista from the means to compensate for the
lack of land. Secondly, the subdivision of small landholdings
increases production costs per produced unit where labour
input price is fixed. The main reasons for this seem to be
that transportation costs increase, and that it becomes difficult to reap economies of scale.[65] The general competitive
position of the minifundio peasant has deteriorated because
the income-generation capacity of his farm has declined over
time both because the land-man ratio has become lower, and
because the farm has been subdivided.

To what extent has the agrarian reform changed this situation? The minifundio complex is mentioned in the Agrarian
Reform Law (D.L. 17716). For example, in article 98 it is
stated that no production unit of less then 3 hectares can

be subdivided. In articles 103-106 inheritance is regulated
so that the process of subdivision is to be stopped upon
the death of the head of a family. Articles 99-102, and
107 deal with the problem of correcting the present system,
of (a) too small production units; and (b) the consolida-
tion of subdivided units.

In practice, however, very little has been done to solve the
minifundio problem. In part, the reason for this can probably be attributed to the fact that the struggle has been
for or against Agrarian Reform. Those in favour have attacked the latifundio system and its negative consequences
on production and income distribution. Those against, the
large landowners and other vested-interest groups, claimed
that land was scarce and advocated two policy options for
increasing the amount of land for the majority of peasants.
The first one was to implement massive colonization programmes, and the second was large-scale irrigation projects.
Both of these "latifundista" solutions were seen as the alternatives to changing the prevailing landownership structure of Peru.

The Belaúnde government attempted to carry out both solutions simultaneously, i.e. agrarian reform and colonization/
irrigation schemes, with the result that little progress
was made in either direction.

One of the alternatives available at the time of the Agrarian reform in 1969 would have been to incorporate the minifundistas and the landless peasants into the expropriated
farms. This alternative was rejected, however, and the reform came to be implemented in such a way that the minifundistas have been excluded from the reform. The legal instruments to carry out the reform including the minifundios

existed, and some attempt of some public officials in the
Agricultural Planning Office (OSPA) to incorporate a larger
number of families on a given expropriated area was stopped
at a higher decision making level. The group was subsequently disbanded and the prevailing agrarian reform pattern became firmly established. Two explanations can be given.

The first one is that the military believed that this "radical" approach could become politically dangerous. It would
have been much more complicated to monitor the reform and
revolutionary changes could have evolved in the process of
peasants' participation and integration. The present pattern, the "reformist" approach, which ultimately became the
predominant one, has created a polarized situation in the
rural areas, where the beneficiaries of the reform and the
non-beneficiaries tend to clash. One important reason is
that the land-man ratio within the reformed sector is
very much higher than outside. The minifundistas and the
landless peasants have in many cases not accepted to be
excluded from the benefits of the reform.

The second explanation is that the lack of growth of agricultural goods in the pre-reform period made it imperative
for the Government to prevent disruptions in agricultural
production. The "radical" approach had an inherent danger
of causing acute shortage of food. This problem could have
been solved through increased imports, but the overall
strength of the Peruvian economy was already becoming
strained. As of 1967 the Peruvian economy entered into a
period of recession and in 1968 there was even a small reduction in GNP. In 1969 the economy started to recuperate.
During the same period the Peruvian development strategy
was challenged by the USA and other capitalist countries
who drastically reduced the inflow of private capital,
and threatened to shut off Peru from access to the interna-

tional capital markets. Viewed against this background, it
is understandable that the Peruvian policy makers were reluctant to implement a "radical" reform which could have
exposed the Peruvian economy to even greater difficulties.

Still, there have been some minor changes which improved
the economic position of some minifundistas. In the case
of tenant farmers, particularly those adjacent to the big
estates, they have received titles to the land, and do not
have to pay rents nor pay for the land they have received.[66]
The prevailing opinion seems to be that large landowners
expelled tenant workers before the reform. In many cases
this has contributed to conflicts between members of the
co-operative enterprises and families outside who claim
land from the enterprises.

These exceptions do not change the overall situation and
the minifundistas faced a very difficult economic situation. There are two important ways in which these could
be benefitted from the present and further reforms. First,
through employment on the co-operative enterprises. Second, through credit and technical assistance which would
enable them to raise output.

Available data do not indicate that the Agrarian Reform has
increased employment opportunities.[67] There are tendencies
for the co-operative enterprises to mechanize agriculture
which most likely would reduce demand from labour outside
these. If this is permitted to happen on a large scale the
agrarian reform could even lead to a reduction of employment.[68]

Also, with respect to technical assistance and credit the
minifundistas are no better off. Ever since the agrarian
reform in 1969 a large part of the administrative capacity

of the Ministry of Agriculture was switched over to agrarian reform activities including assisting the new co-operative enterprises.[69] Credit chanelled through the Agricultural Development Bank was increasingly earmarked for these new enterprises (Table 5.13). No doubt that there was a need to finance these new enterprises, but the effect has been a decreasing share for the medium and small producers. In addition only a few percent of them received credit at all from the public sector.

We have already described how the post reform land ownership will be very uneven. The distribution of this asset will be one of the key factors in determining the future income distribution. The allocation of public sector services, in this case, credit, has not changed the tendency towards an uneven distribution of income.

Table 5.13   Percentage distribution according to size of farms of loans from the Agricultural Development Bank

	1957/58	1968	1972	1973	1974	1975
Co-operative enterprises			49	62	66	66
			74	77	78	79
Large estates	} 84	52	25	15	12	13
Medium estates		19	4	3	4	6
Small producers	16	29	18	16	16	15
Others	--	--	4	4	2	—
	100	100	100	100	100	100

Source: 1972-75: Ministerio de Agricultura (1978);
1957-58:and 1968: Eguren et.al. (1977), p. 248

Note: The Agricultural Development Bank has ceased this classification scheme as of 1976, separating only associated and individual loans.

5.6   SUMMARY AND CONCLUSIONS

In chapter 3 we showed that the average rural income was much
lower than in the urban sector and the income distribution
more skewed. One key development objective of the military
government in 1968 was to redistribute incomes. In order to
accomplish this, rural income distribution had to be changed.
In chapter 4 we discussed how the degree of landownership
and the availability of agricultural land are crucial factors in determining the agricultural income distribution,
and that an agrarian reform is a necessary condition for
improving the rural income distribution.

In this chapter we have shown that land ownership in Peru was
extremely concentrated prior to the reform in 1969. A small
minority of farms occupied the major part of the agricultural land, while the great majority of the Peruvian peasants
survived on small and subdivided farms. Peruvian agrarian
reform attempts prior to the new Agrarian Reform Law in June
1969 were frustrated. In that year agrarian reform commenced
on a massive scale with few precedents in Latin America. At
the end of 1978 practically all big farms in Peru had been
expropriated and almost 50 percent of the agricultural land
in Peru had been involved in this enormous transfer. Most of
this land was handed over to co-operative enterprises. Close
to 400 000 out of 1.4 million families benefitted from the reform. In terms of sheer numbers this was impressive.

The financial system created for the agrarian reform involved
three groups. The beneficiaries of the reform had to pay for
the assets they received. In general the accounting value of
the expropriated assets has been set lower than their commercial value. But, most important, the 20 yearly amortization
and interest payments were not adjusted for inflation, so
that the real value of these rapidly declined. The beneficia-

ries of the reform could even in the short run increase their incomes and there exist considerable possibilities for further increases in the future. The former landowners received some compensation for the expropriated farms, a smaller part in cash and the majority in agrarian reform bonds. These cannot be sold, and again,because of inflation their real value has declined rapidly. The former owners were clearly not "fully compensated". The Government never faced any fiscal problems in financing the agrarian reform.

If on the one hand it can be claimed that an effective agrarian reform was implemented, it can on the other hand be argued that the families benefitting from the reform already belonged to the richer strata in Peru. The evidence available suggests that the incomes of the beneficiaries have increased although there are great differences among reform enterprises and natural regions. The poor majority of Peruvian peasants has only received land, credit and technical assistance to a minor extent. From this point of view, the Peruvian agrarian reform has been a failure in eradicating rural poverty. The overcoming most of the massive rural poverty was and remains a formidable problem. As we discussed in chapter 4 the distribution of land is the crucial factor in determining rural income distribution. In order to overcome rural poverty, land has to be more evenly distributed. Therefore, if the government had decided in 1969 that the expropriated land was to be distributed more evenly, either by incorporating more families on the expropriated estates and/or creating small family farms, more of income in equalities in the rural sector would have been reduced, while production would have been hindered only moderately.

APPENDIX TO CHAPTER 5

The first part of this Appendix gives key data on the advances of the Peruvian agrarian reform on a yearly basis.
The purpose of the second part is to check to what extent the conclusions on the redistributive effects of the reform would be affected if the data were disaggregated. We have therefore checked data with respect to distribution of ownership; of irrigated and non-irrigated land; of livestock; and of different qualities of land.
The third part reviews different estimates of the agricultural population.
The fourth part gives an example of an agrarian reform contract for repayments of the beneficiaries to the Ministry of Agriculture.

NUMBER OF FAMILIES BENEFITTED AND HECTARES ADJUDICATED YEARLY 1967-1978

Table A.5.1   Number of families benefitted yearly by the agrarian reform 1967-1978

Year	Families	
	Number in year	Accumulated
1967	3 593	3 593
1968	7 812	11 405
1969	7 355	18 760
1970	42 343	61 103
1971	18 671	79 774
1972	38 976	118 750
1973	56 496	175 246
1974	42 065	217 311
1975	36 686	253 997
1976	40 550	294 547
1977	21 634	316 181
1978 (Oct)		369 404

Sources: 1967-77: Ministerio de Agricultura (1977:1), Table Reforma Agraria 5; See also Ministerio de Agricultura (1975:1), p. 26. 1978: Ministerio de Agricultura (1978:1), Table 6
Note: The 1977 and 1978 figures are preliminary.

Table A.5.2   Number of hectares adjudicated yearly by the agrarian reform 1967-78

Year	Hectares	
	Number per year	Accumulated
1967	140 219	140 219
1968	182 236	322 455
1969	256 774	579 229
1970	691 697	1 270 926
1971	538 083	1 809 009
1972	1 119 223	2 928 232
1973	1 336 692	4 264 924
1974	865 938	5 130 862
1975	1 083 471	6 214 333
1976	640 253	6 854 586
1977	452 862	7 307 448
1978 (Oct)		8 599 455

Source: See preceeding table
Note: The 1977 and 1978 figures are preliminary

ACCESS TO ASSETS IN PERUVIAN AGRICULTURE

Irrigated land

The lack of sufficient amounts of rain in many regions, plays a decisive role in Peruvian agriculture, where the need for irrigation is high in comparison with for example, Europe and North America. It is, therefore, important to investigate the amount of land with and without irrigation, how this land is owned and whether the Agrarian Reform comprised a large part of this land.

The 1972 Census data are more complete than those in the 1961 Census, and, it is thus difficult to make any in depth analysis on a comparative basis. Rearranging the 1972 Census data it is possible to make a partial comparison between 1961 and 1972 and the results are presented in Table A.5.3.

Table A.5.3   Land with irrigation in 1961 and in 1972

Size of production unit	1961 Area (1000 Ha's)	1961 Distribution (percent)	1972 Area (1000 Ha's)	1972 Distribution (percent)	Difference Absolute (1000 Ha's)	Difference Percent	Area per production unit 1961 (Ha's)	Area per production unit 1972 (Ha's)	Increase in number of production units 1961-1972 percent
Less than 5 Ha's	258	25.4	386	30.3	128	49.6	0.4	0.4	55.0
More than 5 Ha's	759	74.6	889	69.7	130	17.1	5.3	2.9	113.1
Total	1 017	100.0	1 275	100.0	258	25.4	1.2	0.9	64.9

Sources: INP (1965), pp. 100, 110, 118; ONEC (1975), p. 19; Table 5.1

The perhaps most striking result is that while the irrigated area increased 25%, the number of production units rose
by 65%. Another interesting fact is that in the 1-5 Ha's
stratum the average size of irrigated land has remained
practically constant at 0.4 ha, between 1961 and 1972. A
contrary tendency can be noticed among the larger farms
where irrigated land per unit decreased abrubtly, from 5.3
to 2.9 hectares during the same period. The irrigated land
corresponding to this group increased 1.7% while the increase in the number of production units 113%.

It has been argued that the CIDA studies on Peru, and others
have overstated the effects of land concentration by not taking into account the different qualities of land. Douglas
Horton for example has stressed this in several parts in his
report submitted to the World Bank.

> "Land concentration is one of the most salient
> features of Peruvian agriculture, but students
> of the country's agrarian problem have over-
> stated the degree of concentration by failing
> to take into account significant differences
> in land quality on large and small farms".1)

This was discussed above and our findings seem to agree with
the objections raised.

Ownership structure of livestock in 1961 and 1972

In this section we will review census data on the ownership
of livestock.

Before proceeding it is necessary to have an idea of the relative importance of livestock production versus the other
elements in total agricultural production. In the first in-

---

1) Horton (1974), p. iii.

stance the data we have used on Peru excludes fisheries because of its special characteristics and problems. Secondly, although Peru has a vast forestry potential, very little has been exploited, and it only accounts for a few percent of the total value of agricultural production.

Crop production is by far the most important component in total agricultural production, accounting for over 70%, while livestock production accounts for about 25%. However, the rate of growth of the latter has been somewhat higher than for crop production so that a decline in the share of crop and conversely an increase in the relative importance of livestock production can be expected.[2] An additional point merits a careful review of available data. It has been mentioned several times by Peruvian officials that the large farms i.e. those subject to expropriation decapitalized their estates inter alia by slaughtering the cattle and other livestock animals, and/or, they sold part of their livestock to smaller farmers.

On one hand it would seem rather strange that this would occur, since livestock was to be paid in cash when expropriated. The reason for this was exactly to try to prevent the massive slaughtering of livestock. The compensation scheme to the expropriated estate owners contains an important element, confiscation, and to prevent decapitalization of easily transferable capital this was to be paid in cash. It should be remembered that during the whole of this period the Peruvian authorities attempted to control the prices of meat products and the official price was set lower than that which would have prevailed under market equilibrium. The price paid to the expropriated owner was based on this official price. Hence there were moments of excess demand, and

---

2) IBRD (1975), Volume II, Table D.12.

- 180 -

black markets appeared.

To some extent demand pressures were relieved by imports
of subsidized meat. However, several facts contributed in
making it extremely difficult for the government to maintain this policy. On one hand, the domestic price became
successively lower than that prevailing in the world markets and also in neighbouring countries and this has led to
to smuggling of Peruvian cattle to neighbouring countries.
Also, world market prices of meat increased sharply. The
price paid to expropriated owners was based on the official price, and hence lower than that which could be obtained on the black markets which existed in Peru or the
prices in other countries.

Although, the gap between the official meat prices and the
hypothetical equilibrium price increased up until 1976[3]
only some of the effects should have come into full force
by 1972. (The year of the 2nd Agricultural Census). It
should also be remembered that the agrarian reform was
well under way by that time, but the general impression
is that cattle estates entered into the reform process at
a later date. (Priority was given to the Coast where crop
production is the most important).

Finally and equally important, data quality on livestock
is probably relatively poor. The Government has intervened
in many instances and practically always against livestock
producers and/or traders, and this has contributed to a general feeling of scepticism on the part of the farmers.
Farmers' willingness to provide accurate information on
livestock holdings is and probably has been rather limited.

---

3) The price control was eventually supplemented with "meatless days"
   which probably greatly reduced demand for meat.

There are many interrelated factors which both would have
worked towards a reduction of livestock. The outcome of
these cannot be deducted from the policies pursued but
has to be investigated. On the basis of the two censuses
some light can be shed on the complex problem.

The following questions seem important to investigate:
1. Was there a general decline in livestock?
2. What was the ownership structure of livestock?
3. Was there any noticeable change in ownership structure
   between 1961 and 1972?

As can be seen from Table A.5.4 the number of cattle remained practically constant between 1961 and 1972 (increase
of 0.6%).[4] The population of Peru, in the same period, increased 40%. Although there has been no absolute decline in
the cattle stock, on a per capita basis the decline has been
substantial. In this context it is also of importance to
investigate the age structure of cattle since the maximum
possible growth rate will largely depend on the number of
young females in this total stock. While in 1961 the share
of females of 2 years of age and less was 18%, the same group
had a share in 1972 of 20%. However, there is nothing which
can be said about the development   between the two censuses.

According to the census data the evolution of the stock of
pigs was far better and increased some 19% between 1961 and

---

4) A strange phenomenon appeared when the data were analysed. Our first
   calculations were based on a stratified sample of the 1961 census in
   an official Peruvian document. Subsequently, the full 1961 census data were obtained and comparing these it was found that there seems
   to be a systematic and significant difference between the sample data
   and the census data. While for cattle the figures are 3.33 and 3.80
   millions; pigs 1.39 and 1.43 millions; sheep 12.83 and 16.83 for the
   sample and the full census publications respectively. The sampling
   technique used seems to have been incorrect.

Table A.5.4   Cattle: ownership structure in 1961 and 1972

Size of production unit (Ha)	1961				1972			
	Number of units informing	Percent	Number of heads	Percent	Number of units informing	Percent	Number of heads	Percent
Landless	13 294	2.8	136 347	3.6	-	-	-	-
- 1	143 190	29.8	634 386	16.7	181 391	26.0	623 914	16.3
1- 5	236 128	49.1	1 515 224	39.9	325 854	46.6	1 369 331	35.8
5- 20	66 962	13.9	701 369	18.5	145 980	20.9	903 633	23.6
20- 100	14 739	3.1	275 798	7.3	36 370	5.2	437 807	11.5
100- 500	4 360	0.9	215 727	5.7	6 894	1.0	202 426	5.3
500-2 500	1 697	0.4	116 295	3.1	1 742	0.2	112 938	3.0
2 500-	747	0.2	202 836	5.3	498	0.1	169 519	4.4
Others	21	0.0	70	0.0	197	0.0	1 562	0.0
Total	481 138	100.2	3 798 052	100.1	698 926	100.0	3 821 130	99.9

Source: INP (1965), p. 84; ONEC (1975), p. 100

Note: As of September 1978, 252 667 heads of cattle had been expropriated. Ministry of Agriculture (1978), Table 2.

1972. But, again the rate of growth was less than that of the population. The llamas and alpacas increased 23% and the sheep stock declined in a very drastic way by some 17%.

In summary we can conclude that although in general there has been no decline in the stock of livestock, on a per capita basis all of the species investigated have declined. This situation is even more serious if one considers the objectives of the Government to be income redistribution, and the attainment of a higher rate of economic growth, because the elasticity of demand for meat is very high among the lower income groups.

The ownership structure of livestock differs significantly from that of land tenure. However, a smaller complication arises in evaluating the census data. A big farm does not necessarily mean that its economic size is big, or vice versa. In fact, it cannot be excluded that there are small farms in terms of physical extension but big in economic terms, especially in the Lima-Callao area. Farms in this area fatten cattle before they are sent off for slaughtering. In this way very large farms, economically speaking, although their physical area is quite small, can own much livestock. With these comments in mind we note that according to census data in 1961, 60% of the cattle; 56% of the sheep; 58% of the llamas and alpacas; and 79% of the hogs were held on production units of less than 5 Ha's. In 1972 these units had: 52% of the cattle; 53% of the sheep; 53% of the llamas and alpacas; and 65% of the hogs.

A striking result of these data is that the pattern which could be noted in 1961 appears in 1972 again, but in all of the livestock animals considered the Stratum 1-5 Ha's lost in relative importance.

It was mentioned above that there was a general feeling
among Peruvians that many large estates decapitalized
their livestock holdings either by slaughtering and/or
selling their animals. Since the agrarian reform law is
rather generous in its clauses for permitting relatively
extensive holdings of pasture land it seemed correct to
scrutinize the production units of more than 500 Ha's.
As can be seen, while in 1961 they had 8% of the cattle
in 1972 it had dropped to 7%. For llamas and alpacas the
figures were 11% and 16%, for hogs 2% both years and for
sheep 12% and 18%.

In the case of cattle, data support the hypothesis of a
decapitalization. Farmers bigger than 100 Ha's decreased
their stock of cattle heads from 535 to 485 thousand between 1961 and 1972, but data do not support claims of massive decapitalization of cattle. Moreover, livestock production has not been important among the large producers.
Since the smaller strata have lost in their relative importance and also the larger estates in the case of cattle
the medium-size units have gained. In the case of other
livestock products the picture is somewhat ambiguous.

Nevertheless, there is decline in the case of cattle, but
the magnitude indicated by Census data does not indicate
a serious problem. Nevertheless, the data indicate that
the rate of investments in animals has been low among the
larger estates since there has been a decline in the stock
of cattle and a very modest rate of growth for other animals.

What kind of land was expropriated

A first estimate of the scope of the agrarian reform could be to relate total agricultural land to land to be expropriated. Recalling that according to the Census of 1972 total land was 24 million hectares and the "target" was 10 million, it would appear as if the reform only would affect 42 % of the agricultural sector. However, this approach conceals the fact that the land affected by the reform is not of the same quality-structure as in the sector as a whole. In order to provide a better estimate, though still very rough, the targets for agrarian reform in terms of types of land have been related to the data from the 1972 Census. The calculations appear in Table A.5.5.

Table A.5.5 Agrarian reform "targets" by classes of land compared with land available according to the 1972 agrarian census

Class of land	1 "Target" of reform		2 1972 Census		3 1 as percent of 2
	Hectares (1000)	Percent	Hectares (1000)	Percent	
Irrigated	667	6.6	1 274	5.4	52.4
Dry Land	1 045	10.3	2 418	10.3	43.2
Natural Pastures	6 689	65.9	15 129	64.3	44.2
Others[a]	1 755	17.3	4 724	20.1	37.2
Total	10 156[b]	100.1	23 545	100.1	43.1
				Weighted average:	47.9[c]

a) This is mainly land without any value.
b) In 1971 the first estimate was, in thousand hectares, Irrigated 863, Dry land 970, Natural Pastures 6 420. Ministerio de Agricultura (1975:1), p. 22.
c) The following weights were used where: Irrigated land=0.75; Dry Land=0.22; and Natural Pastures=0.03. The sum of weights=1.

Source: ONEC (1975), pp. 18-20; Table 5.1; and Ministerio de Agricultura (1977:1), Table 3

As can be seen from Table A.5.5 the "target" of the reform aimed at better quality land. Thus in the case of irrigated land the "target" figure, 6.6% was higher than that of the census 5.4%. Conversely, the target for marginal land was 17.3% while the census data indicate 20.1%. In summary, the "target" of the reform was to expropriate better quality agricultural land.

These data also permit a rough approximation of the share of production which was generated, by the reformed sector. Applying different weights in Table A.5.5 for taking into account the different qualities of land, and consequently output levels, it can be estimated that the reformed sector generated almost 50% of total agricultural output. The 1961 Census data yield different results and the Reformed Sector would have accounted for not less than 60% of total output. This figure has appeared in different studies or articles, and the reason is quite simple, namely, that the 1972 Census data were not available until 1975. (See for example Cencira estimates in the first half of the 70's).

HOW MANY FAMILIES LIVED IN THE AGRICULTURAL SECTOR IN THE FIRST HALF OF THE SEVENTIES?

In posing this question we immediately face methodological and statistical problems. We would like to have a rough estimate of how many households had agriculture as their main source of income.

A main source of information which cannot be used directly is the Population Census in 1972. The 1972 Population Census gives the following data on the economically active population for the agricultural sector.

Table A.5.6   Agricultural workers economically active
               15 years and older in 1972

	Total	Men	Women
Urban	361 007	334 699	26 308
Rural	1 163 237	1 058 026	105 211
Total	1 524 244	1 392 725	131 519

Source: ONEC (1974), p. 764.

Note: The definition of economically active population is: people who
    work and those unoccupied but looking for work [See ONEC (1974),
    p. xvi]. See also pp. 696-697; 674-675 for a breakdown accord-
    ing to education. The total figure for 15 years and older is,
    however, smaller i.e. 1 502 as compared with 1 524 thousands
    persons.

Two important remarks are: (1) An important portion of agricultural workers lived in urban areas. The census has
been criticized for using a too inclusive definition for
urban area, an agglomeration of a minimum of 100 dwellings.
[See ONEC (1974), p. xv]. (2) The share of women in the
economically active population is very low (9%).

Obviously we cannot directly state that these 1 524 000
workers constitute the same number of agricultural house-
holds/families. E.g. some workers belong to the same family. Some workers were unoccupied and were not looking for
work and thus not registered. Counting only the males,
there would be at least about 1.4 million families.

Another way to look at the data is to investigate the distribution of dwellings, assuming one dwelling corresponds
to one household.

Table A.5.7   Urban and rural distribution of dwellings
               in 1972

	Number (with people living in the dwelling)
Urban	1 539 591
Rural	1 158 993
Total	2 698 584

Source: ONEC (1974), p. 865.

Note: There were, for the rural sector, 66 thousand dwellings where
      the people were absent and 75 thousand uninhabited. These have
      not been included, nor the same categories for urban areas.

But as we saw above, Table A.5.6, a significant proportion
of the agricultural workers live in the urban areas so that
on this ground the 1.2 million would be an underestimate.
Probably most households in the rural areas live from agriculture.

The 1972 Agricultural Census give 1 390 000 production
units. But, many estates have more than one family and on
many small production units the families may have agriculture only as a minor source of income. This suggests that
there are at least 1.4 million families.

Caballero has attempted to estimate the number of families
living in the agricultural sector. [Caballero (1976), p. 11].
According to him there were 938 200 families in the agricultural sector in 1972. The procedure he followed was:
1. Take the Central Bank figure for agricultural labour
   force.
2. Divide this figure with 2.1, the number of workers per
   family, and thus obtain the number of families, which
   was 938 200.

However, several observations should be made. In the first place, the Central Bank figure relied upon the 1961 Population Census. In the second place the females have practically been excluded in the estimate of the labour force. [See Banco Central de Reserva (1976), Notes to Table 10 on p. 31]. So, when Caballero divides the labour force by 2.1 he obviously gets an underestimate. (The 2.1 figure was probably obtained by considering a male as one worker, the female as something less and adding, applying other weights to the children).

A previous study [Convenio (1970:4)] made a great effort in determining the number of families which were eligible to obtain land according to the criteria of the Law 17716. According to this estimate 787 000 families fell into this category in 1967 [Convenio (1970:4), p. 13] and about 973 000 were projected for 1975. It did not, however, estimate the total number of families in the agricultural sector. [See Convenio (1974:4) Appendix A].

The study excluded the agricultural labourers living in urban areas and used the estimates derived from economically active population in agriculture. These two procedures led to an underestimation of the families in the agricultural sector. One important point, stressed in the study, was that adult children should be considered as eligible for land under the Reform, as well as families within the family [Convenio (1974:4), p. 68].

The 1972 Census classification criteria for urban and rural area differ from that of the ENCA study. The National Planning Institute has adjusted the Census figures, using the ENCA criteria for urban areas [2000 persons and more. See INP, (1975), p. 86]. Comparing the revised Census data with the ENCA data, the rural population was 48.8% for the Cen-

sus and 52.7% in the ENCA study [See Amat y León and León
(1977), p. 157]. A similar phenomenon occurs with dwellings. The Census gives 50.4% while ENCA 54.4% for the share
of rural dwellings in total. (Ibidem p. 159). For the procedure carrying out these adjustments of the Census see
INP (1975), pp. 85-89.

For lack of a solution to the problem of estimating the
number of families in the agricultural sector we shall on
the information available make the guess that there were
about 1.4 million in the middle of the 70's.

EXAMPLE OF A CONTRACT FOR REPAYMENTS BETWEEN THE MINISTRY
OF AGRICULTURE AND BENEFICIARIES OF AN ESTATE

Table A.5.8   Value and amortization of assets of a Coastal
               co-operative enterprise (thousand Soles)

Value of land		14 377
Machinery and equipment	2 475	
Cattle	13 394	
Installation	1 200	
		17 069
Subtotal		31 446

Interests

Land (4%)	6 781	
Machinery, equipment, cattle and installa- tion (7%)	15 156	
		21 937
Total		53 383

The beneficiaries received one year of grace (1974), thereafter, the beneficiaries are to pay 2 669 Soles per annum
for twenty years, the total 53 383 000 divided by 20 years
[Source: Eguren (1975), p. 192]. It is not clear, neither
from the law, nor in Eguren's study, nor have I managed to
obtain a clear statement of how interest rates were calculated.

- 191 -

1. In drafting this chapter I have relied extensively on my experiences from my work in Peru 1968-1971 and visits in 1974, 1975 and 1977.

2. Mariátegui (1970).

3. Horton (1976), p. 11; Horton (1974), pp. 32, 42-43. For a discussion of the political scenarios in Peru see for example Astiz (1969). This book contains an extensive literature list on this subject. Also see Owen (1963) for a general description of Peru.

4. See Horton (1974), chapter II; and Horton (1976), Chapter IV.

5. Horton (1976), p. 12. The military junta claimed that hardly any agrarian reform took place before the military take-over in 1968. However, data in the Ministry of Agriculture, see Ministerio de Agricultura (1978); and Ministerio de Agricultura (1975), show that some transfers did take place.

Expropriated*	1962-1968
No. of farms	546-548
Hectares	1,027,649-1,027,650
Heads of cattle	177,712
Adjudications	
Number of families	13,538
Hectares	375,574

*) the differences depend on sources.

Up to June 1969, when the new law was promulgated about 14,000 families had received about 507 thousand hectares. See Alberts and Buechler (1970), and Table A.5.1.

6. Cf. Garcia (1977), chapter 1; Lowenthal et.al. (1975), chapters 1-2; Matos Mar et.al. (1971); Brundenius (1972), pp. 179-203; and Astiz (1969), chapter 12.

7. Mann et.al. (1970), p. 2.

8. Translation taken from Mann and Huerta (1969), p. 3.

9. The law stipulates the following maximum holdings in crop production:

Region	Maximum size of farm (hectares)
Coast	
Irrigated land	150-200
Dry farming	300-400
Sierra and Ceja de Selva	
Irrigated land	30-165
Dry farming	60-330

See Reforma Agraria (1976), the following articles, 28, 30 and 31.

10. It is possible that these difficult Chilean experiences in creating viable reform enterprises inspired the Peruvians to expropriate the whole farm. Based on discussions with agrarian reform officials in Chile and Peru.

11. The importance of various forms of co-operative farms of production is illustrated below; cumulative 31 December 1975:

Forms of Adjudication	Area (1000 Ha's)	%	Families (1000)	%
Individual	136	2.2	19	7.5
Cooperatives	3 012	48.5	124	49.0
Communities	567	9.1	51	20.2
SAIS	2 494	40.2	59	23.3
Total	6 209	100.0	253	100.0

Source: Ministerio de Agricultura (1976:1), p. 67.

Horton (1976), pp. 274-277, identifies the following arguments of the junta for the creation of co-operative farms:
- ideological
- reduce the risk of dislocations in production and marketing
- cut the time and costs necessary for land redistribution
- supposed economies of scale
- reduce future burden of technical assistance and credit

Lipton (1977), p. 107, argues that a co-operative farm is amendable for extracting capital to the urban sector, and therefore popular among urban decision makers. This was also the stated intention of the government. See the introduction to the law 17716.

12. The importance of controlling the water in irrigated agriculture is well known in Peru and dates far back. A senator from Piura, Northern Peru, for example has described how the big estates monopolized the use of water in the 40's. According to him there were two reasons for this: (1) Force the small farmer to sell the land; (2) To reduce competition in the market. Castro (1947), pp. 9-10. See also de Osma (1912), p. 4. In Peru water rights have been as important as the land itself.

13. Practically all studies on the ownership of land in Peru rely on census data. One interesting attempt, using the property registers 1926-30, can be found in Chaplin (1966). Malpica's (1974) work is also important identifying the most important capital owners in Peru and their relationships. See particularly pp. 76-159.

The irrigation authorities also have information on the area irrigated on different farms (Padrón de Regantes).

14. Some information is given on the number of production units being owned or rented, but not enough to permit an analysis of the ownership structure. One example will make the problem clear. Suppose an owner has divided his farm into two estates. The Census data

will register this as two production units, and if one or more parts of this farm is rented new production units will be registered.

15. See FAO (1969), p. ix.

16. See Alberts and Buechler (1970), p. 1.

17. Victor Villanueva, a retired major, has written several works on the role of the military in Peruvian development. One of the prevailing lines of thought among the military was to destroy the landed oligarchy. They believed that an agrarian reform, if it accomplished this, would almost automatically lead to social justice, higher production and industrialization. See Villanueva (1972), particularly p. 177. President Velasco, the son of a small farmer, was also hostile in his speeches attacking the oligarchy for the underdevelopment of Peru. The reduction in target may well be that first priority was assigned to breaking the power of the landed aristocracy. Mounting production problems, rising food imports and prices were probably additional factors in explaining this. See also chapter 2.

18. The reader should keep in mind that the agrarian reform authorities consider the family as the basic unit. In other words the word beneficiary can be substituted with "benefitted family". A benefitted family was interpreted rather loosely by the reform authorities. In general, the number of beneficiaries was overestimated by the junta. For a dicussion of this see Caballero (1976), pp. 1-36.

19. See CIDA study for details on the necessary size for a family farm. See also Appendix to this chapter for details on land tenure, and for estimate of the number of agricultural families.

20. Comparative table of agrarian reform targets and results

	Adjudications
A. Accomplished end 1975	
area (1000 hectares)	6 214
families	251 997
B. Target for end 1976	
area (1000 hectares)	9 631
families	399 311
C. Accomplished end 1976	
area (1000 hectares)	6 855
families	292 547

Source: A. Tables A.5.1 and A.5.2
B. Ministerio de Agricultura(1976:1), Table 8
C. Tables A.5.1 and A.5.2

21. See for example Ministerio de Agricultura (1976:1), pp. 12-15.

22. Ministerio de Agricultura (1978), Table 1. However, Actualidad Económica in its June edition, p. 8, reports that at the end of March 1979, 8.1 million hectares had been adjudicated to about 350 000 families.

23. For a discussion of these issues see Cabellero (1976). Also, Eguren (1975), Valderrama (1976).

24. Vigués (1966), p. 7.

25. Dorner (1972), p. 47.

26. Mann et.al. (1970), p. xiii. Brundenius (1972), pp. 215 and 225-229, considered that the expropriated owners would be very generously compensated.

27. Cf. Vigués (1966).

28. Scott (1971), p. 347.

29. Cf. Carrasco et.al. (1969); and Scott (1971), p. 348. Even during the first years of the military junta this idea prevailed. Valderrama (1976), p. 47.

30. Dorner (1972), pp. 47-48.

31. See for example Eguren (1975), p. 61; Valderrama (1976).

32. The Constitutive Assembly elected in 1978 has proposed to write off the Agrarian Debt, and to make the agrarian bonds marketable. DESCO, Resumen Semanal No 28, 1979, p. 1.

33. Changes in relative prices can of course also occur without inflation.

34. In several Latin American countries where the rates of inflation were high, e.g. Brazil and Chile, indexing systems have been used to adjust the nominal values of bonds, saving deposits, wages etc. In the Chilean Agrarian Reform part of the bonds were adjusted for inflation. Dorner (1972), p. 46.

35. Caballero (1976), pp. 37-39; Mann et.al. (1970), p. xiii. Perhaps, because this is a politically sensitive issue, on one line, in 124 pages, in the Convenio (1970:4) stated that the value for expropriation was only half the market value. p. 50. As Clark and Haswell have pointed out: "The price of land is a consequence of its rent (less tax)...land prices are consequence of rents, not vice versa." Clark and Haswell (1974), p. 164. They also noted that this depends on the rate of return in the economy as a whole and, "...the price of land will depend, not only upon changes in the rate of interest, but also upon the political outlook." Ibidem p. 165. If there had existed a market for land during the reform, the law prohibited the

landowners to sell their land, the price would probably have been
very low, because of the confiscatory elements. Many landowners
had also decapitalized their estates so that the rent from land
had declined. Peruvian scholars writing on the agrarian reform,
influenced by marxism, have attempted to untangle these interde-
pendencies. See for example Caballero (1975:1), and (1975:2).

36. Convenio (1970:4), p. 49. According to the law, (D.L. 17716, Art.
83), the Ministry of Agriculture was entrusted to fix the interest rates and the number of grace years although a maximum of five
years for the latter was law. These figures do agree with those in
Eguren (1975), p. 192. For an example of an agrarian reform contract
of adjudication between the beneficiaries and the Ministry of Agriculture see Appendix. Also Eguren (1975), pp. 190-195.

37. Eguren (1975), pp. 190-195.

38. Van de Wetering (1970), pp. 75-79. The methodology for estimating
the multiplier effects of the income redistribution was a Keynsian
inspired demand multiplier model. The increases thus induced were
not considered here, because we believe that there is a supply constraint. See chapter 6.

39. Some of this will be discussed in chapter 6. On wage increases see
section 5.4.

40. García-Sayán, though, affirms that there were frequent difficulties
to repay the debt. Eguren et.al. (1977), p. 146.

41. Eguren (1975), pp. 155, and 157; Marka No. 44, 1976, in its special
number devoted to the agrarian reform has this on its first page.

42. See Mann et.al. (1970), pp. 74-86.

43. Ministerio de Agricultura (1977:1), Reforma Agraria 5. In the last
two columns the increased value is given. The public sector can
choose among a whole set of policy instruments and it may well increase taxes instead of adjusting the debt. See García-Sayá in Eguren et.al. (1977), pp. 139-216.

44. Ministerio de Agricultura (1975:2), p. 5. On 31 December 1975 the
figure had risen to 23% and it was 4% on 31 December 1974. Ministry
of Agriculture (1976), statistical Table 28.

45. Convenio (1970:4), p. 59.

46. Under the Belaúnde regime, 1964 Law, the bonds could be used to pay
taxes and were negotiable. Mann et.al. (1970), p. 122. For a comparison of the laws see pp. 122-124. They are not correct when stating
that the bonds were accepted at 100% face value for industrial investments.

47. Zaldívar in Lehman ed. (1974), p. 63; Brundenius (1972), pp. 204-229;

Eguren (1975), p. 152; Eguren et.al. (1977), pp. 205-214.

48. Eguren et.al. (1977), p. 212.

49. Ibid. pp. 209-213. Valderama and Ludman (1979), pp. 55-59.

50. Ministerio de Agricultura (1975:1), Table F-2. See also Horton (1976), p. 264.

51. Eguren et.al. (1977), p. 170-177.

52. To what extent high level white collar workers have left the sugar enterprises is not possible to ascertain. During my visits to the sugar estates in 1969 and 1970 there were complaints of this. See also Cáceres (1976); Horton (1976), pp. 302-305.

53. This is reported in Horton (1976), pp. 298-299; Comisión Multisectorial (1975); Roca (1975), p. 33. My field trips in 1969 and 1970 also confirm this. See also chapter 2.4.5.

54. Guillet (1979), p. 193.

55. If we had access to family incomes they would have been higher but for all but the sugar estates the non-monetary income was imputed.

56. In the case of the sugar industry the very rapid increase in wages was possible because of a substantial increase in the world market price of sugar.

Sugar exports 1969-77 volume and value

	Value (US$ 1000)	Volume (metric tons)	Price US$ per metric ton
69	38 926	317 558	123
1970	65 430	523 737	125
71	69 678	532 202	131
72	77 121	552 046	140
73	86 628	548 756	158
74	153 732	486 246	316
1975	295 459	442 455	668
76	92 005	346 581	265
77	83 123	486 743	171

Source: BCR, Memoria (1976), pp. 175 and 173; BCR Memoria (1977), pp. 152 and 154.

The price for domestic consumption was, however, set much lower, and the sugar estates were assigned different volumes to deliver for the domestic market. With this set-up the demand for the domestic market was growing rapidly, faster than production, and the exportable surplus was declining.See Roca (1975); Comisión (1975). What will happen

to the wages of the sugar estates in the future is an open question
and will be influenced by the evolution of the world market price
for sugar and government policies.
At the end of the 70's a serious drought affected Peru and world
market prices for sugar decreased further. As a result the sugar
industry has faced serious difficulties. See Latin American Regional Reports RA-80-02; RA-80-3; and Actualidade Económica, March
1979, pp. 13-14.

57. See Horton (1976), pp. 309-314.

58. Ibid., p. 313. In Tupac Amaru II, a well-run co-operative, sales
    increased substantially between 1971 and 1974. Guillet (1979), p. 190.

59. Cáceres (1976), p. 12. More than half of them had weekly contact
    with agriculture (p. 5), and they were very dissatisfied with how
    the agrarian reform had affected their economic position. Before
    the reform 11% thought that their situation was either bad or very
    bad. In 1975 the figure had risen to 79% and tended to look worse
    for the future (p. 6). This might have influenced their appraisal
    of agricultural production.

60. Horton (1976), p. 30. In Horton (1974), p. xv, he claimed that in
    half of the enterprises visited output and employment had increased
    since the reform, in over two thirds investment had risen. On the
    use of the concept intensive, see footnote 54 in chapter 4. Cáceres
    (1976), p. 14, reports that production had fallen. Guillet (1979),
    p. 201, reports that there is a shift to capital intensive tech-
    niques with negative effects on employment.

61. Fitzgerald (1976), p. 123.

62. Bayer (1975). The same thoughts have been present in Peru in various
    forms. For an interesting analysis of the legal matters of the shift-
    ing and ambiguous policies of the Government see Pásara (1974).

63. Barraclough and Domike (1966), p. 393.

64. See Table 5.1. Bayer (1975), p. 35, on a basis of a case study be-
    lieves that the 1972 Census underestimated the number of minifundistas.

65. Some of the economic effects of fragmentation of land holdings are
    discussed in Lipton (1968).

66. This was decreed in 1973. D.L. 19977 and was valid only for plots up
    to 5 hectares of irrigated land or the equivalent of other types of
    land. See Matos Mar (1976) for a case study. On p. 17 he considers
    that their economic position will improve.

67. Horton (1976), pp. 314-317.

68. Guillet (1979), p. 201.

69. IBRD (1975), p. 24.

6
Stagnation or Growth?

6.1 INTRODUCTION

In chapter 2 we identified two central development objectives of the military government, (i) to re-distribute income and (ii) to increase the rate of economic growth. In
chapter 3 we made a macroeconomic appraisal to what extent the government was successful in implementing these
objectives. We showed that the government maintained a relatively high rate of economic growth in the 1969-75 period, while the results in the 1975-79 period were quite
poor. In part the policies pursued in 1968-75 caused the
poor performance in the second period. Peru had a very
skewed income distribution in the sixties, and in the 1968-
75 period there was no improvement in the overall income
distribution. It may even have deteriorated. Thus in this
area the government was not successful.

In chapters 4-5 our main attention was on the agricultural
sector. In chapter 4 we discussed the relationship between
agricultural income distribution and the concentration of
land ownership. We noted that the higher the degree of land
ownership concentration, and the scarcer land becomes, the
more skewed the agricultural income distribution will be.
Using the framework developed in chapter 4 we proceeded in
chapter 5 to review land ownership concentration before and
after the agrarian reform. These two chapters, 4 and 5, suggest a very uneven income distribution both before and after the agrarian reform, and thus agree with the estimates
in chapter 3.

The main causes of the relatively low average rural income
is the low level of agricultural output and the low rates
of growth of the sector relative to the rest of the economy.

Thus in order to increase rural incomes the rate of agricultural growth has to increase. In this chapter 6 we will review government policies towards agricultural growth and the output performance of the sector. The availability of good quality agricultural land is crucial both in determining income distribution and the rate of growth. The former aspect has been mentioned several times in this study and we will return to it again in this chapter. In chapter 1 we pointed out that agricultural production stagnated before the military coup in 1968. We will in this chapter further investigate this stagnation, its major causes, and investigate closely the development after 1968.

The chapter will be organized in the following way:

The first part will deal with the output performance in Peruvian agriculture before and after 1968. Special attention will be given to the first Development Plan of the junta, 1971-75.

The following parts discus and analyse some of the key factors which can explain the low rate of growth in Peruvian agriculture, such as the resource base, investments and price policies. As will be shown in this chapter one cause for agricultural stagnation prior to the military government in 1968 was government policies towards this sector. Therefore, we will also investigate whether the military government initiated any major change in policy.

The last part summarizes the main findings in this chapter.

6.2   THE SITUATION IN 1968 AND THE PLAN 1971-75

6.2.1 Agricultural production statistics

Production data on the agricultural sector of Peru are usually of poor quality, although several attempts have been made
to improve them.[1] In the sixties the Central Bank, for example, revised the agricultural production data released by
the Ministry of Agriculture, but these estimates were not
used by the Ministry. These Central Bank revisions were made
because of an apparent contradiction between growth in income
and food production. The main argument was that the low rate
of growth in per capita agricultural production was incom-
patible with the growth in demand derived from a higher per
capita income. Therefore, it was argued that agricultural production had been faster than that recorded by official statistics.[2] Thorp disputed this procedure and advanced alternative explanations, among these, that the income distribution might have worsened.[3]

In 1961 an Agricultural Census was carried out, the results
of which led to a major revision of previous estimates of
area, yields and production.[4] Practically all statistical
data on agricultural production rely on this 1961 census
which was published in 1965.[5] Most studies use the 1961,
but frequently their specific source is not mentioned. They
may use preliminary or final figures from the 1961 census, or
even current official production statistics prior to the
census results. The difficulty is compounded when times series are constructed, and it becomes close to impossible to
untangle the original sources used. The difficulty with Peru is how the data were constructed and which were their
original sources.

There is agreement among scholars that these quantitative

data on Peruvian agricultural production are of little reliability.[6] In addition we face the very difficult problems
when we seek to proceed from quantitative data to values.
How can this be done in a country where market prices fluc-
tuate greatly over time and also vary greatly from region
to region? As far as we know, there are no studies available which investigate how this has been done in Peru. For
purposes of analysis we will use, therefore, both aggregated
and disaggregated data on agricultural production.

6.2.2   The military junta's first Plan 1971-75

The agricultural sector and in particular the Coast, was
severely affected by a drought in 1967, and was recuperat-
ing 1968-70. For this and other reasons, when the Reform
came in 1969, many public officials believed that it would
not have any negative side effects on agricultural production. An example of this is that the 1971-75 Plan stated
that while in the period 1960-1970 the value-added of agriculture only grew 1.5 percent per annum in the period 1970-
75 would rise to 4.2 percent yearly.[7]

In fact there existed a general belief that the oppression
of the Peruvian farmer was the main source of poor agricultural growth and that once this ceased the agricultural
sector would more or less automatically increase its rate
of growth.[8] The Plan, for example, stated that the general
supporting services, such as technical assistance, credit, and
production of improved seeds, were central to the success
of the Plan. But, the Plan did not contemplate the major
increase in the overall budget of the Ministry of Agriculture, nor did it relate the production targets to budgetary
allocations. To some extent this can be explained by the lack

of trained economists and planners within the Ministry of
Agriculture, but even the Planning Institute and the Ministry of Finance did not object in substance to the agricultural development Plan.

The Plan explicitly stated that the beneficiaries of the
reform should receive priority in agricultural services.
Since no major increases were foreseen in such services
this meant that officials and technicians were reallocated
to the reformed sector, practically abandoning the rest of
agriculture. Moreover, the administrative procedures.of
the agrarian reform required major re-allocations from
supporting activities to the agrarian reform administration.

Also important is that a major part of the state investments in agriculture was earmarked for irrigation. For the
period 1971-75 no less than 52% was for irrigation.[9] Such
investments have a long gestation period and the possibilities to finance other investment programmes in agriculture were severely constrained.

Our main argument has been that an agrarian reform was a
necessary condition for an equity cum growth strategy, but
it was not a sufficient condition. Since also public investment and services of various kinds were essential, the lack
of agricultural growth was therefore a logical consequence
of lack of sufficient public support of successive governments. Also the military government neglected to give agriculture sufficient support. The effects of this soon became
apparent. In Table 6.1 the situation in 1970, the targets
and the results for 1975 are given.

Table 6.1   Agricultural production. Targets and results
             of key products for the medium-term plan
             1971-75 (1000 metric tons)

| | 1970 | 1975 | | |
	1 Official production	2 Production target	3 Official result	4 Degree of target implementation (percent) (3:2)x100=4
Wheat	138	232	108	47
Corn	615	761	330	43
Rice (paddy)	578	548	400	73
Potatoes	1 896	2 496	1 581	63
Sugar	770	897	986	110
Cotton	244	276	210	76
Coffee	55	68	65	96
Meat	67	84	77	92

Source: The figures for 1970 and targets 1975: INP (1971), Volumen II,
pp. 19, 55, 41.
The figures for 1975 results: Brundenius (1976:1), pp. 58-62;
These are reproduced in Ministerio de Agricultura (1977:1),
Tema II, Table 2. Most of these agree with the data in Ministerio de Alimentación (1976), Tables A-2, A-3 and A-6, except
corn (315) and rice (504). The data for coffee and cotton
agree with Ministerio de Agricultura (1976:1), p. 62.

The output performance is disappointing when evaluated against
the targets of the military junta. In practically all of the
products, output was much lower than planned. What explanations can be given of these differences? We have already
briefly mentioned some reasons above. Most significantly,
the targets were too optimistic given agricultural stagnation and given the limited public resources planned for investment in agriculture. That the plans of the military government were overly optimistic in relation to results can
also be seen from the data on agricultural production com-
piled by FAO. From Table 6.2 it can be seen that total pro-

duction increased slowly 1967-74, but since the middle of
the seventies stagnated. On a per capita basis the long run
trend observed in chapter 1, 1950-68, is continued in the
period 1968-79, during which per capita production decreases
significantly. The drop in 1978 and 1979 can in part be explained by a serious drought in Peru.[10]

Table 6.2   Index number of total agricultural,food pro-
             duction and on per capita basis 1967-79
             (1969-71 = 100)

	Total agricultural production	Food production	Per capita production	
			Total	Food
1967	92	92	101	100
1968	86	83	91	88
1969	95	94	97	97
1970	102	102	102	102
1971	104	104	101	101
1972	102	104	97	99
1973	107	107	98	99
1974	110	112	99	100
1975	106	109	92	95
1976	108	111	92	95
1977	108	110	89	91
1978	103	106	83	85
1979	107	109	83	85

Source: FAO Production Yearbook 1978, pp. 75-81
        FAO Production Yearbook 1979, pp. 75-81

It would, therefore, be possible to argue that agrarian reform caused this poor output performance. However, we have
already mentioned in chapter 1 that per capita output performance possibly started to decline even before the agrarian reform in 1969, and that this process then was continued during the military junta.It is thus difficult to iso-

late what could have been the short-run effects of the reform from the long-run trends towards stagnation. Nevertheless, data do not suggest any abrupt changes during the
agrarian reform.

At least it can be argued that the bias against the agricultural sector relative to public sector investments etc.
was maintained by the military junta. In the remaining part
of this chapter we will analyse more closely some factors
which can explain the low rate of growth of Peruvian agriculture. We will also use another set of data which indicates that the decline in agricultural production may have
been even greater than official production figures would
indicate.

In 1972 another Agricultural Census was carried out, and
again the Census data differ greatly from the current agricultural statistics, published by various public offices.
In this case the difference was even greater, and much work
will be needed to reconcile these diverging sets of data.
In order to assess the great differences let us look at
Table 6.3.

Table 6.3   Comparative table of official current crop
            production statistics and census data in 1972

Product	1 Official current statistics (Average of 1971 and 1972 production)	2 1972 Census data	3 Margin of error [(1:2)−1]×100=3
	———— 1000 metric tons ————		—— percent ——
Rice	511	452	13
Corn	596	458	30
Wheat	138	70	97
Barley	169	106	59
Potatoes	1 796	555	224
Cotton	236	202	17
Sugarcane	8 496	8 333	2
Coffee	66	58	14

Source: 1: See Table 6.1.   2: ONEC (1975), pp. 21-71

These census data, column 2, are practically all significantly below official production statistics, column 1. The
difference between columns 1 and 2 is greatest for typical
Sierra products (potatoes, wheat, barley) and production
data for this region are particularly of low quality. If
these data are more accurate than official current production statistics the situation of agriculture was even worse
than what was commonly believed.

In the next sections of this chapter we will further explore
some of the main causes for stagnation of Peruvian agriculture.

6.3   THE RESOURCE BASE

The basic resource in agricultural production is land. It
is particularly important in developing countries where
both capital investments and technology levels are relatively low. In the case of Peru many have argued that land
is not scarce. Feder, for example has completely rejected
the idea that land is scarce in Peru and claims that much
more land is available than was recorded by the 1961 agricultural census.[11] The demand and supply projections
published in 1969 considered that cultivated area had shown
a remarkable growth in response to population growth.[12]
The Peruvian left has frequently argued that land is not
scarce and that (a) Peru has a large potential and/or
(b) that the big landowners let land be idle.[13]

Our thesis is that land in Peru has been and has become
increasingly scarce in an economic sense. The high cost
of new land will continue to be a major constraint for the
growth of Peruvian agriculture. The remaining part of this
section will discuss this point.

Peru is scarcely populated and the farms of Peru cover only a fraction of total available land. Of the 128 million hectares in the country the farms only cover some 20 million. Judging from this, any hypothesis claiming an absolute scarcity of land must be rejected. Any meaningful discussion of land scarcity must include other criteria than the physical area of the country. Several factors should be considered such as climate, access to markets, transportation costs, and quality of the soil. All these factors are reflected in the price of land on a per hectare basis. Using this approach it is simple to verify that on the Coast land is scarcer than in the Sierra. See Table 6.4.

Table 6.4   The price of agricultural land in Peru (1968)
(current Soles per hectare)

	Irrigated	Dry farming	Weighted average
Coast	20,469	------	20 469
Sierra	9 442	3 553	4 921

Source: Convenio (1970:4), p. 42

The low-cost coastal irrigation projects have largely been implemented. Information available indicates that the marginal cost of incorporating new land through additional irrigation schemes has been rising. (See also chapter 7.3). Demand for land is relatively high but the supply cost is rising.[14]

The lower price of land in the Sierra is a function of: (a) lack of infrastructure such as roads, and irrigation systems; (b) adverse climatological factors; (c) poor access to markets; and (d) poor soil quality. Many of these factors can be overcome through investments most of which must come from the public sector. The marginal cost of

supplying new land of quality is probably lower than on
the Coast, but demand is constrained by high transportation costs for agricultural produce and inputs.

Unfortunately data on land prices are extremely scanty,
but it is probably true that the real price of land has
tended to increase. The reason is that the cost of incorporating new land has increased, and demand for land has
increased. The more relevant issue is the cost of incorporating new land into the market system of Peru. In order to do this investments are needed, and hence the issue
at stake is the production function of new land where
the major input is physical capital. Because capital is
scarce, land becomes scarce and this is the crux of the
matter.[15] Moreover, the issue involves also something
closely related, namely, investment in already available
land evaluated against investment in increasing land area.
Again the great problem is capital scarcity.

A few words on the spatial dynamics of the development of
Peru are necessary. In the past most of the population
was concentrated in the Sierra and successively the Coastal areas have tended to absorb an increasing share of
the population as well as of most economic activities. The
jungle area has been of little economic importance but
during the last decades increasing migratory movements
from the Sierra to the Jungle have been observed.[16]

Both on the Coast and in the Sierra there are no new areas
available for agricultural production without heavy investments. The increase in migration from the Sierra to the
Jungle is an indication that the people face a physical
shortage of land, without access to necessary capital, and
prefer to migrate to the Jungle. This so-called spontaneous
colonization implies using labour to break up new land, prac-

tically without any input of capital. The opening up of new
land on the Coast through irrigation projects has been in
response to the development of the urban centers as well as
easy access to world markets.

Peru is a large country and in 1972 there were only 14 million people. One would, therefore, be tempted to regard the
country as having an abundance of agricultural land. That
this is not the case is easily shown by using international data.

Table 6.5 . Arable land per capita in selected countries

Country	Year	Arable land per capita (Ha's)
Peru[e]	1971	0.18
South America[a]		0.50
Argentina	1968	1.01
Bolivia	1973	0.57
Brazil	1970	0.28
Chile	1973	0.54
Colombia	1970	0.17
Ecuador	1968	0.50
Paraguay	1972	0.31
Uruguay	1970	0.62
Venezuela	1961	0.53
Asia[b]		0.20
India	1972	0.29
Japan	1972	0.04
China	1971	0.16
Europe[c]		0.30
Africa[d]		0.60
North America		
Canada	1971	2.03
USA	1969	0.93
Mexico	1970	0.51

Source: FAO Production Yearbook 1974.
a) 1970 population used; b) 1971 population used; c) 1973 population used; d) 1970 population used; 5) The FAO statistics
do not indicate the source. In 1971 there was no census in Peru
and the data must be based on the 1961 Census in one way or another. Rather than to introduce the 1972 data on Peru the FAO
estimate has been maintained so that the same criteria for international comparison are maintained.
Note: Arable land is defined as "land under temporary crops (double
cropped areas are counted only once), temporary meadows for mowing or
pasture, land under market and kitchen gardens (including cultivation
under glass), and land temporarily fallow or lying idle".

As can be seen from Table 6.5 arable land per capita in Peru is rather small. In comparison with the South American
countries the situation of Perú is the worst with the possible exception of Colombia. Even India appears better off
than Peru and this result is surprising since the general
impression of India is that of an overpopulated country,
while Peru with its vast jungles is not. It seems justified
to conclude from Table 6.5 that on a comparative basis Peru
is characterized by scarcity of land.

As can be seen from Table 6.6 cultivated area per capita in
Peru has declined significantly since 1929. There are two
simultaneous tendencies in land development. One is that marginal land is brought into production and the other is that
capital is substituted for land in agricultural production.
The next step is to compare the two latest censuses, 1961
and 1972, which provide some detailed information on the
quality of land and its use.

Table 6.6   Cultivated area per capita 1929-72

Year	1 Area (1000 Ha's)	2 Area index 1929=100	3 Population index 1929=100	4 Area per capita index 1929=100 (2:3)x100=4
1929	1 513	100	100	100
1961	2 171	143	186	77
1972	2 527	167	260	64

Sources: LAND: 1929 Agricultural Census; 1961 Agricultural Census; 1972
Agricultural Census; See also Thorp and Bertram (1978), pp. 275-
276 for a discussion of land data.
POPULATION: ONEC (1974), p. 172

As can be seen from Table 6.7, while total agricultural land
rose by 33%, the number of production units rose by almost
the double, 65%. This is a partial indication that land has

become increasingly scarce. The cultivated land increased
by only 16 percent. Total area per production unit therefore fell from 21 to 17 hectares between 1961 and 1972,
and cultivated area per unit fell from 2.6 to 1.8 hectares
in the same period.

Table 6.7   Land use in Peru 1961 and 1972 (1000 hectares)

Land used in:	1961		1972		Change between 1961 and 1972	
	1	2	3	4	5	6
	Area	Distri-bution percent	Area	Distri-bution percent	Absolute	$(\frac{5}{1})$ x100=6 percentage
1. "Crop" pro-duction[1]	2 171	12.3	2 527	10.7	356	16.4
2. Natural pas-tures	8 819	49.8	15 129	64.3	6 310	71.6
3. Fallow land[2]	1 726	9.7	1 164	4.9	-562	-32.6
4. Forests and mountains	1 997	11.3	3 069	13.0	1 072	53.7
5. Others[3]	3 008	12.0	1 655	7.0	-1 353	-45.0
Total	17 721	100.1	23 544	99.9	5 823	32.9
Number of produc-tion units (1000)	843		1 390		547	64.9

Source: INP (1965); ONEC (1975)

1) Includes land under temporary and permanent crops, and cultivated
   pastures.
2) The sum of land under temporarily fallow or lying idle.
3) The production unit's land which has not been included in the other
   categories.

The increase in natural pastures seems to be in contradiction with the land scarcity hypothesis. Marginal land may
have been brought into production, and also land cleared

in the Ceja de Selva and the Selva regions which during
the initial years of agricultural production may have been
used for pasture, as is common.[17] The decrease in fallow
land is an indication of pressure on the land, since technology did not change significantly enough to allow for
more intensive cultivation practices (4-5 years of fallow
is required in the Sierra region).[18] The increase in for-
ests and mountains is also an indication of the trend of
incorporating marginal land. Land scarcity is aggravated
by the abandon of agricultural land because of misuse. On
the Coast the use of improper irrigation techniques has resulted in severe.salinity and/or drainage problems.[19] In
the Sierra erosion has also become a problem, although the
extent of erosion is not yet known on a systematic basis.
The cutting of trees for the mines and for household uses
and pressures for new land have aggravated the erosion problem.[20]

The lack of sufficient amounts of rain in many parts of Peru
plays a decisive role in agriculture, where the need for irrigation is very high in comparison with for example Europe
and North America. It is, therefore, important to investigate
the amount of land with and without irrigation. As was mentioned earlier, capital and land are good substitutes in agricultural production. One of the most important kinds of investment is the expansion of irrigated land. The irrigated
area increased 25 percent between 1961 and 1972. Consequently,
the share of irrigated land in cultivated land increased from
46.8 percent in 1961 to 50.5 percent in 1972.[21]

In order to bring more land into production requires as suggested important investments including irrigation, necessary
in Peru. The cost on a per hectare basis is rather high, and
at least on the Coast the marginal cost is increasing. In the

Sierra, the problem seems to be a too intensive use of land, given the technology prevailing and the recorded low levels of investments. The scarcity problem must be analysed in economic terms to enable the policy makers to investigate the proper strategy to pursue - where to invest and in which activities. The land scarcity problem can then be analysed in economic terms and not as something independent of the economic system. The resource base will be discussed further in the next section on investments in agriculture.

6.4   INVESTMENTS IN AGRICULTURE

6.4.1 Private investments

Investments in agriculture may be initiated either in the public or the private sector. There are data for the activities of the public sector, but very few of private sector investments are recorded. In order to arrive at an idea of how private investments in agriculture have developed we will have to rely on indirect methods. Our working hypothesis is that investments in agriculture in the post World War II period have on the whole been low and that they started to decline in the sixties, perhaps earlier.

The reasons for this are basically two. First, the economic policies favoured urban and industrial growth, and had a bias against agriculture. Second, the political circumstances in the 60's, the increasing likelihood of an agrarian reform and political unrest in the countryside rendered investment risky in the agricultural sector. These factors taken together contributed towards a shift of investments out of agriculture.[22]

One way to arrive at an idea of private investments in agriculture is to look at the output performance. We have
already pointed out the low rates of growth of Peruvian
agriculture and that available information tends to indicate that the rate of growth has been falling.[23] Moreover,
the behaviour of commercial credit, for example, is indicative of the behaviour of private investments. Agriculture
has during the years 1950-78 only received a small share
of the credit allocated through commercial banks. In the
50's there was an increase, both absolutely and proportionately; in the 60's the share allocated to agriculture
drops, first proportionately and subsequently absolutely.
After 1975 total credit decreased and agriculture continued
to receive a decreasing share.

Table 6.8   Outstanding credit of commercial banks
             (Million 1970 Soles)

	1 Agriculture	2 All sectors	3 Agriculture share in total (percent) (1:2)x100=3
1950	1 120	9 094	12.3
1955	2 505	15 389	16.3
1960	2 379	16 507	14.4
1965	2 539	22 999	11.0
1970	1 541	23 632	6.5
1975	1 076	32 486	3.3
1976	889	29 549	3.0
1977	712	25 373	2.8
1978	459	21 707	2.1

Source: BCR, Boletín November (1976) and May (1979). For
        deflator used see Appendix to this chapter.

At the time of the agrarian reform it was discovered that
many of the sugar industry complexes were using very old

machinery which needed replacement showing low levels of
capital investment in an important agricultural sub-sec-
tor. The low and decreasing levels of investments in agriculture are also corroborated by data from the evaluation
procedures of the agrarian reform. In 1969-70 a study of
the book-keeping value of machinery and buildings of the
expropriated farms indicated that they represented only
0.5-1.5 percent of the farm value.[24] The regional imbalance is also confirmed by these data since these investments were 4 times higher on the Coast than in the Sierra,
on a per hectare basis.

Indicative is also that in the period 1961-1972 the number
of cattle practically remained constant. Beef production,
however, increased during the same period.[25] Moreover,
scrutinizing the 1961-72 data it can be observed that for
farms above 100 Ha's there was a marked drop in the number
of cattle, from 535 to 486 thousand heads. This information
suggests that the big landowners shifted assets out of agriculture to other economic sectors.[26]

What is also important in Peruvian agriculture, is that big
producers, particularly those on the Coast, also had important economic interests outside agriculture, e.g. banking,
housing and industry.[27] The economic interests outside agriculture can probably be explained by the fact that at least
a part of the profit was invested outside the agricultural
sector. The transfer of profits out of agriculture was probably accelerated in the 60's. Horton writing on the Belaúnde agrarian reform has stated that: "Fearing expropriation,
landowners 'mined agriculture', extracting surplus for investment elsewhere in the economy and failing to conserve
or improve their estates' land, equipment, and installations."[28]

These indicators all point in the direction of very low levels of investment, declining in the 60's. Notwithstanding, some indicators point to a slow but significant contrary evolution. For example in the 1961 Census a maximum of 61,000 production units used guano or chemical fertilizers while in 1972 this figure had risen to over 200 000. The efforts of the Peruvian government in introducing modern methods of cultivation have in this respect met with some success.

The figures are also corroborated by studies on fertilizer consumption. In general Peru is using little of fertilizers. For example in the 60's Western Europe consumed 120 kgs of fertilizers per hectare while in Peru it was only 34 kgs.[29] This situation is changing. The use of nitrogen, for example, has increased significantly in a relatively short time span. See Table 6.9.

Table 6.9   Nitrogen use in Peruvian agriculture

Period	1 Yearly average (1000 metric tons)	2 Area (1000 Ha's)	3 Kg/Ha (1:2)=3
1957-59	41	-	-
1960-62	54	2 171	25
1971-72	86	2 527	34

Source: 1: Naciones Unidas (1966), pp. 6-7; FAO (1975), p. 253.
        2: Table 6.6

However, as of 1973 the consumption dropped significantly as a result of the drastic increases in world market prices for fertilizers.[30]   As of June 1975 the Government started to subsidize fertilizers in order to combat the fall in their use. The policy has been, however, only to subsidize fertilizers in food production.[31]

Table 6.10 Consumption of **fertilizers** (1000 metric tons of nutriments)

	1973	1974	1975	1976	1977	Cultivated Area* 1972 (1000 Ha's)
Coast	n.a.	74	84	105	115	620
Sierra	n.a.	19	21	24	29	1 407
Total	100	93	105	129	144	2 027

Source: Pacora (1978), Table 7; ONEC (1975)

*) Includes land under temporary and permanent crops, and cultivated pastures.

Table 6.10 shows how consumption of fertilizers quickly increased again after 1975. It also demonstrates clearly how total consumption is greater on the Coast than in the Sierra. The consumption per unit of area is much higher on the Coast than in the Sierra.

During the reform period 1969-75 the pattern of investments is somewhat contradictory. The big owners decapitalized whatever possible. The beneficiaries, taking over these run-down estates, seem to have invested, or have been induced to do so through the controlling function of the state. Horton has claimed that: "Most cases studied show impressive rates of   capitalization. On the Coast, nearly all enterprises visited had purchased tractors, field machinery, and trucks. In the Highlands, livestock numbers had increased markedly."[32]

With respect to the small- and medium-size farms the situation has been changing. During the first years of the agrarian reform it was uncertain how they would be affected by the reform. These farmers felt a great deal of uncertainty, and were reluctant to invest and expand production. As it was becoming clear that the agrarian reform only would ex-

propriate the big farms,different measures were introduced
to guarantee these farmers security of tenure. Since 1973
the government increased the issuing of certificates of non-
expropriation.[33]

With the present agrarian reform transfer processes being
concluded in 1979, one important task of the government
will be to stimulate investments in agriculture so as to
break the Post-World-War II pattern of low and declining
investments in agriculture. Since agriculture is a bottleneck in overall growth, investments in agriculture could
have a high return.

6.4.2 Public sector investments

The public sector has had to deal with two long term tendencies. First, development accelerated on the Coast, and in
part this was financed through agricultural exports. This
Coastal growth vis-a-vis the stagnatory tendencies in the
Sierra region, and the increase in the rate of population
growth triggered off extensive migration from the Sierra
to the Coast. In addition, the post-Second-World-War
emphasis on industrialization concentrated on the Lima-Callao area triggered off a very high rate of urbanization.[34]
Also, the agricultural exports of the Coast financed in part
the Coastal and especially the Lima-Callao area. The public
sector became an active supporter of this Coastal development, and geared its resources to support the agricultural
development of the Coast especially for export commodities.
This emphasis on investments on the Coast contributed to
the stagnation and loss in economic importance of the Sierra.[35]

Second, the agricultural sector had difficulties to provide

food for the increasing large urban conglomorate. The stagnation in output has forced the public sector to take measures to attenuate this evolution.[36] Now, agricultural production can be increased through an expansion of land and/or increases in yield per hectare. To increase land under cultivation requires investments and yield increases can be accomplished through more labour input per hectare and/or the increased use of non-traditional inputs such fertilizers and improved seeds.

However, as explained, the marginal cost of expanding land under irrigation on the Coast is increasing, and on the whole the production from the Coast tends successively to be more costly vis-a-vis output expansion in the Sierra and the High Jungle areas. Therefore, in a longer perspective the present Coastal/Lima-Callao development pattern may well have to be changed. But let us investigate the data available to see the pattern which has developed.

It is possible to construct some long-time series on public sector expenditures. On the basis of data collected, the following Table 6.11 was constructed. (It should be noted that the fisheries sector is included in the Ministry of Agriculture up to 1969).

As can be seen in column 4, the Ministry of Agriculture has only managed to capture a minor share of the national budget.[37] This shows that the agricultural sector has not been a priority sector.

However, the trend is increasing at least up to 1975. From 1950 to 1975 the share of the Ministry of Agriculture in the national budget increased from 1.7% to 8.1%. It is too early to comment on whether the decline after 1975 reflects the beginning of a reduced priority for agriculture. These

Table 6.11 Indicators of public sector expenditures in agriculture 1950-77 (1970 million Soles)

Year	1 Ministry of Agriculture a)	2 World Bank estimate for public sector outlays for agriculture	3 Central Government budget	4 Agriculture share in public expenditures (1:3)x100=4	5 Agriculture share in public expenditures (2:3)x100=5	6 Iowa mission estimate
1950	152.3		8 712.4	1.7		
1955	169.8		10 292.7	1.6		
1960	497.8		13 429.4	3.7		1.8
61	749.5		16 804.6	4.5		3.1
62	766.7		17 534.0	4.4		2.6
63	939.1		29 640.6	3.2		3.0
64	1 026.8		29 917.7	3.4		3.2
1965	1 210.6	1 831.7	31 617.8	3.8	5.8	3.3
66	1 073.5	2 527.7	34 670.7	3.1	7.3	2.9
67	1 383.5 b)	2 438.2	45 767.3	3.0	5.3	3.0
68	208.4 b)	1 526.8	32 435.4	0.6	4.7	
69	1 633.2	1 678.6	28 663.9	5.7	5.9	
1970	2 824.6	2 450.0	45 502.9	6.2	5.4	
71	2 433.3	2 915.7	42 957.1	5.7	6.8	
72	3 707.2	3 980.8	64 662.2	5.7	6.2	
73	3 543.1		64 571.0	5.5		
74	4 492.2		63 137.9	7.1		
1975	5 313.9		65 912.3	8.1		
76	4 766.8		66 329.5	7.2		
77	3 267.2		61 262.9	5.3		

Source: Ministerio de Economía y Finanzas, various years; Iowa (1967), p. 235; IBRD (1975), Vol. II, Tables H.5 and H.6; Ministerio de Agricultura (1977:1), Table "Inversión 2"

a) Until 1969 the fisheries sector was part of the Ministry of Agriculture.
b) This figure is probably wrong.

Note: The figures in columns 1 and 3 refer to resources allocated, but not necessarily spent.

data support the idea that the agricultural sector became
a bottle-neck for the overall growth of the economy, and
suggest that the government had to re-appraise its role.
The very substantial increase as of 1969, however, should
be interpreted with caution, because, public sector outlays
for compensation payments in agrarian reform are included
as well as the associated administration costs and food subsidies. The beneficiaries' payments to the public sector
are not included.

If we also consider the agricultural sector's contribution
in taxes in relation to the public sector's expenditures in
agriculture a slightly different pattern emerges. While in
the 50's agriculture contributed significantly more in taxes
than what it received, the trend has been towards a balance.
See Table 6.12.

Table 6.12 Comparison of public sector receipts from
            and expenditures for agriculture 1956-70
            (Current billion Soles)

| | Public sector | | |
Year	1 Outlays in agriculture	2 Receipts from agriculture	3 1:2=3
1950	0.03	0.3	0.1
1955	0.05	0.4	0.1
1960	0.2	0.6	0.3
1965	0.8-1.2	1.1	0.7-1.1*)
1970	2.6-2.8	2.7	0.9-1.0

Source: 1. Table 6.11
        2. Data provided by BCR

*) Domike and Tokman estimated that in the period 1966-68 the Agri-
   cultural Sector received 0.62 of what it contributed to the Public Sector. See Griffin (1971), p. 128.

The agricultural sector has received an important share of central government investments. See Table 6.13. First it should be noted that the share of investments in total public sector expenditures never was very large, practically always below 15%. Second there is no systematic trend, although it can be noted that as of 1969 investments increased from an all-time low of 8 percent to almost 14 percent.

The predominance of irrigation schemes, practically all on the Coast, can be appreciated. Moreover, there are cyclical swings in investments in irrigation, and they seem to last about five years. The most probable reason for this is that once a project has commenced it has a construction phase of about 5-6 years.

It is interesting to note that the military junta, initially, gave low priority to irrigation schemes, 1969-72, but thereafter the share of irrigation schemes in public sector investments rose from 7 percent in 1970 to over 30 percent in 1974. The investments are basically practically all earmarked for the Coast.[38]

Before proceeding it should be observed that the data in Tables 6.11 and 6.13 are somewhat contradictory. During several years, especially in the fifties, investment in irrigation, Table 6.13 was larger than the budget of the Ministry of Agriculture, Table 6.11. The most probable reason is that the administrative set-up has changed so that during certain time periods investments in irrigation have been included in the budgets of public entities outside the Ministry of Agriculture and vice-versa.

Investment in the road system may stimulate agricultural development. There is no consistent long term trend in the share allocated to roads. But there is a significant

Table 6.13   Total central government investments 1950-74

(Million current Soles)

Year	Irrigation 1 Absolute	Irrigation 2 Percent of total (1:7)x100	Roads 3 Absolute	Roads 4 Percent of total (4:7)x100	Others 5 Absolute	Others 6 Percent of total (6:7)x100	Total 7 Total government investments 1+3+5=7	8 Total expenditures of government	9 Investments as percent of total exp. (7:8)x100
1950	47	28.3	44	26.5	75	45.2	166	1 642	10.1
51	70	34.5	45	22.2	88	43.3	203	2 107	9.6
52	103	20.6	216	43.2	181	36.2	500	2 566	19.5
53	88	19.1	221	48.0	151	32.8	460	2 966	15.5
54	30	7.9	117	30.8	233	61.3	380	3 001	12.7
1955	191	20.8	285	31.1	441	48.1	917	3 918	23.4
56	285	36.4	142	18.2	355	45.4	782	4 738	16.5
57	179	25.9	187	27.1	324	47.0	690	5 058	13.6
58	212	25.1	316	37.4	316	37.4	844	5 474	15.4
59	111	17.6	278	44.1	241	38.3	630	6 377	9.9
1960	27	4.6	327	55.3	237	40.1	591	7 236	8.2
61	75	6.5	484	42.1	591	51.4	1 150	9 270	12.4
62	107	7.4	645	44.6	695	48.0	1 447	10 978	13.2
63	164	18.6	261	29.5	459	51.9	884	13 195	6.7
64	129	7.9	553	33.7	958	58.4	1 640	17 672	9.3
1965	342	12.1	926	32.8	1 551	55.0	2 819	22 914	12.3
66	671	17.9	1 662	44.3	1 421	37.9	3 754	27 563	13.6
67	657	19.7	1 254	37.5	1 429	42.8	3 340	31 647	10.6
68	533	18.7	1 068	37.4	1 253	43.9	2 854	35 664	8.0
69	414	11.8	1 171	33.4	1 919	54.8	3 504	37 149	9.4
1970	439	7.4	1 594	26.8	3 905	65.8	5 938	45 196	13.1
71	642	8.9	1 689	23.5	4 858	67.6	7 189	52 889	13.6
72	964	11.6	1 905	23.0	5 427	65.4	8 296	59 766	13.9
73	1 971	24.4	1 633	20.2	4 485	55.4	8 089	72 290	11.2
1974	3 819	30.1	1 787	14.1	7 090	55.8	12 696	92 317	13.8

Source: 1950-1966: BCR (1968), p. 35; 1967-1974: BCR (1976), p. 35

change as of 1968 when it starts to decline from about 37%
to 14% in 1974. This corresponds to a shift in emphasis
in priority. During the Belaúnde regime the highway along
the high jungle was assigned high priority which was completely reversed during the military junta. There are no
data available on the spatial allocation of investments in
roads. A slightly different approach will be followed to
obtain some indicators on where the Government have invested in road construction.

Already at the beginning of the sixties investments in roads
had been on the Coast. Practically 85% of all the paved
roads can be found on the Coast. See Table 6.14. Some data from 1971 indicate the effects on freight charges of
these investments. It costs about twice as much to transport a given quantity of agricultural products a given
distance in the Sierra as it does on the Coast. If transportation costs from the farm to the highway system were
considered the difference would be even greater. If freight
charges vary from 1 000 Soles for a ton of potatoes per
1 000 kilometers on the Coast to about 2 000 Soles per ton,
the importance of the relative differences in quality in
the road system can be appreciated.[39] Prices for transport also increase drastically during periods of peak demand for transport.

Another indicator of how the public sector has allocated its
resources among the three regions is the credit allocated by
the Agricultural Development Bank.[40] The increasing rate of
inflation has led to a situation where the real rate of interest has become negative. In other words, the Government
has subsidized the credit, and because of this, it seems justifiable to assume that in the 70's the allocation of credit
to a larger extent than before reflected the government's
control of the supply and is hence indicative of the government's development policies.

Table 6.14 Indicator of spatial allocation of public
sector resources: roads

Region	Cultivated area 1964 (1000 Ha's)	Population 1961 (1000)	Kilometers of roads		Kilometers of roads per culti- vated ha		Kilometers of roads per 1000 persons	
			paved	gravel	paved	gravel	paved	gravel
Coast	669	3 920	3 550	1 450	5.3	2.2	0.9	0.4
Sierra	1 701	5 495	640	3 840	0.4	2.3	0.1	0.1
High Jungle	235	399	10	1 250	0.0	5.3	0.0	4.2
Low Jungle	130	607	7	230	0.1	1.8	0.0	0.4

Source: Coutu and King (1969), Tables, 3.2, 3.8 and 3.11

As can be seen from Table 6.15 while the share of the Coast
in total cultivated area was 25% in 1972 it received 61%
of governmental agricultural credit. The Sierra, which had
56% of the cultivated area received only 12% of credit. The
portion of the Jungle area was more balanced, having 20% of
the area and receiving 27% of the credit. The development
of credit over time has been somewhat unstable from year to
year. Still the long-run trend has been that the Coast has
reduced its share in credit from about 80% in the sixties
to about 65% in the seventies. The completion of the irrigation schemes in the pipe-line on the Coast will drastically increase demand for agricultural credit for a number
of years. The allocation to the Sierra has remained fairly
stable, 10-15 percent, though it had over half of the cultivated land.

Table 6.15   Spatial allocation of agricultural credit
              (percent)

Year	Region		
	Coast	Sierra	Jungle
1962	88	10	2
1963	77	15	8
1969*	61	12	27
1970	59	11	30
1972	61	12	27
1973	68	12	20
1974	67	15	18
1975	68	13	19
1976	65	15	20
Distribution of cultivated land 1972	25	56	20

Source: 1962-63: IBRD (1975), p. 96; 1969-70: Various Memorias of the
         Agricultural Development Bank; 1972-76: Ministerio de Agricul-
         tura (1978); Cultivated land: Tables 6.9 and 6.10

*) October 1968 - December 1969.

The Selva region has increased its share from a few percentage points to about 20%. It is curious to note that
the credit expansion in the Selva occurs simultaneously
with a reduction in the share of public sector investments for roads in this region. It is possible that the
road building activities in the period 1957-1969, part
of which should have benefitted the Selva region, are
having a strong impact on Selva development. However,
detailed studies are needed before a definite answer
can be given.

At the beginning of this chapter it was mentioned that
the commercial banks reduced their allocation of credit

to agriculture. This evolution as well as the lack of growth of agricultural production probably forced the Government to step up its lending activities to attenuate these adverse factors. At the end of the forties and at the beginning of the fifties the commercial banking system provided the major part of institutional credit. From Table 6.16 it can be seen that as of 1955 the situation had reversed and the public sector became the most important source. At the end of the seventies the commercial banks played only a minor role in agricultural credit.

Simultaneously there is a very rapid increase in the rate of growth of public sector credit to agriculture in _real_ terms, increasing over ten times in two decades. For details see Table 6.16. In the period after 1975, inflation accelerated and there was a significant fall in credit in real terms.

Table 6.16   Increasing role of public sector credit in agriculture, total outstanding credit end year (Million 1970 Soles)

Year	1 Agricultural Development Bank	2 Percent of total (1:5)x100	3 Commercial Banks	4 Percent of total (3:5)x100	5 Total 1+3
1950	617	35.5	1 119	64.5	1 736
1955	2 800	52.8	2 505	47.2	5 305
1960	3 985	62.6	2 382	37.4	6 367
1965	4 601	64.4	2 538	35.6	7 139
1970	7 384	82.7	1 541	17.3	8 925
1975	9 546	89.9	1 076	10.1	10 622
1979	7 022	94.6	401	5.4	7 423

Source: BCR Boletín February (1977), pp. 25 and 28, and March (1982), pp. 31 and 33.

The evolution of the share of agriculture in all credit allocated through all State Development Banks has been irregular. Still, it must be stressed that agriculture has received a major share, about 60 percent in the pe-period 1950-70, but thereafter continuously falling to 32 percent in 1979.[41]

Long term loans, mainly for investments purposes have also increased in importance over time until the agrarian reform in 1969. In 1960 about 30% of total outstanding credit was for investments, and this rose to about 45% the years before the reform.[42] Since then there has been a major change particularly after the agrarian reform.

In the period 1958-70 the share of long-term credit drops from 19 percent to 7 percent. As of 1971 there is an increase until 1974.[43] See Table 6.17.

Table 6.17   The share of investments in yearly allocated credit of the Agricultural Development Bank

Year	Share of investment in total credit allocated yearly (percent)
1958	19.3
1960	14.4
1965	10.4
1970	7.2
71	10.2
72	12.9
73	17.7
74	15.7
1975	8.8
1976	5.2

Source: Appendix

Although investment credits have increased during the
first years of the agrarian reform they were inadequate
for playing a significant role in financing agricultural
investments. To indicate orders of magnitude the size of
the Gross value of agricultural production can be related
to the value of these long-term loans. In 1970 the gross
value of agricultural production was about 40 000 million
Soles while long-term credit of the Bank was only 355 million. Guesstimating a marginal capital-output ratio in
agriculture of 2 and a target rate of growth of agricultural production of 4 percent, the investment level would
have to be in the order of magnitude 3 200 million Soles.
The Bank's contribution in this respect is clearly insufficient.

6.4.3 Summary

This section has investigated in some detail the investments in agriculture. Most data indicate that private investments have fallen significantly. The exact evolution
over time is impossible to establish, but it seems as if
in the decade of the sixties this process was started.
This fall in the rate of investments should to a large
extent explain the declining rate of growth of Peruvian
agriculture, and the tendency for secular stagnation.

The public sector has assigned low priority to agriculture, and it seems as if in the fifties only a fraction
of the budget was earmarked for this sector. Emphasis has
historically been laid upon increasing land under irrigation and improving the road systems, mainly on the Coast.

The declining rate of growth of agricultural output and

of private investments induced the Government to step up
its resource allocation to agriculture. There seems, however, to be a substantial time lag between on the one hand
the fall in performance of agriculture, and on the other
hand increasing the share of public sector resources allocated to agriculture. As of 1969, the beginning of the
new agrarian reform activities, the public sector increased
the share of its resources allocated for agricultural development. After 1975 it drops again.

To complete the analysis two additional considerations have
to be made. Firstly, the public sector has increased its
total expenditures rapidly since 1950. Therefore, although
the share allocated to agriculture has been rather small
there has been a rapid expansion in absolute terms until 1976.
Moreover, agriculture has changed from a net contributor to
the national budget to a net receiver.[44] On a net flow
basis, the agricultural sector has strengthened its relative priority position in the overall development strategy formulations of different governments, at least until
1976.

6.5 PRICE POLICIES

6.5.1 Introduction

This section will be divided into two separate parts. The
first one will deal with the overall development strategy
of import-substitution pursued since the late fifties, its
effects on the Peruvian price system and especially on
agricultural prices. The second part will analyse in some
detail the agricultural price policies pursued by different Peruvian governments and review those of the military
junta in order to establish if, and to what extent there

was a change in price policies under the military government. The overall effects on agricultural prices of the
strategy of import substitution have been overlooked by
the policy makers in Peru and scholars writing on the
agricultural development of Peru.

6.5.2 Some comments on the import substitution strategy

The basic elements of the strategy of import substitution
in Peru have been: (a) raised tariffs on imported manufactured goods; (b) stimulation of industrial investments.
This was accomplished by favourable financial treatment -
low taxes, low rates of interest charged on loans from the
public sector, special favourable conditions for imports
of capital goods, and to some extent also for intermediary
inputs. This kind of import substitution policy has an inherent bias against agriculture. A series of studies sponsored by OECD came to this conclusion. This was confirmed
by Little et.al., where it states, "...industry has been
over-encouraged in relation to agriculture..."[45]

Some of the mechanisms for this bias in development are as
follows. Many manufactured goods markets are not competitive in Peru which can be ascribed to the limited size of
the markets and certain monopolistic practices. Markets
in Peru for manufactured goods are relatively small because
the size of population and aggregate output are small and
income distribution is extremely skewed. On the one hand
this last aspect tends to favour industrialization through
import substitution, since a more symmetrical distribution
of incomes would lead to an expansion of demand for food
and would reduce the market for consumer durables. On the
other hand the possibilities for industrialization become
rapidly exhausted because the market for any isolated good

is relatively small. Thus, economies of scale cannot be
taken full advantage of and average costs tend to be high
relative to fully industrialized economies.[46]

Due to small, segmented markets, only a small number of
enterprises can produce efficiently in any one line of production. Consequently, monopolistic practices are characteristic of Peru, as well as of other small Third World
countries embarking on import substitution policies. Such
practices could hardly exist if free trade prevailed. The
high import tariffs and import restrictions have permitted
the firms in Peru to charge high prices. Moreover, imports
of manufactured goods have also been curtailed by quantitative import restrictions.[47] All this implies a general
and steady increase in the prices of manufactured goods
vis-a-vis agricultural products since the end of the fifties. However, it is not possible to estimate with reasonable accuracy the development of terms-of-trade between the
agricultural sector and industry with available data.
Goods formerly imported, now produced domestically under
the import substitution scheme, are defined as new goods
in official price indices and there are no specific indices for industrial goods.

Thorp and Bertram writing on Peru have estimated the terms-
of-trade between (i) food and other economic sectors and
(ii) export crop and general wholesale prices. They claim
that for the period 1930-77,

> "In addition to the long-standing role of
> export agriculture as a net supplier of
> funds for investments in other sectors,
> agriculture in general (including the tra-
> ditional sector) had been subjected over
> the long term to a steady squeeze on its
> surplus as the terms of trade shifted in
> favour of urban sectors."[48]

This long-run change in the structure of the price system
in Peru had important effects. The change in relative output prices has affected the rate of return on invested
capital in different sectors. The relative increase in the
prices of manufactured goods made it more profitable to
invest in the industrial sector than in agriculture. Moreover, the favourable conditions for investments in industry,
created by the import substitution strategy mentioned above,
should also have had a strong positive impact on the level
of expected rate of return.[49]

The firm commitments of successive governments to indust-
rialize Peru, the policies implemented, and the fact that
an agrarian reform was becoming increasingly necessary,
lowered the expected rate of return drastically in agriculture vis-a-vis industrial and urban investment ventures.
The urban sector grew, because practically all industries
were located in the urban centers, especially Lima-Callao.

The expansion of industrial activities had important link-
age effects such as attracting people to the cities, construction activities etc.[50]

Little has argued, "The discouragement of exports is inherent in the policy of protection, quite apart from actual
inefficiencies in its operation, or from any exessive discrimination against agriculture."[51] In general, an import
substitution strategy may tend to create or aggravate balance-of-payment difficulties and a common solution to
these has been to impose various kinds of exchange rates
controls and frequently the result has been an overvalued
national currency.[52] Peru has increasingly imposed strict
controls over foreign exchange transactions and also overvalued the national currency - the Sol, during the period
1968-77. In addition a host of regulations and rules have

been implemented, especially under the military government
as of 1969, to stimulate the industrialization and ration
scarce foreign exchange to industrial development. As a
result of these effects agricultural export prices have
tended to be lower, since prices are given at world market
prices and for each dollar converted to Soles less is obtained than if the Sol were not overvalued. Foreign exchange policies were thus transmitted to the domestic market, causing a downward press on agricultural prices.

Moreover, the lack of development of the agricultural sector forced the Government to import ever-increasing quantities of food. Since the national currency was overvalued,
and there were low tariffs on these goods, the prices of
imported agricultural goods were low relative to manufactured goods and also had the effects of exerting a general
downward pressure on agricultural prices. With these remarks in mind we will turn to the price policies before and
during the military government.

6.5.3 Agricultural price policies 1950-75

In the post-World-War II era price policies have been increasingly geared towards low food prices to the urban consumers.[53] The predominant feature has been, at least until 1977, that the Government has intervened directly and
indirectly in the price system. The most common practice
has been to fix legal maximum and at times minimum retail
prices. Sometimes prices have been set throughout the marketing chain, down to the local farmer. It seems as if
this tendency has been increasing over the years since
the beginning of the sixties, although variations can be
found from year to year.

The main hypothesis concerning the cause of the establishment of price controls is that the high rate of urbanization and economic growth caused a rapid increase in demand for food and for marketing services. As we have already discussed in this chapter, there were problems in increasing agricultural production, and difficulties to ensure that the production reached the consumers. The demand for marketing services thus increased rapidly. As we have already mentioned several times in this study, the economic center shifted away from the Sierra and down to the Coast and was concentrated in the Lima-Callao area. This development obliged successive governments to attempt to supply food at relatively low prices to the cities.

Abstracting from the government's direct intervention, the price levels to the consumers tended to increase because of the tendency for demand to grow faster than supply, and because marketing costs were increasing.

Recurring rapid price changes of agricultural commodities forced governments to take actions to dampen the effects of these price changes.[54] When prices decreased, in general, the urban consumers benefitted from lower prices. In cases of price increases, frequently governments imposed price controls, again benefitting the urban consumers. The effects of these measures were rarely analysed in a longer time perspective, and at times the desirable short-term effects - maintaining food prices low - were probably detrimental for long-run agricultural growth. The peasants price expectations were influenced negatively, and consequently also the expected rate of return of investment in agriculture.

Another important effect of price controls, but frequently overlooked, is that relative prices tend to become distor-

ted and so do the signals they provide in resource allocation. Moreover, price controls practically always result
in black markets, and speculative economic activities become increasingly profitable. The benefits of high black
market prices are not necessarily passed onto the producers,
the profits may instead remain within the marketing system.
Also, scarce resources could be allocated to such activities
and hence reduced in others. These distortions in the resource allocation tend to produce negative long-run effects
on the rate of growth.

It may in this context be mentioned that a careful study of
the price policies in Chile raises an important point, namely
that,

> "...relative price policies have been fre-
> quently used as a substitute for taxation
> in underdeveloped countries, where the tax
> systems are characterized by their inflexi-
> bility and inefficiency. Although in econo-
> mic terms this may be a very poor way of
> extracting income from some groups to bene-
> fit others, in many instances is the only
> alternative that is politically feasible."55)

The Iowa Universities Mission to Peru has published a series of articles and papers on the price policies in Peru.
The World Bank and the International Monetary Fund have
also been critical of the Peruvian price policies. Since
in the opinion of many Peruvians these bodies are associated with accepting the capitalist mode of production and
the power structure in Peru, their conclusions have often
been rejected. Advocating a policy for higher producer
prices, may have short- and medium-term effects of increasing the profits in commercial farming, while negatively affecting large segments of the urban poor. Moreover, since the concentration of landownership has been
very high in Peru, the benefits of higher prices for agri-

cultural products would have improved hardly at all the incomes of the rural poor.

However, much criticism has been raised against the price policies in Peru. Some studies will be cited to illustrate this and we will moreover show that basically the same policy was continued during the military Government 1968-75.

In 1967 Shephard and Dale published a study on the legal and economic aspects of price controls in Peru. One of the main conclusions was that,

> "...the present laws on the concentration of establishments, price controls and the regulations on trade in general are outside the economic reality of Peru...almost all basic food stuffs sold in Peru are subject to, in one form or another, price controls."56)

The same basic conclusions appear in another study from the same year.

> "Policy-makers are not always clear as to whether prices ought to be controlled for stabilization purposes, for production incentives or for consumer welfare. The latter goal appears to have ranged very high among Peru's objectives during the last few years."57)

The authors argued that the policies benefitted mainly the urban consumers.

> "In other words, the generally strong balance of payments position and the relatively high level of foreign exchange reserves which have characterized the Peruvian economy from 1960 to 1966 have made it possible to keep prices down for those products which are, in part, imported. As a consequence, the general rise in consumer food prices has been kept lower thus benefitting the coastal urban (Lima) con-

sumption groups."58)*)

The devastating critique continues: "The problem arises because overvaluation of the exchange rate, a recurring phenomenon in most underdeveloped economies, leads to periodic
subsidization of food imports at the expense of production."[60]
What is so disturbing is the fact that many of the commodities for which price controls and/or low price imports have
taken place are produced in the Sierra. The major Sierra
products - beef, potatoes and wheat - have been particularly
subject to discriminatory actions and as a result the output performance has been very poor. In the case of beef production it was noted that the larger farmers have tended to
abandon beef production.

Turning to the situation during the military government
1968-75, we will see that the price policies were continued. A 1975 World Bank report was also critical of the
price policies in Peru with respect to agricultural goods.

> "Prices of half a dozen basic products are
> set at producer, wholesale and consumer le-
> vels; prices of most other commodities are
> free, though subject to Government-set mar-
> keting margins...The present situation is
> further characterized by numerous measures
> to control the movement of produce, frequent

---

*) The negative effects on production are also stressed.
"Looking back to 1950, the negative aspects of a policy
of keeping consumer food prices down through imports can
be easily seen in the case of beef. Consumer prices can
ᴗe kept down through imports only as long as foreign exchange is available. From 1950 to 1960, two foreign exchange crises (1953 and 1958/59) forced devaluations. Consequently, substantial prices increases of imported products and of foods which were partly imported took place.
The fact that beef prices were kept relatively stable by
legally-imposed price controls during periods of balance
of payments strength and were allowed to rise only in periods of foreign exchange scarcity must have been an important detriment to the development of domestic beef
production."59)

> localized shortages, large operating losses
> on EPSA's*) wholesale activities, and a (re-
> portedly) widespread black market."61)

The World Bank is careful to spell out that non-price policy instruments should also be used and that the inci-
dence of raising agricultural prices must be determined.
The argumentation follows closely the recommendations contained in the book "Redistribution with Growth".[62] In
substance, the urban and rural poor are to be given special treatment. High income consumers and producers are
to assume a proportionately higher cost. Still, production incentives are to be considered against welfare implications.

The price policy tended to become more complex and less
coherent in the period 1970-75. At the beginning of the
seventies the Peruvian currency increasingly became overvalued. See Figure 6.2. Instead of devaluation, the Peruvian policy makers opted for a complex system which in
essence amounted to the same as using multiple exchange
rates. One feature in this policy package was to subsidize export of so called non-traditional exports. The exchange rate applied to agricultural exports was in general the most unfavourable one.

Even, with the increase as of 1973 in the world market
prices for many agricultural products, the policy of the
Government was to attempt to maintain food prices constant. Figure 6.1 gives details of world market prices for
some important traded agricultural goods. The amount of
subsidies spent by the public sector in maintaining low
consumer prices has sometimes been very high.

---

*) EPSA is a public enterprise set up by the military go-
vernment to administer wholesale markets, slaughter fa-
cilities and carry out wholesale operations.

Figure 6.1   World market price index of major agricultural goods 1970-77 (1970 = 100)

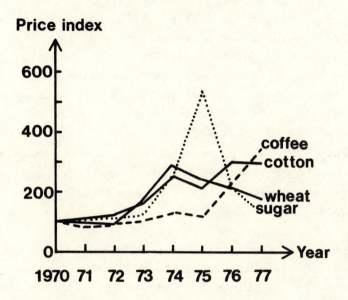

Share in Agricultural trade in 1970 (percent)

	Imports	Exports
Wheat	36	--
Sugar	--	36
Coffee	--	26
Cotton	--	31

Source: BCR(1977), pp. 152 and 154; Pacora (1978), table 9; IBRD (1975), Volume II, Table E.4.

The case of wheat is illustrative, wheat being also the most important food imported. In 1972 and 1973 the price of imported wheat delivered to the Peruvian mills was set at about 70 US dollars per metric ton. During this period the CIF price of wheat reached over 200 US dollars per metric ton. As a result, the difference had to be fi-

nanced and the subsidy amounted to over 4 200 million Soles in 1972 and during the first 10 months in 1973 to almost 4 000 million Soles.[63] Another estimate gives the
figure of 40.2 million US dollars which would amount to
about 1 548 million Soles of wheat subsidies in 1973.[64]
This situation was continued in 1974 and it was estimated
that the subsidy for wheat imports "...will cost the Trea-
sury at least as much as 2 400 Soles (US $ 60 million)."[65]
These subsidies might be related to total public sector
expenditures during 1973, which amounted to 72 290 million Soles. (Table 6.13). In other words about 3 percent
of these had to be earmarked for wheat imports. Other products have been subsidized as well, for example meat, rice
and potatoes.[66]

Thus the effects on domestic agricultural prices have obviously been quite significant. The Government did maintain relatively low prices for food indicated by the official price series. For details see Figure 6.2. In spite
of the poor performance of the agricultural sector and the
drastic increases in agricultural prices on world markets,
the food and beverages component in the general price index only increased slightly until 1974. To construct these
price indices official price indices had to be used rather
than those prevailing in the markets. Thus, they tend to
underestimate the actual price increases for food.

It may be noticed that during the period considered non
registered trade and smuggling were frequent. The case of
sugar is an interesting example of how attempts to maintain
low domestic prices in Peru was counteracted with smuggling which tended to force up the Peruvian domestic price.
The domestic sugar price was almost kept constant in the
period 1973-75, when the world market price increased

Figure 6.2 <u>Consumer price index, food and beverages</u>
<u>price index and exchange rate index</u>
1970=100

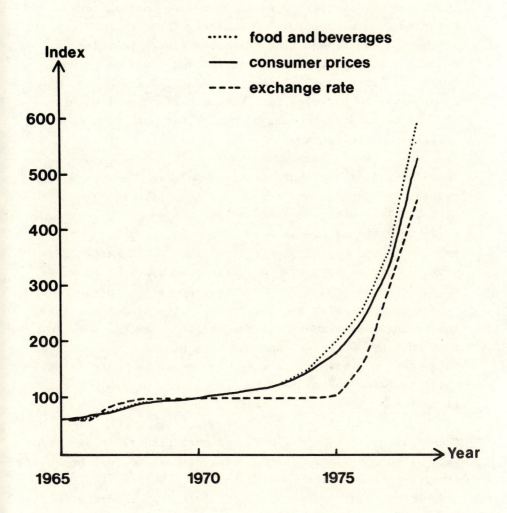

Source: BCR, Boletín (1979:February), pp. 25 and 32;
(1976:December), p. 35; (1968:January), p. 31;
and Memoria (1975), p. 115.

several times. See again Figure 6.1. To secure supply for
the domestic market, where prices were significantly lower,
the sugar complexes were ordered to market pre-established
quotas on the domestic market. This also contributed to
maintain food prices low.[67] However, the city of Piura is
close to Ecuador, and also to Peru's sugar producing regions. Because of this the price of sugar was 14 percent
higher in Piura than in Lima. In the case of the city of
Puno, close to Bolivia, the price was 41 percent higher
than in Lima.[68] It should be noted that both Ecuador and
Bolivia exported sugar.[69]

These data indicate that the price policies have been successful in keeping consumer prices down principally in the
Lima-Callao region. They also represent strong pieces of
evidence that the overall level of producer prices was
kept at a considerably lower level than world market prices. To some extent this was attenuated by the influences
of extra-legal trade. Scarce resources were channelled to
this end. Ironically enough, the policies also meant that
the Peruvian Government was subsidizing the consumers in
neighbouring countries, and was straining its own balance
of payment position to do this. Moreover, the effects of
these policies in the 1970-75 period were probably not an-
ticipated by the decision makers.

The price policies for imports of agricultural inputs have
varied, but in general there does not seem to have been any
excessive bias against the agricultural sector. In the sixties there were additional import duties on imported fertilizers to protect domestic production. These additional
revenues from fertilizer imports were handed over to domestic producers who consequently were subsidized. One
study reports that, "Prices of domestic products vary from
30% to 50% more than similar imported products. These

higher prices have been possible because of import restrictions and/or high tariffs."[70] My study on rice production in the Northern part of Peru in 1970, Agrarian Zone II, did not produce any evidence of a systematic price discrimination in fertilizer distribution. As of 1969 the farmers could import their own fertilizers and this together with a fairly competitive situation resulted in favourable prices. Still domestic producers of fertilizers were to be protected, import duties amounted to 35-45 percent, and import licences were required.[71]

As of 1975 fertilizers in food production were subsidized to combat the rapid increase in world market prices.[72] This together with an overvalued exchange rate suggest that with respect to input prices the agricultural sector was in a better position than with respect to output prices.

6.5.4 Summary

Governments before the military junta in 1968 implemented price policies against the agricultural sector, and this general policy was continued by the military. In fact in several cases they even aggravated the pre-existing tendencies. This bias against agriculture has developed in two distinct, although interrelated ways.

First, the overall and increasing emphasis on industrialization has changed the terms-of-trade rapidly against the agricultural sector. Manufactured goods are produced at very high costs and often of poor quality protected by high tariffs, while there have been systematic attempts to curtail price increases of food.

Second, one of the main objectives of different Govern-

ments has been to protect the urban consumers, particularly in Lima, against food price increases. The emphasis
has been on short-run solutions to problems and on an isolated, commodity-by-commodity, basis. Dynamic considerations in the design of a particular price policy have been
rare. The types of policies vary from legal price controls,
subsidies, forced deliveries and even to the imposition of
detailed production orders with little attention paid to
the economic consequences.[73] Moreover, price policies
have been subject to frequent changes, and strong uncertainty influences farmers' production decisions.

Each of these factors would by itself be a major impedi-
ment to private investments in agriculture. Together they
presumably represent a formidable obstacle to agricultural
growth.

As of 1975 there was a change in government, and the economy entered into a serious depression in 1977-78. The military opted to return to civilian rule, and as of 1980,
Belaúnde returned to the Presidency. It is probable that
when the balance-of-payment situation improves the urban
bias in price policies will be continued.

6.6   SUMMARY

The stagnation, and possibly decline, in per capita agricultural production in the 50's and 60's commented on in
chapter 1 continued in the 70's. During the period 1969-
75 most of the agrarian reform was carried out. According
to official production data it is not possible to detect
any decline in production during these years. On this account the reform was quite successful, even if disappointing in terms of expectations of the government. However,

the 1972 agricultural census indicates that there was a
significant decline in production in the 70's, but statistical data are not good enough to permit any final comment.

There are several interacting factors which explain agricultural stagnation. First, land has been and is becoming
increasingly scarce. Cultivated land has increased in Peru, because increasingly, marginal land has been brought
into production in addition to investments in irrigation.
Agricultural land has been lost through improper irrigation
techniques on the Coast and through erosion in the Sierra.

Second, private investments have been low in agriculture
and started to decline in the 60's. There are some signs
that this process was reversed in the 70's, particularly
on the expropriated farms. The public sector has historically neglected agriculture, and only a minor part of the
national budget was earmarked for this sector. The military junta did not, in this respect, introduce any fundamental new approach to overall development.

Third, different governments have discriminated against
agriculture through various price policies, ranging from
price controls to import subsidies. These policies were
continued by the military as of 1968.

These factors, scarcity of land, government neglect of
agricultural development, and discriminatory price policies existed during previous regimes, and were continued
during the military junta. Taken together they represent
a formidable obstacle to agricultural growth, and the
1950-1979 record is a logical result of this set of policies.

Accelerating agricultural growth in the post-agrarian-reform period, therefore, requires at least a significant
increase of resources allocated to agriculture, and a set
of price policies conducive to growth.

APPENDIX TO CHAPTER 6

Because of the rapid inflation in the Peruvian economy
we have in this study converted most values from current
prices to 1970 prices. There are two long price series
which we could use. The first is a consumer price index
and the second one is the implicit GNP deflator. These
two series have been reproduced in Table A.6.1 and the
period 1960-1976 in Figure A.6.1. As can be seen, the
two series follow each other quite well. Thus it would
not matter which serie we use. We have chosen the consumer price index because it is published earlier.

Table A.6.2 was used to construct Table 6.17 and give
data on agricultural credit allocated through the Agricultural Development Bank. Long-term credit is mainly
credit for more than one year of duration.

Table A.6.1   GNP implicit deflator and consumer price
               index deflator to convert current into
               1970 Soles

Year	1 GNP Deflator	2 Consumer price index deflator
1950	0.183	0.193
1955	0.254	0.275
1960	0.396	0.411
61	0.411	0.436
62	0.432	0.465
63	0.458	0.493
64	0.517	0.541
1965	0.586	0.630
66	0.658	0.686
67	0.738	0.753
68	0.870	0.896
69	0.938	0.952
1970	1.000	1.000
71	1.045	1.068
72	1.110	1.144
73	1.262	1.253
74	1.473	1.465
1975	1.769	1.811
76	2.377	2.417
77	3.291	3.337
78	5.322	5.267
1979	9.413	8.833

Sources: Column 1; For the period: 1950-66, BCR (1968), p. 26
                                    1967-70, BCR (1976), p. 26
                                    1970-76, BCR (1974), pp. 29 and 265
                                    BCR, Memoria (1975), p. 114
                                    Memoria (1980), p. 126
         Column 2; For the period: 1950-55, Thorp and Bertram (1978),
                                             p. 227; Iowa Mission (1967),
                                             p. 169
                                    1960-66, BCR, Boletín (1968: January),
                                             p. 31
                                    1967-79, BCR, Boletín (1978: November),
                                             p. 31; BCR, Memoria (1980),
                                             p. 135.

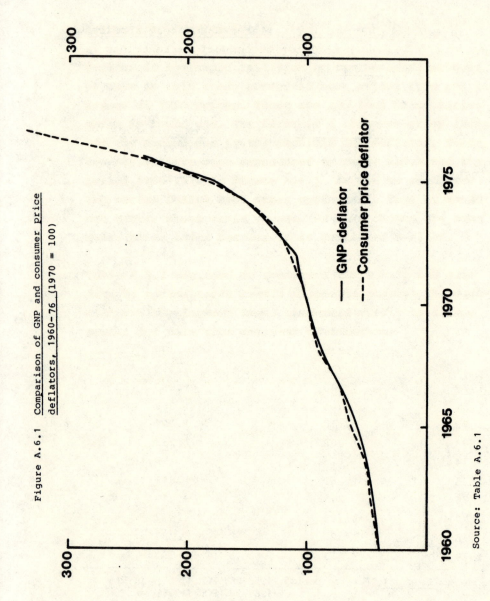

Figure A.6.1 Comparison of GNP and consumer price deflators, 1960-76 (1970 = 100)

—— GNP-deflator
‑ ‑ ‑ Consumer price deflator

Source: Table A.6.1

Table A.6.2 The share of long term credit in total yearly credit of the Agricultural Development Bank (Current Soles x 10^6)

Year	1 Total	2 Long term credit	3 Long term credit share in total (percent) (2:1)x100=3
1950	116	n.a.	n.a.
51	154	"	"
52	185	"	"
53	250	"	"
54	276	"	"
1955	318	"	"
56	421	"	"
57	519	"	"
58	641	124	19.3
59	737	112	15.2
1960	910	131	14.4
61	1 094	172	15.7
62	1 205	156	12.9
63	1 271	150	11.8
64	1 575	187	11.9
1965	1 764	183	10.4
66	2 035	254	12.5
67	2 223	264	11.9
68	2 860	315	11.0
69	4 731	441	9.3
1970	4 920	355	7.2
71	5 883	599	10.2
72	6 510	838	12.9
73	8 790	1 552	17.7
74	10 959	1 720	15.7
1975	14 842	1 298	8.7
1976	22 010	1 151	5.2

Source: Agricultural Development Bank, various reports;
Ministerio de Agricultura (1977:1);
Alberts and Buechler (1970);
Turner (1974).

1. Convenio (1967), pp. 44–46, and 130–134; Thorp (1969); and IBRD (1975), Statistical Appendix D, and Hopkins (1979).

2. Thorp (1969); BCR (1968), note 2 p. 17; and BCR (1976), note 2 p. 19.

3. Food prices might have risen relative to other prices. Production statistics may be wrong. Income distribution might have worsened and per capita income figures may be wrong. Thorp (1969), pp. 230–231.

4. INP (1965); See again Convenio (1967), p. 133 for a comparison of cultivated area.

5. The Convenio study (1967), p. 133, suggests that the final census data were revised in the light of some contradictions in the results. However, in the introduction to the final Census results no such indications are given. Moreover, it states that a random sample of the Census was published in November 1963. It should be noted that many studies on Peru relied on the preliminary 1963 results among which the important CIDA study, both the draft version (1965) and the final version (1966) used the 1963 sample.

6. Thorp (1969), pp. 230–231; Thorp and Bertram (1978), p. 274–276; IBRD (1975), Statistical Annex D; and Fitzgerald (1976), Appendix IV.

   To show the influence of the 1961 Census the following table relying on Brundenius (1976) and Ministry of Agriculture data in 1977 has been constructed. Brundenius (1976) has fused scattered data on agricultural production, citing sources which at times rely on data among themselves e.g. BCR cite the Ministry of Agriculture and vice versa. His 1961 data for a sample of products are as follows:

1961 production data (1000 metric tons)		
Brundenius*	Diagnostico*	Census 1961
Rice	290	290	289
Corn	469	469	469
Wheat	150	150	150
Barley	180	180	180
Potatoes	858	858	713
Cotton	361	361	361
Coffee	40	40	40

   *) They cite the same sources, and it is possible that the Diagnostico used the Brundenius data.

7. INP (1971) Vol. II, pp. 9 and 18.

8.   See note 17 in chapter 5.

9.   INP (1971) Vol II, p. 109.

10. Latin American Regional Report RA-80-02 and RA-80-03.

11. Feder (1972), p. 48.

12. Convenio (1969)

13. Mariátegui (1970), pp. 50-104; De la Puente (1966), p. 114-117; Eguren (1975), p. 10; and Espinoza and Malpica (1970), pp. 369-371.

14. The weighted average construction costs per irrigated hectare in 1966 prices was 29500 Soles since 1945. The new projects considered at the end of the sixties show generally considerably higher costs for the Coast.

Name of Project	Construction costs per hectare (Soles)	Prices of year
Large & Medium size		
Olmost	49 300	1966
Majes	64 900	1965
Choclacocha	24 500	1965
Chira	36 800	1967
Moquequa	43 000	1965
Tumbes	34 600	1965
Small size		
El Cural	36 100	1965
La Cano	43 900	1965
El Huevo	38 600	1965

Sources: McGaughey (1970), p. 81; Iowa (1967), p. 206.

15. Bottomley (1971), pp. 37-40.

16. See chapter 1, Table 1.2.

17. Feder (1971), p. 48, rejected the land scarcity hypothesis because of this increase in pastures, but fails to recognize that population pressures have led to an extension of the agricultural frontier through marginal land. This land is also aggravating the erosion problem in the Sierra.

18. IBRD (1975), Annex 2 p. 9.Lundahl (1979) has described the process of falling rural incomes in Haiti. Soil destruction was generated by population growth. See particularly chapter 5. Boserup (1965), has argued that population growth is conducive to technological innovations. The process of agricultural development in Peru seems more to correspond to that described by Lundahl (1979).

19. Ministerio de Agricultura (1976:1), p. 50 reports that 247 000 Ha's out of 721 094 Ha's investigated had such problems. The World Bank (1975) General Report p. 19, reported that 150 000-200 000 Ha's were affected by salinity.

20. IBRD (1975), Annex 2, p. 7.

21. Table A.5.3, and Table 6.6.

22. An interesting model has been developed by Kelley et.al. (1972), chapter 7. It formalizes the behaviour of private investors and the distribution of capital between agriculture and the rest of the economy.

23. See chapter 1 and section 6.2. See also Thorp (1969), and Thorp and Bertram (1978).

24. Convenio (1970:4), pp. 41-44.

25. IBRD (1975), Volume II, Table D.10.

26. For livestock numbers see Appendix to chapter 5.

27. Malpica (1974), pp. 76-159 and Bayer (1975), pp. 16-18.

28. Horton (1976), p. 12. See also Mejía (1978), p. 180. Figueroa in an article on agrarian reform in Latin America notes that: "The first problem of capital formation that arises in connection with land reform programmes is the possibility of an immediate decrease in capital stock. Landlords may react to expropriation by dismantling and selling existing equipment, cattle and forest. The gradualness of expropriation procedures provides the opportunity for doing so. This has been the case in Peru, where many farms were transferred to peasants with no capital goods except a house (with no doors and windows) and the land". Figueroa (1977), p. 162. Thorp and Bertram (1978), p. 283.

29. Naciones Unidas (1966), pp. 5-7 and Table 6.6.

30. See for example CEPAL (1976), p. 12.

31. Ministerio de Alimentación (1976), p. 14.

32. Horton (1976), p. 312, and Guillet (1979), p. 188.

33. IBRD (1975), p. 25; Horton (1976), p. 313.

34. See Tables 1.2 and 3.1.

35. Thorp and Bertram (1978), chapter 13.

36. Ibidem.

37. In order to check the data, the BCR Cuentas Nacionales del Perú 1950-1967 was used. In Table 6.12 the National Accounts data are reconciled with those of the Budgetary Accounts of Peru. Those figures agree almost completely with those used by us. They refer to Total expenditures for the years 1963-66.

38. McGaughey (1970). See also chapter 7.3.2.

39. IBRD (1975), Annex 6, pp. 15-17.

40. Based on interviews with Bank officials in 1969 and 1970. Ministerio de Agricultura (1974), pp. 2 and 5. Ministerio de Agricultura (1975:3), pp. 2, 8, 6, 13 and 15.

41. BCR Boletín May (1979), p. 44; and March (1982), pp. 33 and 34. It should be noted that the rate of interest charged by the Agricultural Development Bank has been significantly smaller than the rate of inflation. For example in 1974 the interest rate charged varied from 7 to 13%, while the rate of inflation was about 17%.

42. IBRD (1975), Table G.1.

43. See note 41.

44. See Table 6.12.

45. Little et.al. (1970), p. 1; and Lipton (1977).

46. The military government believed that this was the situation in Peru in 1968. This was discussed in chapter 2. The introduction of the agrarian reform law, referred to in chapter 5.2.1 states the need for income redistribution as a measure to enlarge the markets for industrial goods. The military government was strongly influenced by the ECLA doctrine. See Delgado ed. (1965), pp. 29-35 and Thorp and Bertram (1978), p. 300.

47. Thorp and Bertram (1978), pp. 261-274. Shunt in Lowenthal et.al. (1975), chapter 8. The economic programme for 1978-80 included the abolition of price controls and a reduction of import tariffs. The Peruvian manufacturing industry has opposed this strongly. In 1980 the Latin America Weekly Report (WR-80-10) reports that: "Local industrialists have been able to use their influence in the cabinet to block the import programme sponsored by finance minister Javier Silva Ruete and central bank president Manuel Moreyra; the latter claims that the maintenance of high protective barriers is helping to fuel the inflation rate, while keeping profit rates high." (p. 1). See also Fitzgerald (1976), pp. 64-66.

48. Thorp and Bertram (1978), p. 278. See also Oman (1978), p. 313.

49. Kelley et.al. (1972), chapter 7.

50. INP (1971), Vol I , pp. 54-62; and Thorp and Bertram (1978), p. 327.

51. Little et.al. (1970), p. 10.

52. Little et.al. (1970), chapters 2, 3 and 5.

53. For the 50's see Thorp and Bertram (1978), pp. 276-282; and Oman (197 p. 313.

54. For seasonal variations in prices see for example Robertson (1967); and Ministerio de Alimentación (1976), pp. 26-35.

55. Echeverria (1969), p. 197.

56. Shepherd and Dale (1967), p. v; See also (1968), pp. 33-38.

57. Iowa mission (1967), p. 167.

58. Ibidem, p. 171.

59. Ibidem.

60. Ibidem, p. 172.

61. IBRD (1975), Volume I, p. 27.

62. Chenery et.al. (1974).

63. Unpublished study of the Ministry of Agriculture, November 1973.

64. Ministerio de Agricultura (1974), p. 129.

65. IBRD (1975), Volume I, p. 28.

66. IBRD (1975), Volume II, Annex 6. Ministerio de Agricultura (1974), pp. 139-140. It can be seen that the CIF price of meat increased 59% between 1970 and 1973 while the retail price was maintained constant.

67. Comisión Multisectorial de la Problemática Azucarera (1975), pp. 8-9.

68. Ministerio de Alimentación (1976), Table A-26.

69. CEPAL-FAO (1976), p. 126.

70. Robertson (1968), p. 35.

71. Cabrera (1970), and Alberts (1977), pp. 5-59.

72. Lipton (1977), p. 17, claims that in general rich farmers benefit from such a subsidy.

73. The following is illustrative of the attitudes prevailing in the Ministry of Agriculture in 1975, "...several agrarian co-operatives,..., have substituted the production of sugar for cotton, without the authorization have sown 79 hectares with sugar, others,...disobeying instructions of Agrarian Zone IV and have stated that to cultivate cotton involves economic problems which can only be solved by cultivating profitable crops such as in the case of sugar cane." (My underlining). Ministry of Agriculture (1976:1), p. 3. Note in Figure 6.1 that the price evolution in 1975 was highly favourable for sugar. In 1976 the cotton price increased while the sugar price fell.

7
Summary and Conclusions

7.1   OUR MAIN FINDINGS

The renewed interest in the development literature about growth
with economic redistribution and also in favour of economic redistribution per se, culminated in the 1970's with many studies.
One of the most important of these was the World Bank publication of Redistribution with Growth. Agrarian reform was here as
well as in the earlier literature considered as a necessary
condition for an equity-cum-growth strategy[*]. In 1968 a military government installed itself in Peru and launched an am-
bitious development programme towards equity and growth. An
important part of this policy implemented during the 1968-75
period was a radical agrarian reform which aimed at both re-
distributing incomes and wealth, and accelerating the rate of
growth of the agricultural sector.

The Peruvian attempts to transfer its economic system through
agrarian reform were consonant with the ideas generated in
the international discussions on the necessary conditions for
an equity-cum-growth development. We have in this study concentrated on the changes within the agricultural sector, where
income distribution has been more skewed than in the rest of
the economy. The rate of growth has been low and average rural income significantly lower than in the rest of the economy.
This study examined the military government's agrarian reform
and its impact in two areas: (i) in the redistribution of incomes and wealth and (ii) in the increase of the rate of growth
in agriculture.

---

[*] In the fifties the situation was quite different and
Doreen Warriner then said, "Professional economists neglect
the subject of land reform,..."[1]. Today, as we saw in chapter 4, agrarian reform is no longer neglected and many economists consider it to be necessary for rural development.

In chapter two we reviewed planning documents and speeches
of the military junta, documenting that the Government intended to alter the prevailing income and wealth distribution through a major agrarian reform. We also pointed out
that although this basic decision was clear there were shift-
ing ideas and statements on how the agrarian reform was to
be carried out, and of how far reaching it was going to be.
The discussions and the policies actually implemented by
the government suggest that the policy makers had no clear
ideas what they wanted. In part this was a reflection of different opinions or of different ideological conceptions within
the military. In part it was also due to a lack of knowledge
of the fundamental economic tendencies and problems affecting
Peruvian agriculture.

Therefore, contradictions between overall development objectives and measures used to implement these objectives were
frequent. When, in the end, the agrarian reform was seen to
benefit only half a million families, thus leaving out about
one million poor families, the explanation can be found in
these two sources of ambiguity mentioned above. It could also at times appear as if the military thought that once the
big landowners were expropriated the rest would solve itself.

In chapter three we analysed the overall performance of the
Peruvian economy. Peru has had a relatively good economic
performance since 1950, the rate of growth of production being well above that of population. In 1967 and particularly
in 1968 economic problems were mounting so that in 1968 GDP
remained practically constant. The very rapid recuperation
of the economy in 1969 and 1970 was probably the main factor
behind the very optimistic growth rate targets of the first
five year plan of the junta, 1971-75. While the planned rate
of growth was as high as 7.5%, the junta managed 5.5%. Although this figure was below the planned one, it can still

be considered as a relative success. This was accomplished
mainly through fortuitous external factors. While the volume
of exports hardly increased, the export prices moved very favourably for Peru during this period.This fortunate development tended to conceal the profound disequilibria in the economy. Actually the rate of investments fell in spite of considerable increase in public sector investments. Foreign borrowing increased substantially. The difficulties in the 1975-
79 period implied that the relative economic success during
the first phase of the military junta had to be replaced by
austerity measures through inter alia successive devaluations,
cutting of public expenditures, including subsidies, and a
general squeeze on real wages.

In chapter three we also showed that data on income distribution in Peru are of relatively low reliability. Still the
basic pattern is sufficiently clear, namely, that income
distribution has been extremely skewed, and that urban incomes and standards of living were on the whole significantly
higher than in rural areas. Moreover, the income distribution
was more skewed in rural than in urban areas. The data available do not indicate that the income distribution improved
between 1961 and 1972, in fact the data suggest a deteriora-
tion in the distribution of income. Since rural incomes
were so much lower than urban incomes, the income redistribution objectives should have included either a massive transfer of incomes through a change of relative prices and/or
fiscal policy from the urban to the rural areas, and/or a
strategy to accelerate the rate of growth of agriculture to
raise rural incomes. We will return to this question when
commenting chapter six.

In chapter four we commented on the importance of ownership
of land in income distribution. We noted that in areas where
land is relatively scarce rents are relatively higher than

in areas where land is relatively abundant. Since land is an important production factor not least of all in developing agriculture, it seemed appropriate to analyse the ownership of land. One may also use the ownership variable as a proxy for the skewedness of the income distribution. We also pointed out that non competitive elements can contribute to a very high rent share and that such elements have been frequent in Peru.

The theoretical considerations in chapter four are background for our analysis in chapter five, where we investigate in some detail the structure of land ownership before and after the agrarian reform, implemented in June 1969. Prior attempts at such a reform were largely frustrated. We showed that land ownership in Peru was extremely concentrated, a fact which was also confirmed by the data on rural income distribution in chapter three. The Peruvian agrarian reform in absolute numbers may at first instance seem impressive. By the end of 1978 almost 50 percent of the agricultural land had been handed over to, primarily, co-operative enterprises and close to 400 000 families had benefitted. If we instead relate these accomplishments to the general objective of social equity the results are far less impressive. There were about 1.4 million families living in the agricultural sector and among these we find the great majority of poor minifundistas, scratching out a meagre living on fragments of land. The majority of the peasants have hardly received any benefits from the reform. The beneficiaries of the reform, in many cases, belonged to the upper-income group in the rural areas and in the case of the sugar estates to the highest-income groups in Peru. The agrarian reform has therefore been a failure with regard to the aim of redistributing incomes on a massive scale within the agricultural sector.

In chapter six we analysed the output performance of the agricultural sector. The sector has long been a problem in Peru

and the data from 1950 up to the military coup in 1968 suggest that output has barely been at pace with the population
growth, and the growth in demand has been met by increases in
imports and decreases in exports of agricultural goods. The
statistical data indicate that this process was continued during the 1971-75 planning period, and some data even suggest that the situation deteriorated. The policy makers were
obviously dissatisfied with the production results since they
tended to have a naive belief that once the big land owners
were removed, the major obstacle to agricultural growth would
also have been removed and that agricultural production would
grow at a higher and sustained rate of growth. Still viewed
against the background of a radical agrarian reform programme
the production results were quite good during the 1969-75 period. However, the tendency towards stagnation in agricultural production soon became apparent and during the second phase
of the military government, 1975-79, per capita agricultural
production fell, aggravating the economic crisis during these
years.

Two main reasons for the poor performance of agriculture in
the 1950-79 period were the lack of land and the economic policies of various governments in Peru. First, as was discussed
in chapter six, Peru is a large and scarcely populated country.
Still most of its population is concentrated on the Coast and
in the Sierra regions where the possibilities to increase the
amount of agricultural land are quite restricted. The amount
of cultivated land per capita has been decreasing since the end
of the twenties in Peru. To open up new land, either through
irrigation schemes and/or colonization programmes, large investments from the public sector were required, and the actual
investments were not enough to offset the declining trend.

The second reason is that subsequent governments have neglected

the agricultural sector, and extracted its surplus to finance
industrial-urban growth. This has been accomplished through
various discriminatory price policies and a lack of public
sector allocations to agriculture. This trend was continued
during the military junta 1968-77 although there have been
some changes which indicate that the public sector is slowly
coming to realize that agricultural growth requires some
priority. We have argued that from the point of view of
creating necessary conditions for agricultural growth the
resources allocated to agriculture have been insufficient
and that the price policies have discriminated against the
sector. If we now also consider the overall objective of income redistribution and recall that rural incomes were significantly lower than urban incomes, the failure to implement an equity-cum-growth strategy becomes apparent.

From the preceding it is clear that the agrarian reform did
not accomplish a radical and lasting improvement in the degree of equity within the agricultural sector. The economic
policies implemented by the military government were not conducive to agricultural growth nor did they accomplish any-
thing towards reducing the urban-rural income gap.

7.2   SOME FURTHER REFLECTIONS ON THE PERUVIAN AGRARIAN
       REFORM

In the discussion on redistribution with growth,one important question has been,to what extent is it possible to carry
out planned radical reforms without the violence and other
characteristics of a revolution? In the case of the agrarian
reform in Latin America there are only two cases where radical reforms were carried out without a revolution. The first
is the agrarian reform which was effectively commenced in
Chile during the Christian Democratic presidency of Eduardo Frei

1965-70 and which was mainly implemented during the presidency of Salvador Allende, 1970-73. Salvador Allende, the
first elected marxist president, was killed in a bloody
military coup d'etat in 1973. The Chilean development since
1973 seems to be the antithesis of an equity-cum-growth strategy.

The other is the Peruvian agrarian reform which has certain
similarities with that in Chile. The land ownership was extremely concentrated prior to the reform, agricultural production was stagnating and food imports increasing.[2] It was
commenced during president Belaúnde, 1964-68. In both the
case of Chile and Peru during these first years of relatively
low activity in agrarian reform, valuable administrative experience was gained. Agrarian reform officials were trained
and a lot of basic data collected. For a rapid and a planned
agrarian reform these are essential. Thus during the second
phase of the agrarian reform, 1970-73 in Chile and 1969-78
in Peru, it was possible to increase the rate of implementation dramatically. See Table 7.1.

Table 7.1   Peru and Chile. Acceleration in agrarian reform
             implementation

	Percent of agricultural land expropriated per period
Peru	
1962-68	9
1969-78 (Oct.)	91
Total	100
Chile	
1965-70 (Sept.)	31
1970 (Oct.) - 73 (Sept.)	69
Total	100

Source: Peru: Chapter 5 note 5; Ministerio de Agricultura
             (1978:1), Table 1
        Chile: CIESA (1975),pp. 53, 189,and Annexes, p. 205

Some important differences are worth mentioning. Both reforms compensated the former landowners and both compensation schemes were quite complex. Still, in general, the Chilean system tended to compensate the former owners more generously than the Peruvian reform, because in Chile there was 1) no maximum set for amortization on bonds and 2) part of the value of the bond was readjusted for inflation.[3] Moreover, in Chile the landowners could retain the best of the agricultural land and other capital assets, leaving the beneficiaries with limited possibilities to increase production. Moreover, the maximum a landowner could possess was 80 hectares of very good irrigated land and when other land was converted into irrigated land equivalents very big farms were left intact.[4] In Peru the limits were generally set lower.[5] Thus, the agrarian reform in Peru was more extensive than in Chile.

In Chile the beneficiaries were heavily subsidised by the state, mainly through non-repayments of yearly credit and negative real rates of interest, while in Peru the Government was strict in the beneficiaries complying with the repayments of credit and the agrarian debt.[6] While in Chile the agrarian reform efforts aggravated the deficit of the national budget in Peru the agrarian reform did not play any significant role in the national budget.[7]

Both reforms in Chile and Peru benefitted mainly the permanent workers living on the expropriated big estates.[8] This fact became, in the case of the Chilean agrarian reform, a matter of increasing concern among policy makers towards the end of the Allende government. Particularly the landless workers' ('afuerinos') situation was debated. I believe that there were two important reasons why the permanent workers were favoured. The first was that in Peru and

Chile the landowners wielded power and a first necessary step for the governments was to break this power. Thus it seemed logical to concentrate on expropriation first, with less consideration of how and to whom to adjudicate the land. The second reason was linked to the slogan of land-to-the-tiller. Administrative expediency may have been another reason, because it was simpler to remove the landowner, and hand over the land to the permanent workers, than to re-organise the access of land to the rural population.

It is difficult to say how much the Peruvian agrarian reform officials and policy makers learnt from the experience of the Chilean agrarian reform. At least there were contacts between Chilean and Peruvian officials. At time Peruvian officials compared the reforms with those of Chile, proudly claiming that the Peruvian reform was more radical and better implemented.

Table 7.2   Peru and Chile. Comparative agrarian refrom data

	Chile (Sept. 1973)	Peru (October 1978)
1. Percent of total agricultural land expropriated	32	47
2. Percent of irrigated land expropriated	58	52*
3. Percent of families in the agricultural sector benefitted	13	26

*) Target for the reform. 68 percent was accomplished as of July 1976. Ministerio de Agricultura (1976), p. 5.

Source: Chile: 1. CIESA (1975), p. 189
             2. Ibidem
             3. CIESA (1975), Annexes p. 207

        Peru: 1. Ministerio de Agricultura (1978:1), Table 1
             2. Table A.5.5
             3. Ministerio de Agricultura (1978:1), Table 6; Appendix chapter 5

From Table 7.2 it can be seen that both reforms were radical in that a major part of the agricultural land was expropriated. Still, only a small part of the agricultural population received land. In Peru, though, a quarter of the total number of families benefitted (26% versus 13% in Chile).The type of reform in Peru and Chile tends to run contrary to one stream of thinking among development economists. The idea is that man/land ratios are higher on the small farms than on the bigger farms, and labour input per hectare and output per hectare is greater on the smaller farms. Thus giving more land to the small farms would increase aggregate output as well as improve income distribution.[9] However, the type of agrarian reform in Chile and Peru tends to preserve relatively high land/man ratios on the big farms leaving the landless and small farms without any new land.

Therefore, it seems that a great deal of the literature has focused on the need for agrarian reform. In their discussion of the different effects of the reform in relation to production, employment, investments, labour input and marketable surplus, economists have taken for granted that the land/man ratios on the expropriated farms would be significantly reduced; i.e. they have overlooked the fundamental and practical problems of how to distribute the land during the reform process.

If Chile can be considered as an example of a failure to carry out a planned major agrarian reform without a revolution, (partly because of the military coup in 1973), Peru remains the only important Latin American example that has endured time. To what extent this can be repeated elsewhere is of course an open question. I think that the historical circumstances in 1969 were very specific in Peru so that generalizations on this question are difficult. However, one of the lessons is, as just mentioned, to try to avoid that the "permanent workers" are more or less the only beneficiaries. No doubt, slogans like "land-to-the-tiller" will be heard in other places. Other problems that might reappear are for example that big estates sell out cattle, do not maintain agricultural machinery and, in general, divest. Such a process seems to commence even before agrarian reform is implemented, and is aggravated during the reform. In both Peru and Chile there was a lack of a clear policy to increase investments in agriculture. Thus the pre-reform agriculture stagnation was continued during and after the reform.

We have in this study argued that the Peruvian agrarian reform failed to eradicate rural poverty. There are two reasons for this. One is the subsequent governments' neglect of the agricultural sector in their overall economic policy as discussed in chapter six. The other is that the land was distributed to the poor peasants only on a very limited scale. The question one immediately poses, was it possible in 1969 to better spread the benefits of the reform. I believe that there existed such possibilities and these were never tried, though some minor attempts were made. One such attempt was made in Piura region to proceed according to the PIAR model, Integrated Rural Settlement Scheme.[10] In essence this scheme proposed to proceed with the reform on an area basis instead of expropriating farm by farm. It was however soon abandoned. I believe that had the Government chosen this strategy it would have been possible to restructure the land ownership in a way which would have accounted for the equity objective more effectively than was the case.

As has been mentioned in this study the Government could have expropriated most agricultural land according to the law. Moreover, the Government's show of force in June 1969 to occupy

militarily   the sugar complexes crushed the hopes of the
landowners   to sabotage the reform.   By carrying out
the reform in a given area, determining the existing situation, identifying possible solutions to the agrarian problem
in that area, the Government should then have proceeded to
expropriate and adjudicate. As was mentioned above the process followed was to expropriate the big farms and then
identify those who were eligible to receive land and adjudicate to them. In this way the pre-reform tenure was largely   maintained, except that the owners were removed.

In 1963 president Belaúnde promised to fight poverty, illi-
teracy and hunger. By 1968 when he was ousted in a military
coup little had been accomplished. During these years of military rule, 1968-80, important changes have occurred in Peru, not least of which,the agrarian reform. In 1980 Belaúnde
was again elected president and rural poverty remains an un-
resolved problem. In the next section we will briefly outline two basic development options for the coming decades.

7.3   TOWARDS YEAR 2000. REDISTRIBUTION WITH GROWTH

7.3.1 Introduction

We have in this study examined agricultural development in
Peru over a time span of more than 25 years. The emerging
trend is not a promising one. The rate of growth of agriculture is falling below that of population growth. Overall income distribution may have deteriorated at the end of the
seventies as a consequence of the austerity measures in the
economy introduced during the second half of that decade.[11]
About 800 000 agricultural families continue to survive on
small and fragmented pieces of land, and might migrate to
the urban areas "voting with their feet", aggravating the

slum and unemployment problems there.[12] The struggle in
Peru for a more equitable distribution of incomes surely
will be one of the controversial issues to be resolved in
this century. Though the redistribution objective has become increasingly verbally supported since the end of the
Second World War, actual policies implemented have benefitted the poor relatively little.

Any new government in Peru must face two urgent questions.
The first one is, how to increase agricultural production
and the second, how to distribute incomes and wealth more
evenly. Rather than to discuss each of these objectives se-
parately as we have done throughout this study, we will
concentrate on two strategic options available to the Peruvian government for the agricultural sector. We will call
the first one a growth strategy, and the second one equity-
cum-growth strategy. These two do not pretend to encompass
all alternatives available, but we believe that they reflect
two distinct approaches relevant in the actual discussion
about Peruvian agricultural development. Before discussing
these two options it is important to recapitulate some major
findings and policy implications of this study.

1. Good quality land is becoming increasingly scarce. There
   are no large areas of land which can be opened up at low
   costs. Any strategy must accept the basic fact that important increases in agricultural production will require
   major investments. The alternative of increasing output
   per unit of land will also require significant investments.
2. The price policies pursued in the post-World-War II era
   involving low food prices have been detrimental to long-
   run agricultural growth. Since investment decisions lie
   in the hands of the peasants, a favourable price policy
   is necessary to stimulate investments in agriculture.
   Clearly, a programme to raise the relative price of food

and to stabilise prices is needed and such schemes in-
cur costs in terms of personnel and capital. Such a programme would also directly raise average rural income.
Price policy should thus be used as an instrument to obtain agricultural growth. Price policies must be established with a long-term purpose and ad-hoc manipulations
should be the exception rather than the rule.

3. While large agricultural investments are needed both for
   increasing output per unit of land, and also land under
   cultivation, the present credit system is inadequate, as
   it is unable to cope with a large number of loans efficiently.[13] Ways of channeling credit from the urban to the
   rural sector have to be found, and also means to insure
   that savings within the agricultural sector are re-invested
   in agriculture.

4. Throughout this study we have argued that land and capital
   are scarce. Labour, however, is not a major constraint for
   agricultural growth. If this is a realistic description
   there are good grounds to argue that a lot can be gained
   by reducing the high birth rate. The population of Peru is
   presently growing at about 2.9 percent per annum. That
   means that by year 2000 the Peruvian population will be
   77 percent higher than in 1980. From this follows that
   agricultural production must also increase 77 percent just
   to maintain the per capita level in 1980. (See Table 7.3,
   column 2).

In the last years, the agricultural growth rate has been less
than 3 percent per year. Assuming an agricultural growth rate
above that of population, say 3.5 percent, by year 2000 per
capita agricultural production would have increased from 100
to 112. (See Table 7.3, column 5). If the population growth
could be reduced from 2.9 percent to 2.5 percent, the additional
improvement in per capita agricultural production, from 112 to
121, would almost be as great as that obtained by a ceteris

paribus 3.5% rate of growth of agricultural production over a time span of 20 years. Clearly this reasoning suggests that because land and capital are scarce, a reduction in the rate of growth of population would permit a higher rate of growth of per capita production. Such an increase in per capita production would permit a substantial improvement in the nutritional levels of Peru, particularly if the benefits of increased growth per capita were, through the economic policy, earmarked for the poorer strata.

Table 7.3   Per capita agricultural production 1980-2000
(1980=100)

Year	Population growth. rate 2.5% 1	Population growth. rate 2.9% 2	Agricultural production growth rate 3.5% 3	Per capita production (3:1)x100 4	Per capita production (3:2)x100 5
1980	100	100	100	100	100
1985	113	115	119	105	103
1990	128	133	141	110	106
1995	145	154	168	116	109
2000	164	177	199	121	112

These findings explain the central elements in a strategy for accelerating agricultural growth. In the following discussion we will inter alia use the low population growth rate hypothesis.

Let us now turn to the two basic strategies available. Johnston has developed an analytical framework which is useful in this context. He distinguishes two types of agricultural development strategies.

"The most fundamental issue of agricultural strategy faced by the late developing countries is to

> choose between a bimodal strategy whereby resources
> are concentrated within a subsector of large, ca-
> pital-intensive units or a unimodal strategy which
> seeks to encourage a more progressive and wider dif-
> fusion of technical innovations adopted to the factor
> proportions of the sector as a whole."14)

In the Peruvian context we can distinguish the following strategies.

The growth strategy, largely seen, continues the development
policy of Peru in investing and expanding land under irrigation
on the Coast. It seeks as before to direct most public investments to this region, stimulating and improving its extension
services, research and road system.

The equity cum growth strategy which to a comparatively larger
extent focuses investments on human capital. It breaks with
the present spatial development pattern by assigning higher
priority to the development of the Sierra and the Jungle regions. Instead of large capital-intensive investment schemes,
(capital deepening), it seeks more to spread investments. Let
us consider each strategy in turn.

7.3.2 The growth strategy

The Coast is a big desert and agricultural production can
mainly be expanded here through increasingly large irrigation
projects. What are the possibilities to physically obtain
enough land through these irrigation projects? In Table 7.4
we have added land under irrigation in 1972, under construction in 1975, and under study in 1975. On this account there
could be an increase of about 43 percent between 1980 and
2000. There are also possibilities to improve the present
irrigation system and in 1975 there were about 190 000 hectares being improved, and another 353 000 hectares under
study. These have not been considered in Table 7.4.15)

Table 7.4   Possibilities to expand irrigated land in
             Peru, 1981-2000   (thousand hectares)

1. Land with irrigation 1972   1 273
2. In construction 1975   36
3. 1+2=3 Total available 1980   1 309
4. In study   558
5. 3+4=5 Total   1 867
6. Percent increase $\left(\frac{5-3}{3}\right) \times 100 = 6$ 42.6

Source: 1. Table A.5.3
        2 and 4. Pacora (1978), Table 14

From Table 7.3 we get that if the growth of population is
2.5 percent the Peruvian population would increase 64 percent between 1980 and 2000. Such an expansion of irrigated
land as indicated in Table 7.4 has certain characteristics
such as (1) concentration on the Coast; (2) production becoming increasingly capital intensive, i.e. capital-output
ratios are increasing and investment projects larger and
thus more difficult to finance. Let us consider each factor
in turn.

An inventory of possible irrigation projects in 1970 provides important information. Out of 16 irrigation projects
13 are for the Coast and 3 are for the Sierra. Summing new
irrigated land to the amount of land to be improved we obtain that 98.6 percent of the area is located on the Coast
and only 1.4 percent in the Sierra. Moreover, no less than
99.7 percent of the investments are for the Coast and only
0.3 percent for the Sierra.[16] The cost of extending the
area of irrigated land has increased rapidly. While in the
period 1945-65 the average cost per hectare was 1 100 US
dollars, the projected average cost per hectare for eleven
new irrigation projects was, in 1970, 2 100 US dollars.

(Both figures in 1965 prices).[17)

There has been a tendency to build ever bigger and more capital-intensive irrigation projects in Peru. One important
reason for this is that the most natural and cheapest irrigation projects have already been carried out on the Coast.
There is besides a tendency for investment cost per hectare to
increase and also for the economic return to become smaller.[18)
The fact that new investment projects tend to be bigger is
not seen to reverse this trend. Figure 7.1 depicts the relationship between the capital-output ratio on the y-axis
and the benefit-cost ratio on the x-axis. As can be seen the
more capital-intensive the project, the lower the rate of
return will be. It should be added that the largest projects
are also the most recent.

Figure 7.1   <u>Relationship between capital-output ratio and
              benefit cost coefficient</u>

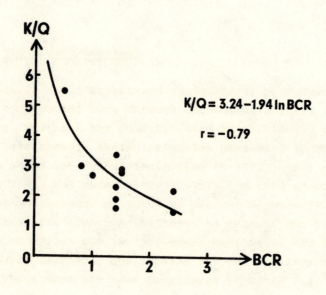

Source: See data below

Name of Project	Capital-output ratio K/Q	Benefit-cost ratio BCR*
1. Antara	2.2	2.4
2. Huanscolla	1.5	2.4
3. Chococo	2.8	1.5
4. El Cural	1.6	1.4
5. La Cano	2.3	1.4
6. El Huevo	1.9	1.4
7. Olmos	3.4	1.4
8. Choclacocha	2.9	1.5
9. Chira	5.5	0.5
10. Moquegua	2.7	1.0
11. Tumbes	3.0	0.8

*) At market prices. 10 percent discount rate.

Investment costs per hectare   (US dollars, 1965 prices)

Small Sierra	670
Small Coastal	1 570
Medium Coastal	1 530
Large Coastal	2 780

Source: McGaughey and Thorbecke (1972), pp. 33-35

What will be the price to incorporate new irrigated land in
Peru? Doing a bit of guesstimating we can give some ideas of
the costs involved. We have already mentioned that the cost are
increasing and that this trend probably will continue. Let
us suppose that the cost to produce one hectare of irrigated land was 3300 US dollars in 1980, in 1970 prices.[9]
We assume that land under irrigation is to grow at the same
rate as the lower hypothesis for population growth, i.e.
2.5 percent and annum. From Table 7.4 we have that the total
amount of irrigated land was 1.31 million hectares in 1980.

Assuming a yearly rate of growth of 2.5 percent, we get the amount of irrigated land which has to be produced in column 1 in Table 7.5. If there would be no increases in the costs to produce irrigated land, column 2 in the same table gives the annual investment costs. We have discarded this hypothesis above. We elaborate on two alternative hypotheses. The first is that the costs increase 5 percent per annum, called the low hypothesis, and at 10 percent per annum called the high hypothesis. The results are given in columns 3 and 4 in Table 7.5.

Next we have calculated the budget of the Central Government and the Ministry of Agriculture and the results are reproduced in Table 7.6. Investments in irrigation have to become a very high share both in the budget of the Ministry of Agriculture but also in the total budget of the Central Government if this growth scenario is followed. For example, if the total budget of the Ministry of Agriculture would grow at 10 percent as of 1975, in 1985 it would be 316 million US dollars. In that year 61 percent of the budget of the Ministry of Agriculture would have to be earmarked for irrigation investments in the high hypothesis.

In order to justify these high costs per hectare the value of the agricultural production obtained from this land must be very high. This in turn will require high levels of non-traditional inputs, in particular fertilizers. Therefore, this development strategy will demand large amounts of additional credit.

We have thus far shown that this growth strategy will require significant and rapidly increasing investment expenditures to increase production. As the effects of increasing costs to sustain this strategy are felt in the national budget, policy makers probably will shift to another development strategy.

Table 7.5   Investment in irrigated land 1981-2000

	Irrigated land to be produced (hectares)	Investments (US million dollars, 1970 prices Yearly price increases per hectare		
		0%	5%	10%
	1	2	3	4
1981	32 750	108	113	119
82	33 569	111	122	134
83	34 408	114	131	151
84	34 268	116	141	170
1985	36 150	119	152	192
	172 145	568	659	766
86	37 054	122	164	217
87	37 980	125	176	244
88	38 929	128	190	275
89	39 903	132	204	310
1990	40 900	135	220	350
	194 766	642	954	1 396
91	41 923	138	237	395
92	42 971	142	255	445
93	44 045	145	274	502
94	45 146	149	295	566
1995	46 275	153	317	638
	220 360	727	1 378	2 546
96	47 432	157	342	719
97	48 618	160	368	811
98	49 833	164	396	914
99	51 079	169	426	1031
2000	52 356	173	458	1162
	249 318	823	1 990	4 637
Total:	836 589	2 760	4 981	9 345

Note: the average cost in 1965 prices was 2060 US dollars per hectare. Assume that the effects of inflation and real costs of constructing one hectare increased 10% per annum in the period 1965-79 we obtain the average cost of 3 300 dollars in 1970 prices.

Table 7.6   A. Government budget and investments in irrigation
                (Million US dollars 1970 prices)

Year	Ministry of Agriculture	Central Government
1965	28	729
1970	65	1 048
1975	122	1 519
1977	75	1 411

            B. Investments in irrigation (yearly average)
                (Million US dollars 1970 prices)

Period	High	Low
1981–85	153	132
1986–90	279	191
1991–95	509	276
1996–2000	927	398

Source: Table 6.11 and Table 7.5
We have deflated the budgets in current Soles to obtain 1970
Soles, and converted at the exchange rate of 1970.

Before turning to our second alternative, let us consider
the effects on equity. We have throughout this study argued that the rural income distribution will largely be
determined by the distribution of land. In this growth
strategy, the main addition to land will be through irrigation projects. There are different options available to
distribute this addition of land. See Table 7.7.

In the mid-seventies there were about 1.4 million families
in the agricultural sector of which at least 800 000 were
living at very low-income levels. Assuming that the agricul-

tural population is growing at about 2 percent per annum,in
the period 1981-85, 161 000 families will be added to the
agricultural population by 1985. The CIDA study referred to
several times in the present work considered that the minimum
size of a family farm on the Coast is 3 hectares.[20] Only if production units of 1 hectare each are formed will this strategy
be able to supply the increase in the agricultural population
with land. Since this strategy is geared to supply the urban

sector with food it is probable that larger units will be
formed to secure a high level of marketable surplus. A
smaller area per family means smaller family incomes and
a higher proportion of the income spent on food. For a given production, less will be marketed.

Table 7.7   Number of families to be benefitted by the
             growth strategy, 1981-85

1. Increase in irrigated land (hectares)	172 145	172 145	172 145
2. Allocated land per family (hectares)	20	3	1
3. Number of families to be benefitted 1:2=3	8 600	57 400	172 100
4. Growth in agricultural families 1981-85	161 000	161 000	161 000
5. Absorption (3:4)x100=5	5%	36%	107%

Source: See Table 7.5

In summary, the growth strategy is one which has considerable support in the current policies in Peru. Large-scale
investment projects in irrigation have been carried out and
several are in the pipeline. It would seem as if this strategy can be continued until the year 2000, because the fi-

nancial constraint does not seem to be binding. It is, however, possible that during this period, 1981-2000, a basic
change in the growth strategy will come about as a result
of increasing costs of irrigation schemes. The Coastal area
is a big desert, while the Sierra has some growth potential.
Probably the Jungle region, though, will increasingly become
the new growth pole in Peruvian development. This process
has already started shown in the data on population growth
in chapter one, and the data on income distribution in chapter three.

This growth strategy, large irrigation schemes, has little
if any direct benefit for the rural poor. Scarce resources
are allocated on a relatively small area, deepening capital,
thus leaving the majority of peasants with little access to
the means to increase their production. We will now consider
some elements in the equity-cum-growth strategy.

7.3.3 Equity-cum-growth strategy

The growth strategy will not reduce income differences within
the agricultural sector. It is a feasible strategy though
increasingly costly. An equity-cum-growth strategy would differ in many respects. It would need another study to analyse the content and consequences of such a strategy. However, some of the elements of such a strategy will be suggested for future research.

In designing a Peruvian development strategy there is always
an important spatial dimension to consider. As we have mentioned several times throughout this study, the development
of the urban-coastal areas triggered off migration to this
region. This, in turn, created pressures to expand agricultural land on the Coast, in addition to the pressures gene-

rated by the export demand for Peruvian agricultural export goods produced there. While under the growth strategy this process is to be continued, the equity-cum-growth strategy concentrates or allocates a greater share of investments to the Sierra region and successively more to the Jungle region. There are two basic reasons for this. The first one is that the bulk of the population is living in these regions and, in the Jungle region, migrating there. The second one is that the agricultural growth potential seems relatively greater in these regions due to the rising costs for increasing irrigated land on the Coast. There exists some possibilities to expand new land in the Jungle area instead of carrying out expensive colonization schemes which could be another kind of bimodal strategy, due to elevated infrastructure investments. The Government could opt for supporting spontaneous colonization which has taken and is taking place. In addition small irrigation schemes could be developed in the Sierra.

Another important aspect of this strategy which makes it differ significantly from the growth strategy is that, instead of concentrating large sums on a relatively small area and a quite limited number of families, the equity strategy purports to spread the investments across a larger area and a larger number of people. As an illustration of the differences we can use the example in Table 7.7 on the growth strategy. Assume that on an average each family receives 3 hectares. Thus 57 400 families would benefit. This represents a total investment in irrigated land of 766 million US dollars, high hypothesis. (Table 7.5). Per family this amounts to about 130 000 US dollars. In chapter three we estimated the average rural household income per month. Converting this into a yearly income in 1970 prices, the average

rural household income was about 570 US dollars. If these
766 million US dollars instead were distributed evenly among
1.5 million rural families, on an average each would receive
about 510 US dollars. Such an investment pattern, spreading
investments, would still represent a significant sum when
compared to the average rural annual income, 570 US dollars
and should permit a relatively rapid rate of agricultural
growth.[21] Closely related to this aspect is that the strategy allocates a significantly higher proportion of investments to the formation of human capital instead of to physical capital and land formation. Because of the type of
investments proposed for the public sector, an important
part of the increased production will come from an increase
in output per labourer and per unit of land in agriculture,
particularly in the Sierra and subsequently in the Jungle
area.

The post-agrarian-reform land ownership is still characterized by great inequalities. There will still remain the
need to give the great majority of peasants access to more
land. There still is the option to distribute more land for
the peasants outside the reformed sector by reducing the
land available to those already benefitted by the reform.
One such solution would be to increase the number of families on the reformed units. Another approach would be to
expropriate more land.

This strategy has far-reaching implications for agricultural research, extension services, education, credit and so
forth. At present these only reach a small proportion of
the rural population. To engage almost the whole agricultural population in the agricultural growth process requires
a fundamental change of policy.

Herein are some of the more important aspects of necessary
conditions for an equity-cum-growth strategy. It is based
on a belief that the peasant family has the capacity to rapidly increase production and its income and well-being if
given the possibility to do so.

The urban bias in development is one outstanding characteristic of post-World-War II Peruvian development. If the agrarian reform of 1969 destroyed the landholding classes,
it has not, however, been conducive to the creation of strong
peasant organizations capable to articulate the interests of
the peasants. Therefore, the peasant barely surviving from
the food produced on fragmented and depleted soils has but
one option, namely, to "vote with his feet" joining the ranks
of the urban poor.

Peruvian agriculture will remain an obstacle to development
as long as a majority of the peasants are not integrated in
the development processes and given a fair chance to share
the fruits of progress.

1. Meier (1976), p. 607.

2. CIESA (1975).

3. Based on my own calculations at ECLA and ICIRA. See also Lehman (1974), pp. 70-119.

4. CIESA (1975), pp. 46-63; 133-194; Annexes pp. 95-102; Lehman (1974), pp. 70-119.

5. See note 9 in Chapter 5; and CIESA (1975), pp. 46-48.

6. CIESA (1975), pp. 266-278.

7. Based on my own calculations at ECLA. Cf. Table 5.9.

8. CIESA (1975), pp. 431-468.

9. See Chapter 4.3.

10. See Chapter 2.4.5.

11. The evolution of real wages of workers was as follows; taking 1970=100

1970	1971	1972	1973	1974	1975	1976	1977	1978	1979
100	106	110	116	106	101	89	77	63	61

    Source: Desco (1980:67), p. 9.

12. The expression"voting with the feet"taken from Lipton (1977), p. 217.

13. Recalling that there were about 1.2 million production units in 1972 the number of loans approved by the Agricultural Development Bank is clearly insufficient:

1969	1970	1971	1972
53 000	52 000	50 000	53 000

    Source: IBRD (1975), Volume II, Table G.3. See also Turner (1974).

14. Johnston in Meier (1976), p. 594.

15. Pacora (1978), Table 14.

16. McGaughey (1970), p. 81.

17. McGaughey and Thorbecke (1972), p. 33; Iowa (1967), p. 206.

18. The Majes project was not included in the sample of figure 7.1. It has the highest costs of all and the expected returns were quite poor. See McGaughey (1969). It was still decided to proceed with the project. In 1978 I was told by an engineer of the consortium implementing the project that it was becoming more costly than expected, and that there were serious delays in the implementation of the project.

19. See note to Table 7.5.

20. See Table 1.6.

21. The following hypothetical example illustrates the potential impact on
    the peasant income and on production of such an investment:

		US dollars (1970 prices)
1. Peasant family income before investment		570
2. Investment		
2.1 Government financed	510	
2.2 Peasant's own contribution	510	
Total		1 020
3. Capital-output ratio:2		
4. Increase in production 2:3=4		510
5. Additional expenditures on purchased inputs		210
6. Peasant additional income 4-5=6		300
7. Percentage increase in peasant's income (6:1)x100=7		53

The value of Peruvian agricultural production was about 1 000 million
US dollars at the end of the 70's. (Tables 5.5 and 6.2). The aggregate
increase in production from this hypothetical example would be 765
million US dollars, or about 77 percent.

Bibliography

Acción Popular. Propuesta de Plan de Gobierno 1980-1985. Resumen. Lima, 1980.

Actualidad Económica. Lima, various issues.

Adelman, Irma. Development Economics - A Reassessment of Goals, in American Economic Review, May 1975, pp. 302-309.

———   Growth, Income Distribution and Equity - Oriented Development Strategies, in World Development, February-March 1975, pp. 67-76.

Adelman, Irma and Morris, C.T. Distribution and Development: A comment, in Journal of Development Economics, Vol 1, No 4, February 1975, pp. 401-402.

———   Economic Growth and Social Equity in Developing Countries. Stanford University Press, Stanford, 1973.

Adelman, Irma and Robinson, Sherman. Income Distribution Policy in Developing Countries. A Case study of Korea. Stanford University Press, Stanford, 1978.

Adelman, Irma and Thorbecke, Erik (eds). The Theory and Design of Economic Development. The John Hopkins Press, Baltimore and London, 1966.

Agricultural Development Bank. Memorias. Lima, various years.

Ahluwalia, M.S. (1976:1) Income Distribution and Development: Some Stylized Facts, in American Economic Review, May 1976, pp. 128-135.

———   (1976:2) Inequality, Poverty and Development, in Journal of Development Economics, 3 (1976), pp. 307-342.

Ahluwalia, Montek et.al. A Comment, in IDS Bulletin, August 1975, Vol 7, No 2, pp. 17-18.

Aitchison, J and Brown, J.A.C. The Lognormal Distribution. Cambridge University Press, 1963.

Alberts, Tom. "Disguised Unemployment" i den traditionella sektorn i u-länderna. Nationalekonomiska Institutionen. Mimeo, Stockholm University, Stockholm, 1969.

———   Draft Plan for the 1970-71 Rice Campaign in Agrarian Zone II. Unpublished study. Ministerio de Agricultura, Oficina Sectorial de Planificación Agraria, Lima, 1969.

———   Fallstudier i Utvecklingsplanering. Föreningen Nationalekonomer i Lund. University of Lund, Lund, 1977.

Alberts, Tom and Brundenius, Claes. Growth Versus Equity: The Brazilian

Case in the Light of the Peruvian and Cuban Experiences. Discussion Paper No 126, RPI, University of Lund, Lund, 1979.

Alberts, Tom and Buechler, Peter. Agrarian Reform Data. Memorandum to a UNDP-FAO mission. Mimeo, Lima, 1970.

Allen, R.G.D. Mathematical Analysis for Economists. MacMillan and St. Martin's Press, New York, 1967.

Alvarez, Elena. Política Agraria y Estancamiento de la Agricultura, 1969-1977. Instituto de Estudios Peruanos, Lima, 1980.

Amat y León, Carlos. Analysis de los Variables de la Demanda en el Perú. Estudio Económetrico. 4 Funciones de Consumo de Alimentos en la Zona Urbana. Convenio para Estudios Economicos Basicos, Lima, 1970.

Amat y León, Carlos and León, Héctor. Estructura y Niveles de Ingreso Familiar en el Perú. Ministerio de Economía y Finanzas, Lima, 1977.

Amat y León, Carlos et.al. Realidad del Campo Peruano Después de la Reforma Agraria. 10 Ensayos Criticos. Centro de Investigación y Capacitación, Lima, 1980.

Astiz, Carlos A. Pressure Groups and Power Elites in Peruvian Politics. Cornell University Press, Ithaca, 1969.

Bamat, Thomas Patrick. From Plan Inca to Plan Tupac Amaru. The Recomposition of the Peruvian Power Bloc, 1968-1977. PhD thesis, Rutgers University, 1978.

Barraclough, Solon and Collarte, Juan Carlos. El Hombre y la Tierra en América Latina. Resumen de los informes CIDA sobre tenencia de la tierra. ICIRA, Editorial Universitaria, Santiago de Chile, 1972.

Barraclough, Solon and Domike, Arthur. Agrarian Structure in Seven Latin American Countries, in Land Economics, November 1966, pp. 392-424.

Baster, Nancy. Distribution of Income and Economic Growth: Concepts and Issues. UN Research Institute for Social Development (UNRISD), Geneva, 1970.

Bayer, David L. Reforma Agraria Peruana. Descapitalización del Minifundio y Formación de la Burgesía Rural. CISE, Universidad Nacional Agraria La Molina, Lima, 1975.

BCR, Banco Central de Reserva del Perú. Boletín del Banco Central de Reserva del Perú. Lima, various issues.

——— Cuentas Nacionales del Perú 1950-1967. Lima, 1968.

——— Cuentas Nacionales del Perú 1960-1974. Lima, 1976.

——— El Desarrollo Económico y Financiero del Perú 1968-1973. Lima. Without date referred to as BCR(1974).

BCR, Banco Central de Reserva del Perú. Memoria. Lima, various years.

---   Renta Nacional del Perú 1942-1959. Lima, 1967.

Beckerman, Wilfred. Some Reflections on "Redistribution with Growth", in World Development, Vol 5, No 8, August 1977, pp. 665-676.

Béjar, Hector. Peru 1965. Anteckningar från en gerilla erfarenhet. Rabén och Sjögren, Stockholm, 1970 (In Spanish: Peru 1965: Apuntes sobre una Experiencia Guerrillera. Instituto de Libro, Havana, 1969).

Best, Michael H. Uneven Development and Dependent Market Economies, in American Economic Review, May 1976, pp. 136-146.

Blanco, Hugo. Land or Death. The Peasant Striggle in Peru. Pathfinder, New York, 1972. Jord eller död. Bokförlaget Forum AB, Stockholm 1974.

Bliss, Christopher and Stern, Nicholas. Productivity, Wages and Nutrition, in Journal of Development Economics, Vol 5, No 4, December 1978, pp. 331-398.

Blomström, Magnus and Hettne, Björn. Beroendeskolans Uppgång och Fall. Göteborgs Universitet, Avdelningen för freds- och konfliktforskning, Göteborg, 1979.

Bogdanowicz-Bindert, Christine A. Portugal, Turkey and Peru: Three Successful Stabilization Programmes Under the Auspices of the IMF, in World Development, Vol 11, No 1, 1983, pp. 65-70.

Boserup, Ester. The Conditions of Agricultural Growth. The economics of agrarian change under population pressure. George Allen and Unwin Ltd, London, 1965.

Bottomley, Anthony. Factors Pricing and Economic Growth in Underdeveloped Rural Areas. Crosby Lockwood & Son Ltd, London, 1971.

Brady, Eugene. The Distribution of Total Personal Income in Peru. International Studies in Economics, Monograph No 6, Iowa State University, Ames, 1968.

Bronfenbrenner, Martin. Income Distribution Theory. Aldine Publishing Company, Chicago, 1971.

Brundenius, Claes. Imperialismens ansikte. 400 år av underutveckling i Peru. Bokförlaget Prisma, Stockholm, 1972.

---   (1976:1) Patrón de Crecimiento de la Economía Peruana. Mimeo, INP/OIP Informe No 041-76/INP-OIP. Lima, 1976.

---   (1976:2) Structural Changes in the Peruvian Economy 1968-1975. Discussion Paper No 104, RPI, University of Lund, 1976. See also Spanish translation published in Peru: Los Cambios Estructurales en la Economía Peruana y el Fracaso del Populismo Militar (68-76). Instituto Cultural José María Arguedas, Lima, 1977.

---   (1976:3) Remúneraciones y Redistribución del Ingresos. Mimeo, INP/OIP Document: Informe No 037-76/INP-OIP, Lima, 1976.

Byres, T.J. Review Article of Neo-Populist Pipe Dreams: Daedalus in the Third World and the Myth of Urban Bias, in *The Journal of Peasant Studies*, Vol 6, No 2, January 1979, pp. 210-242.

Caballero, José María. (1975:1) Aspectos Financieros en las Reformas Agrarias: Elementos Teóricos y Experiencias Históricas en el Perú. Serie Documentos de Trabajo, No 25, CISEPA. Mimeo, Universidad Católica, Lima, 1975.

—— (1975:2) Notas sobre la Renta de Tierra. Serie Ensayos Teóricos, No 4, CISEPA. Mimeo, Universidad Católica, Lima, 1975.

—— Reforma y Reestructuración Agraria en el Perú. CISEPA. Mimeo, Universidad Católica, Lima, 1976.

Caballero, José María and Alvarez Elena. Aspectos Cuantitativos de la Reforma Agraria (1969-1979). Instituto de Estudios Peruanos, Lima, 1980.

Cabrera, Raul Munoz. Legislación Básica que Sanciona el Régimen de Liberación en las Importaciones de Insumos Agropecuarios. Mimeo, Ministerio de Agricultura en colaboración con la Misión de las Universidades de Iowa en el Perú, Lima, 1970.

Cáceres, Ps. Baldomero S.M. Opiniones de Profesores Universitarios de Ciencias Agrarias sobre la Prebolemática del Campo. CISE. Mimeo, Universidad Nacional Agraria La Molina, Lima, 1976.

Cairncross, Alec and Puri, Mohinder (eds). Employment, Income Distribution: Problems of the Developing Countries: Essays in Honor of H.W. Singer. Holmes and Meier, New York, 1976.

Carrasco, Gamaliel; Kozub, Jacques; Strasma, John and Domike, Arthur. Mobilización de Recursos Financieros y Económicos para la Reforma Agraria Peruana. CIDA, Trabajo No 13, Editado por Unión Panamericana. Versión Preliminar, Washington DC, 1969.

Castro, Hildebrando Pozo. El Yanaconaje en las Haciendas Piuranas. Azangare, Lima, 1947.

Catacaos: Comunidad Propriedad Social. Mimeo, Piura (?), February 1973.

Catacaos una Experiencia de Lucha. Mimeo, Piura (?), December 1972.

CEPAL, Comisión Económica de las Naciones Unidas para América Latina. Perspectivas del Consumo y la Producción de Fertilizantes en América Latina. CEPAL-FAO Conference document LARC/76/7(d). Santiago de Chile, 1976.

—— Long-term trends and projections of Latin American Economic Development. Mimeo, Document E/CEPAL/1027, 1977.

Chand, Sheetal K. and Wolfe, Bertran A. The Elasticity and Buoyancy of the Tax System of Peru 1960-71: An empirical analysis. International Monetary Fund. Fiscal Affairs and Western Hemisphere Departments, Washington DC, 1973.

Chang, Pei-Kong. Agriculture and Industrialization. Greenwood Press, New York, 1949.

Chaplin, David. Industrialization and the Distribution of Wealth in Peru. Land Tenure Center. Research Paper No 18, University of Wisconsin, Madison, 1966.

Chenery, Hollis. Structural Change and Development Policy. A World Bank Research Publication. Oxford University Press, 1979.

Chenery, H. et.al. Inkomstfördelning under tillväxt. Panel Discussion in Ekonomisk Debatt, No 8. Stockholm, 1976.

——— Redistribution with Growth. Oxford, 1974.

Chiriboga, Carlos Collazos et.al. The Food and Nutrition Situation in Peru. Ministerio de Salud Pública y Asistencia Social and Interamerican Co-operative Service of Public Health, Lima, 1960.

CIDA, Comité Interamericano de Desarrollo Agrícola. Perú - Tenencia de la Tierra y Desarrollo Socio-Económico del Sector Agrícola. Mimeo, OEA-BID-FAO-CEPAL-IICA, Washington DC, 1965.

——— Perú - Tenencia de la Tierra y Desarrollo Socio-Económico del Sector Agrícola. Unión Panamericana, Washington DC 1966.

CIEPA, Centro de Investigación Económica para la Acción. Informe de la Economía Peruana 1978. Lima, 1979.

CIESA, Centre International d'Etude des Structures Agraires. La Reforme Agraire Chilienne Pendant l'Unité Populaire. CIESA, Montpellier, 1975.

Clark, Colin and Haswell, Margaret. The Economics of Subsistence Agriculture. Fourth edition, MacMillan and Co., London and Basingstoke, 1970.

Cline, William R. Potential Effects of Income Redistribution on Economic Growth Latin American Cases. Praeger Publishers Inc., New York and London, 1972.

——— Income Distribution and Development in Journal of Development Economics, February 1975, pp. 359-400.

——— Economic Consequences of a Land Reform in Brazil. North Holland Publishing Company, 1970.

Comisión Multisectorial de la Problemática Azucarera. Informe General de Base sobre la Problemática Azucarera. Resumen. Mimeo, Comité Permanente de Trabajo. Lima, 1975.

CONVENIO, Convenio para estudios económicos basicos. (1970:1) Requerimentos Mensuales de Mano de Obra para la Agricultura por Hectarea, por Cultivo, por Provincias y para la Actividad Pecuaria. Año base 1967. Mimeo, Lima, 1970.

CONVENIO, Convenio para estudios económicos basicos. (1970:2) La Fuerza
Laboral Agrícola Actual y Proyectada por Sexo y Grupos de Edad,
por Provincias, Departamentos y Regiones. Mimeo, Lima, 1970.

— (1970:3) Primera Estimación de Sub-empleo de la Población Economica-
mente Activa Agrícola en Areas Rurales, por Meses Provincias y Regiones en el Año 1967. Mimeo, Lima, 1970.

— (1970:4) Aspectos Sociales y Financieros de un Programa de Reforma
Agraria para el Período 1968-1975. Mimeo, Lima, 1970.

Convenio de Cooperación Técnica. Peru: Proyecciones a Largo Plazo de la
Oferta y Demanda de Productos Agropecuarios Seleccionados 1970-1975-
1980. Programa Iowa-Peru, Estudio No 11, Lima, 1969.

Couriel, Alberto. Perú: Estrategia de Desarrollo y Grado de Satisfacción de
las Necesidades Básicas. OIT. Programa Regional del Empleo para América
Latina y el Caribe (PREALC), Santiago de Chile, 1978.

Coutu, Arthur J. and King, Richard A. The Agricultural Development of Peru.
Praeger Special Studies in International Economics and Development,
New York and Longon, 1969.

Currie, Lauchlin. Is There an Urban Bias? Critique of Michael Lipton's "Why
Poor People Stay Poor", in Journal of Development Studies, Vol 6,
No 1, May 1979, pp. 86-105.

Cutivalú, Carlos. Por el Sendero de las Luchas Populares: Comuneros Cam-
pesinos. Ediciones Sincuenta, Piura, 1977.

De Las Casas, Moya P.L. A Theoretical and Applied Approach Towards the For-
mulation of Alternative Agricultural Sector Policies in Support of
the Peruvian Agricultural Planning Process. PhD thesis. Iowa State
University, 1977.

Decreto Ley 17716. Reforma Agraria. El Peruano. Lima, 1969.

Delgado, Oscar (ed). Reformas Agrarias en la América Latina. Procesos y Perspectivas. Fondo de Cultura Economica, Mexico City, 1965.

Desco. Resumen Semanal. Lima, various issues.

Dorner, Peter. Land Reform and Economic Development. Penguin Modern Economics
Texts, 1972.

Echeverría, Roberto D. The Effects of Agricultural Price Policies on Inter-
sectoral Income Transfers. Latin American Studies Program. Cornell
University, Dissertation Series No 13, Cornell, 1969.

ECLA, Economic Commission for Latin America. Long Term Trends and Projections of Latin American Economic Development. Mimeo, Document E/
CEPAL/1027, Santiago de Chile, 1977.

Eguren, Fernando Lopez. Reforma Agraria Cooperativización y Luchas Campe-
sinas. El Valle Chancay-Huaral. Desco, Lima, 1975.

Egur n, Fernando Lopez; García-Sayán, Diego; Pease, Henry García and Rubio, Marcial Correa. Estado y Politica Agraria. 4 Ensayos. Desco, Lima, 1977.

Ellman, Michael. Socialist Planning. Cambridge University Press, 1979.

Encuesta Nacional de Consumo de Alimentos (ENCA). ENCA-Diseño Muestral. ENCA Publication No 2, Lima, without date.

Espinoza, R. and Malpica, Carlos. El Problema de la Tierra. Amauta SA., Lima, 1970.

FAO. The Impact on Demand of Changes in Income Distribution, in Monthly Bulletin of Agricultural Economics and Statistics, March 1972.

———   Informe de la Misión de la FAO para Evaluar los Requerimentos de Asistencia Técnica para la Reforma Agraria Peruana. Mimeo, Draft, Santiago de Chile, 1969.

———   Production Yearbook. Rome, various years.

Feder, Ernest. Poverty and Unemployment in Latin America: A Challenge for Socio-Economic Research, in The Rural Society of Latin America Today. Scandinavian studies on Latin America No 2. Almqvist and Wiksell, Stockholm, 1973.

———   Violencia y Despojo del Campesino: El Latifundismo en América Latina. Siglo Veintiuno, Mexico, 1972 (A shortened version in English: The Rape of the Peasantry: Latin America's Landholding System, Anchor Books, Garden City, 1971).

Figueroa, Adolfo A. Agrarian Reform in Latin America: A Framework and an Instrument of Rural Development, in World Development, Vol 5, Nos 1&2, January-February 1977, pp. 155-168.

———   Income Distribution, Employment and Development: The case of Peru. PhD thesis, Vanderbilt University, Nashville, Tennessee, 1972.

Fitzgerald, E.V.K. The Political Economy of Peru 1956-78. Economic development and the restructuring of capital. Cambridge University Press, 1979.

———   The State and Economic Development of Peru since 1968. Cambridge University Press, 1976.

Flores-Saenz, Otto. An Historical Analysis of Peru's Agricultural Export Sector and the Development of Agricultural Technology. PhD thesis, University of Wisconsin-Madison, 1977.

Foxley, Alejandro (ed). Distribución del Ingreso. Fondo de Cultura Economica, Santiago de Chile, 1974.

———   Income Distribution in Latin America. Cambridge University Press, 1976.

Foxley, Alejandro et.al. Chile: The Role of Asset Distribution in Poverty-Focused Development Strategies, in World Development, January-February 1977, pp. 69-88.

Frank, Charles R. and Webb, Richard C. (eds). Income Distribution and Growth in the Less-Developed Countries. The Brookings Institution, Washington DC, 1977.

García, Antonio. Agrarian Reform and the Peruvian Model of Development, in Trimestre Económico, 1974, pp. 439-457.

García, Raúl. La distribución del ingreso por niveles en el Perú. San Marcos University, Lima, 1967 (not published) cited by Webb and Figueroa (1975), p. 28.

Gavilán, Marcelino Estelat. Perú: Legislación de Reforma Agraria. ICIRA, Santiago de Chile, 1969.

Georgescu-Roegen, N. Economic Theory and Agrarian Economics, in Oxford Economic Papers, February 1960.

Giles, Antonio S. Planificación Regional de Base Agropecuaria: "Programas Integrados de Desarrollo" (P.I.C.). Ministerio de Agricultura, Lima, 1972.

Goldsmith, William W. The War on Development, in Monthly Review, March 1977, pp. 50-56.

Griffin, Keith. International Inequality and National Poverty. MacMillan Press Ltd, London and Basingstoke, 1978.

——   Land Concentration and Rural Poverty. MacMillan Press Ltd., London 1976.

——   The Political Economy of Agrarian Change. An essay on the Green Revolution. MacMillan Press Ltd., London and Basingstoke, 1974.

——   Under-Development in Spanish America. George Allen and Unwin Ltd., London, 1969.

Griffin, Keith (ed). Financing Development in Latin America. MacMillan St. Martin's Press Ltd., London and Basingstoke, 1971.

Guillet, David. Agrarian Reform and Peasant Economy in Southern Peru. University of Missouri Press, Colombia and London, 1979.

Handelman, Howard. Struggle in the Andes: Peasant Political Mobilization in Peru. Latin American Monographs No 35, University of Texas, Austin, 1979.

Henderson, James M. and Quandt, Richard E. Microeconomics Theory. A mathematical Approach. International Student Edition, McGraw Hill Inc., 1958.

Hirschman, A.O. and Rotschild, M. Changing Tolerance for Inequality in Development. Quarterly Journal of Economics, November 1973.

Hopkins, L. Raul. La Producción Agropecuaria en el Perú, 1944-1969: Una aproximación estadística. Documento de Trabajo No 42. Mimeo, Instituto de Estudios Peruanos, Lima, 1979.

Horton, Douglad E. Haciendas and Cooperatives:A study of Estate Organization, Land Reform and New Reform Enterprises in Peru. PhD thesis, Cornell University, 1976.

――― Land Reform and Reform Enterprises in Peru. Report to the Land Tenure Center and to the World Bank. University of Wisconsin, Madison, 1974 (2 volumes. Vol 1-main report, vol 2-appendix A and B).

IBRD, International Bank for Reconstruction and Development. Agricultural Sector Survey Peru. Volume I: General Report; Volume II: Annexes. Washington DC, 1975.

ILO, International Labour Office. Poverty and Landlessness in Rural Asia. ILO, Geneva, 1977.

INP, Instituto Nacional de Planificación. (1975:1) Estudio de Consumo. Lima, 1975.

――― (1975:2) Plan Nacional de Desarrollo 1975-1978. Editorial Universo SA, Lima, 1975.

――― (1976:1) Algunas Consideraciones sobre el Sector Externo. Oficina de Investigaciones de Planificación (OIP). Informe No 039-76/INP-OIP, Lima, 1976.

――― (1976:2) Comentarios acerca de la Participación del Sector Público en la Economía Peruana. Mimeo, Informe No 036-76/INP-OIP, Lima, 1976.

――― Estrategia del Desarrollo Nacional a Largo Plazo. Resumen. Lima, 1968.

――― Plan De Desarrollo Economico y Social 1967-70. Plan Sectorial Agropecuario. Volumen II. INP, Lima, 1967. (Printing date not on the document.

――― Plan Nacional de Desarrollo para 1971-1975. Volumen I: Plan Global; Volumen II: Plan Agropecuario, Plan de Pesqueria, Lima, 1971.

――― Primer Censo Nacional Agropecuario. Lima, 1965.

Iowa Universities Mission to Peru. Peruvian Macro-Economic and Agricultural Prospects and Strategy, 1967-1972. Economic Report No 3, Lima, 1967.

Jacoby, Erich H. Människan och Jorden. Raben och Sjögren, Stockholm, 1971. English version: Man and Land. André Deutsch Ltd., London, 1971.

Jain, Shail. Size Distribution of Income. A compilation of Data. World Bank, Washington DC, 1973.

Johnson, Harry G. The Theory of Income Distribution. Gray-Mills Publishing Ltd., London, 1973.

Jolly, Richard. Redistribution with Growth - a reply, in *IDS Bulletin*, August 1975, Vol 7, No 2, pp. 9-17.

Kay, Cristóbal. Achievements and Contradictions of the Peruvian Agrarian Reform, in *The Journal of Development Studies*, Vol 18, No 2, 1982, pp. 142-170.

Kelley, Allen C; Williams, Jeffrey G. and Cheatham, Russel J. Dualistic Economic Development. Theory and History. The University of Chicago Press, Chicago and London, 1972.

Kendrick, John W. Productivity Trends in the US. National Bureau of Economic Research. Princeton University Press, Princeton, 1961.

Kilty, Daniel R. Planning for Development in Peru. Frederick A. Praeger Publishers, New York and London, 1967.

Kravis, Irving B; Kenessey, Zoltan; Heston, Alan and Summers, Robert. A System of International Comparisons of gross Product and Purchasing Power. A World Bank Study. Published by the John Hopkins Press, Baltimore and London, 1975.

Kuznets, Simon. Economic Growth and Income Inequality, in *American Economic Review*, March 1955, pp. 1-28.

—— Economic Growth of Nation: Total Output and Production Structure. The Belknap Press of Harvard University Press, Cambridge, Massachusetts, 1971.

—— Quantitative Aspects of the Economic Growth of Nations: VIII. Distribution of income by size, in *Economic Development and Cultural Change*, Vol XI, No 2, Part II, January 1963, pp. 1-80.

Lal, Deepak. Distribution and Development: A Review Article, in *World Development*, September 1976, pp. 728-738.

Latin America Weekly Report. Latin American Newsletters Ltd., London, various issues.

Latin American Regional Reports. Latin American Newsletters Ltd., London, various issues.

Lehman, David (ed). Agrarian Reform and Agrarian Reformism. Studies of Peru, Chile, China and India. Faber and Faber, London 1974.

—— The Death of Land Reform: A Polemic, in *World Development*, Vol 6, No 3, 1978, pp. 339-345.

Leibenstein, Harvey. The Theory of Underdevelopment in Backwork Economies, in *The Journal of Political Economy*, April 1957.

Leys, Colin. The Politics of Redistribution with Growth. The 'target group' approach, in *IDS Bulletin*, August 1975, Vol 7, No 2, pp. 4-8.

Lincoln, Jennie May Kah. Land to the Peasants: The Peruvian Military in Action: An Agrarian Reform Policy Study. PhD thesis, Ohio State University, 1978.

Lipsey, Richard G. and Steiner, Peter O. Economics. Harper International edition, 1966.

Lipton, Michael. The Theory of the Optimizing Peasant, in *Journal of Development Studies*, Vol 4, 1968:1, pp. 327-351.

— Why Poor People Stay Poor. Urban Bias in World Development. Maurice Temple Smith, London, 1977.

Little, I.M.D; Scitovski, T. and Scott, M. Industry and Trade in Some Developing Countries. A comparative study. OECD, Oxford University Press, London, 1970.

Lowenthal, Abraham F. (ed). The Peruvian Experiment. Continuity and change under military rule. Princeton University Press, Princeton, 1975.

Lundahl, Mats. Peasants and Poverty: A study of Haiti. Croom Helm Ltd., London, 1979.

Malpica, Carlos. Los Duenos del Perú. 7th edition. Ediciones Peisa, Lima, 1974.

Mann, Fred L. and Huerta, John (translators). Text of Decree Law No 17716. Agrarian Reform Law. Iowa-Peru Mission, Program Reports T-5. Ministry of Agriculture, Lima, 1969.

Mann, Fred L; Huerta, John; Morrisey, Dennis et.al. Preliminary Analysis. Agrarian Reform Law No 17716 enacted on 24 June 1969, Peru. Iowa-Peru Mission Reports T-4, Lima, 1970.

Mariátegui, José Carlos. 7 Ensayos de Interpretación de la Realidad Peruana. 18th edition. Editora Amuta, Lima, 1970.

MARKA. Reforma Agraria. No 44, Lima, 1976.

Matos Mar, José. Yanaconaje y Reforma Agraria en el Perú. Perú Problema No 15. Instituto de Estudios Peruanos, Lima, 1976.

Matos Mar, José and Mejía, José M. La Reforma Agraria en el Perú. Perú Problema No 19. Instituto de Estudios Peruanos, Lima, 1980.

Matos Mar, José et.al. Perú: Hoy. Siglo Veintiuno Editores S.A., Mexico, 1971.

McGaughey, Stephen Eugene. Criterios de Inversion para la Evaluación y Planificación de Proyectos de Irrigación en el Perú. Iowa Universities Mission to Peru, Study 13, Lima, 1970.

— Proyecto de Irrigación de Majes. Beneficio, Costos y Tasa Interna de Retorno. Ministerio de Agricultura, Lima, 1969.

McGaughey, Stephen and Thorbecke, Erik. Project Selection and Macroeconomic
   Objectives: A Methodology Applied to Peruvian Irrigation Projects.
   American Journal of Agricultural Economics, No 54, 1972, pp. 32-40.

Mejía, José M. Acerca de los Avances de la Investigación sobre Reforma
   Agraria en el Perú, in *Estudios Rurales Latinoamericanos*, Vol 1,
   No 2, Bogotá, 1978.

Mejía, José M. and Diaz, Rosa. Sindicalismo y reforma agraria en la valle
   de Chancay. Instituto de Estudios Peruanos, Lima, 1975.

Mesa-Lago, Carmelo. Estraficación y Desigualdad en la Seguridad Social La-
   tinoamericana: Peru. Center for Latin American Studies. Occasional
   Paper No 11, University of Pittsburgh, Pennsylvania, 1975.

Ministerio de Agricultura. (1975:1) Working Document without title. Lima,
   1975.

———   (1975:2) Análisis de la Situación actual y Perspectivas del Finan-
   ciamiento del Proceso de Transferencia de Propriedad de la Tierra.
   Internal Memorandum, Lima, 1975.

———   (1975:3) Evaluación 1974. Lima, 1975.

———   (1976:1) Informe de Evaluación. Plan Bienal del Sector Agrario
   1975-76. Período Enero-Diciembre 1975. Lima, 1976.

———   (1976:2) Delimitación Geográfica de las Zonas Agrarias por Oficinas
   y Agencias Agrarias. Lima, without date, referred to as (1976:2).

———   (1977:1) Diagnóstico de la Agricultura Peruana (Información Preliminar). Lima, 1977.

———   (1977:2) Exposición del Director Superior del Ministerio de Agricultura ante el Consejo de Ministros (May 1977). Lima, 1977.

———   (1978:1) Reforma Agraria en cifras. Working Document of DGRA no 10-78.

———   Informe del Sector Agropecuario. Evaluación 1973. Cuarto Trimestre.
   Lima, 1974.

———   Statistical tables. Referred to by year.

Ministerio de Alimentación. Informe del Sector Alimentacion. Evaluación Sectorial Año 1975. Lima, 1976.

Ministerio de Economía y Finanzas. Cuenta Nacional de la Republica. Lima,
   various years.

Mirrlees, J.A. A Pure Theory of Underdeveloped Economies, in Reynolds, L. (ed)
   Agriculture in Development Theory. Yale University Press, New Haven,
   1976.

Montoya, Rodrigo. A Propósito del Carácter Predominantemente Capitalista de la Economía Peruana Actual. Teoría y Realidad, Lima, 1970.

Naciones Unidas. El Uso de Fertilizantes en América Latina. New York, 1966.

——   Proyecto de Desarrollo de las Cuencas de los Rios Huallaga Central, Chiriyacu y Nieva. Diagnóstico Económico y Social. II Aproximación. Mimeo, UNDP, FAO and the Ministry of Agriculture, Tarapoto and Lima, 1970.

——   Situación y Evolución de la Agricultura y la Alimentación en América Latina. Mimeo, CEPAL-FAO Document LARC/76/2, Santiago de Chile, 1976.

Oman, Charles P. The Formation of Capitalist Society in Peru: "Dualism" and Underdevelopment. PhD thesis, University of California, Berkeley, 1978.

ONEC, Oficina Nacional de Estadística y Censos. II Censo Agropecuario 1972. Resultados Definitivos. Nivel Nacional. Lima, 1975.

——   Censos Nacionales. VII de Poblacion. II de Vivienda. 4 de Junio de 1972. Resultados Definitivos. Nivel Nacional. Lima, 1974.

——   La Población del Perú. Lima, 1974.

ONERN, Oficina Nacional de Evaluación de Recursos Naturales. Capacidad de Uso de los Suelos del Perú. Tercera Aproximación, Lima, 1971.

de Osma, Don Felipe. Informe que sobre Las Huelgas del Norte. Presenta al Gobierno du Comisionado Don Felipe de Osma. Casa Nacional de Moneda, Lima, 1912.

Owens, R.J. Peru. Oxford University Press, London, New York and Toronto, 1963.

Pacora, Lander Coupen. Perú Agropecuario: Década del 80. Speech given at the 12th annual meeting of executives, (CADE), in 1978. Mimeo, Instituto Peruano de Administración de Empresas, Lima, 1978.

Pásara, Luis H. Reforma Agraria: Derecho y Conflicto. Mimeo, Versión Preliminar. Lima, 1974.

Paukert, Felix. Income Distribution at Different Levels of Development, in International Labour Review, August-September 1973, pp. 97-125.

Pease García, Henry. El Ocaso del Poder Oligárquico. Lucha política en la escena oficial 1968-1975. Desco, Lima, 1977.

Peru. Major Development Policy Issues and Recommendations. IBRD, Washington D.C., 1981.

Pinto, Honorio. El Primer Censo Agropecuario del Perú (1929). Mimeo, Lima, 1972.

PREALC, Programa Regional del Empleo para America Latina y el Caribe. PERU:

Estrategia de Desarrollo y Grado de Satisfacción de las necesidades
Basicas. ILO, International Employment Programme. Work document,
final version. PREALC/127, 1978.

de la Puente, Uceda Luis F. La Reforma de Agro Peruano. Industrial Grafica
SA, Lima, 1966.

Pyatt, Graham. Review Article: Economic Strategies for Growth with Equity,
in *Economic Development and Cultural Change*, Vol 25, No 3, April
1977, pp. 581–587.

Reforma Agraria. The set of agrarian reform laws in force in 1976. INKARI,
Lima, 1976.

Reseña Económica. BCR, Lima 1982.

Robertson, Thyrele. Analisis de Precios de Productos Agricolas en el Perú.
Estudios Económicos por la Misión Iowa, No 2, Lima, 1967.

—— The Peruvian Fertilizer Industry - present situation and future
prospects. Iowa Universities Mission to Peru, Lima, 1968.

Robinson, Sherman. (1976:1) Toward an Adequate Long-run Model of Income
Distribution and Economic Development, in *The American Economic
Review*, May 1976, pp. 122–127.

—— (1976:2) A note on the U Hypothesis Relating Income Inequality and
Economic Development, in *The American Economic Review*, June 1976,
pp. 437–440.

Roca, Santiago. Las Cooperativas Azucareras del Perú. Distribución de Ingresos
Esan, Lima, 1975.

Roel, V. Historia Social y Económica de la Colonia. Editorial Gráfica Labor,
Lima, 1970.

Samuelson, Paul A. Economics: An Introductory Analysis. Sixth edition. McGraw
Hill Book Company, International Student Edition, 1964.

Scott, Juan Felipe. A Self-financing Strategy of Agrarian Reform: The case
of the Peruvian Sierra, in *Socio-Economic Planning*, Vol 5, 1971,
pp. 347–361.

Sen, Amartya. Ethical Issues in Income Distribution: National and Internationa
Institute for International Economic Studies, Stockholm, 1978.

Shepherd, Geoffrey. Low Income People in Peru Need more Proteins: Here is
how they can get it. Mimeo, Iowa Universities Mission to Peru, Lima,
1966.

Shepherd, Geoffrey and Furnish, Dale B. La Economía y Aspectos Legales del
Control de Precios en la Agricultura Peruana. Iowa Universities
Mission to Peru, Lima, 1967.

———   Price Policy for Beef in Peru. Iowa Universities Mission to Peru.
Special Report No 8, Lima, 1968.

Shoup, Carl S. Production from Consumption. Public Finance 1/2, 1965,
pp. 173-202.

Spalding, Karen. De Indio a Campesino. Cambios en la estructura social del
Perú Colonial. Instituto de Estudios Peruanos, Lima, 1974.

Stewart, F. and Streeten, P. New Strategies for Development: Poverty, Income Distribution and Growth, in Oxford Economic Papers, November
1976, pp. 381-405.

Stiglitz, Joseph E. The Efficiency Wage Hypothesis, Surplus Labour, and
the Distribution of Income in the LDC's, in Oxford Economic Papers,
July 1976.

Strassman, Paul W. Economic Growth and Income Distribution, in Quarterly
Journal of Economics, August 1956, pp. 425-440.

Strauss, Eric. Soviet Agriculture in Perspective. George Allen and Unwin
Ltd., London, 1969.

Suárez, Germán and Tovar, Mario. Deuda Pública Externa 1920-1966. Mimeo,
Banco Central de Reserva del Peru, Departamento de Estudios Económicos, Lima, 1967.

Thorbecke, Erik. A Methodology to Estimate the Relationship between Present
and Future Output and Employment, Applied to Peru and Guatemala.
OECD, Paris, 1969.

Thorbecke, Erik and Condos, Apostolos. Modelos Macroeconomicos de Crecimier
y Desarrollo de la Economía Peruana. Mimeo, Iowa Group at Universit
of San Marcos, Lima, 1965.

Thorp, Rosemary. A Note on Food Supplies, the Distribution of Income and Na
tional Income Accounting in Peru, in Bulletin of the Oxford University, Institute of Economics and Statistics, Vol 31, November 1969,
No 4, pp. 229-241.

———   The Post-Import-Substitution Era: The case of Peru, in World Develc
ment, Vol 5, Nos 1/2, 1977, pp. 125-136.

Thorp, Rosemary and Bertram, Geoffrey. Peru 1890-1977. Growth and Policy ir
an Open Economy. The MacMillan Press Ltd., London and Basingstoke,
1978.

Thorp, Rosemary and Whitehead, Laurence (eds). Inflation and Stabilisation
in Latin America. Holmes and Meier Publishers Inc., New York, 1979.

Tostlebe, Alvin S. Capital in Agriculture: Its Formation and Financing sinc
1870. National Bureau of Economic Research, Princeton University
Press, Princeton, 1957.

Turner, George. El Credito Agrícola y la Reforma Agraria Peruana. Mimeo, Paper presented to the FAO conference on agricultural credit in Latin America. Quito, 1974.

Turnham, David assisted by Jaeger, Ingelies. The Employment Problem in Less Developed Countries. A Review of Evidence. OECD, Paris, 1971.

Valderrama, Mariano. 7 Años de Reforma Agraria Peruana 1969-1976. Pontifica Universidad Católica del Perú, Lima, 1976.

Valderrama, Mariano and Ludmann, Patricia. La Oligarquía Terrateniente Ayer y Hoy. Universidad Católica del Perú, Lima, 1979.

Van de Wetering, H. La Reforma Agraria: Un Enfoque Dirigido a Medir su Impacto en la Economía Provincial. Convenio para Estudios Economicos Basicos, Lima, 1970.

Vigués, Enrique Roig. Inversión de los Bonos de la Deuda Agraria en la Industria. Iowa Universities Mission to Peru, Boletin No 1, Lima, 1966.

Villanueva, Victor. El Caem y la Revolución de la Fuerza Armada. Instituto de Estudios Peruanos, Lima, 1972.

Wachtel, Nathan. Sociedad e Ideología. Ensayos de Historia y Antropología Andinas. Instituto de Estudios Peruanos, Lima, 1973.

Wald, Haskell P. (ed). Papers and Proceedings of the: Conference on Agricultural Taxation and Economic Development. Cambridge, Massachusetts, 1954.

Webb, Richard C. Government Policy and the Distribution of Income in Peru 1963-73. Harvard University Press, Cambridge, Massachusetts and London, 1977.

Webb, Richard C. and Figueroa, Adolfo. Distribución del Ingreso en el Perú. Instituto de Estudios Peruanos, Lima, 1975.

Williams, Lynden S. Land Use Intensity and Farm Size in Highland Cuzco, Peru, in Journal of Development Areas, January 1977, pp. 185-204.

Yotopoulos, Pan A. and Nugent, Jeffrey B. Economics of Development: Empirical Investigations. Harpers and Row, New York, 1976.